GREAT
ZULU BATTLES
1838–1906

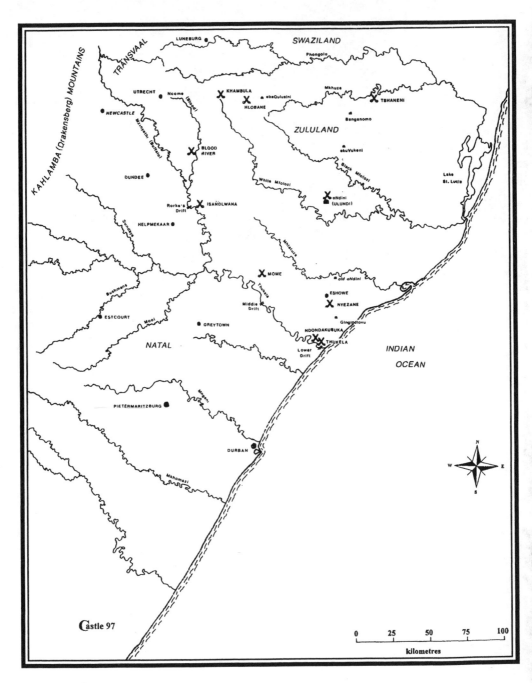

ZULU BATTLES 1838–1906

GREAT ZULU BATTLES 1838–1906

IAN KNIGHT

CASTLE BOOKS

This edition published in 2003 by Castle Books ®,
A division of Book Sales Inc.
114 Northfield Avenue
Edison, NJ 08837

This book is reprinted by arrangement with
Orion Publishing Group Ltd.
Orion House, 5 Upper St Martin's Lane, London WC2H 9EA

British Library Cataloguing-in-Publication Data : a
catalogue entry for this book is available from the British
Library

ISBN: 0-7858-1569-4

Printed in the United States of America

Designed and edited by DAG Publications Ltd.
Designed by David Gibbons; layout by Anthony A. Evans;
edited by John Gilbert.

CONTENTS

INTRODUCTION

There is a story which is widely known in Zululand, even today, about the last moments of the great King Shaka kaSenzangakhona. It was Shaka who created the old Zulu kingdom, by binding together a variety of disparate chiefdoms, and infusing them with a common sense of nationhood. It had not always been a peaceful process, and King Shaka is variously remembered as a conquering hero or a ruthless tyrant, according to your point of view. He had scarcely completed the process when the first white men, a handful of predominantly British traders and adventurers, arrived at his court, seeking his protection. When, four years later, King Shaka was assassinated in a coup orchestrated by members of his own family, he is said to have made a prophecy. Even as the assassins struck at him with broad-bladed stabbing spears, Shaka is supposed to have said: 'Sons of my father, you will not rule this land when I am dead, for it will be ruled by the white people who come from the sea.'

The story may, of course, be apocryphal, but it is interesting to note that it was current even before the Anglo–Zulu War of 1879, when the kingdom which Shaka had created finally buckled beneath the forces of white colonial expansionism. The fact that the story had already become part of the folklore of the Zulu kingdom suggests the extent to which most Zulus saw the arrival of the whites as foreshadowing the ruin of their political and economic independence. Indeed, there is another variation of King Shaka's prophecy which has come down to us, and that is equally revealing. In this version, he prophesies the destruction of the kingdom not through the coming of the whites, but through the quarrelsome nature of the royal family itself: 'Are you stabbing me, kings of the earth?', he asked them. 'You will come to an end through killing one another.'

The coming of the whites and the royal rivalries proved to be the twin curses of the nineteenth-century Zulu kingdom. Driven by an undercurrent of long-term consequences engendered by the rise of King Shaka's state, exaggerated by internal political tensions, and by the undermining of traditional patterns of life by European economic pressures, almost all the spectacular outbreaks of violence which scarred the history of the old Zulu kingdom could be ascribed to one cause or the other.

Furthermore, this pattern of conflict came to assume a geographical context, with many of the political rivalries falling either side of a north–south divide. The history of Zululand and its southern neighbour, Natal, has always been inextricably mixed, and the physical boundaries between them blurred. During the latter part of his reign, King Shaka attempted to extend Zulu influence south into Natal. He was only partly successful in this, and his failure determined the political allegiances of the groups who resisted him for generations to come.

The situation became more acute with the advent of colonial rule in Natal. An area in which Zulu rule had been tenuous now became a focus of potential opposition to Zulu domination. This opposition developed into open hostility when the British went to war with the Zulu kingdom in 1879. Following the British military victory, the tide was turned, and the south – Natal – came gradually to swallow up the north. Where once Natal had been part of the Zulu sphere of influence, now the reverse situation applied.

Although Britain refused to accept the political responsibilities of its actions in 1879, most of the subsequent bloodshed in Zululand can be traced to the operations of British agents, and is part of a broader pattern of the breakdown of traditional life under the assault of colonialism. Indeed, this conflict still resonates today; in the new, post-apartheid world of free South Africa, many of the political rivalries in modern KwaZulu/Natal revolve around whether the new administrative capital should be Pieter-maritzburg or Ulundi. In a more extreme form, this debate would have been all too familiar to successive generations of Zulu kings.

In the nineteenth century, few British administrators in Natal would have doubted that a clash between Natal and the Zulu kingdom was eventually inevitable; for them, the cultural differences were too extreme for the two states to live indefinitely side by side in harmony. They characterised this as a struggle between 'civilisation and savagery', between progress and inertia. In retrospect, it might be possible to argue that the European understanding of progress inflicted untold misery on the indigenous population of southern Africa, yet it is hard to deny that the two political philosophies were essentially incompatible.

The very fact that the Zulu kingdom was robust, powerful, and largely self-sufficient made it resistant to any sort of colonial exploitation. It was a potent symbol of the independence of the African spirit, and the fact that it functioned perfectly well without European interference was precisely why the Europeans deemed it necessary to overthrow it, if their own economic needs were to be satisfied. Even after half a century of penetration by white traders and missionaries, the Zulu kingdom retained its essential autonomy. That is why the British were compelled to use military force to break it; that explains, too, the British aversion to the Royal House which characterised their policies in the post-war years.

All ten of the battles in this book fit into this broader pattern of conflict. It was at the battle of the Thukela in 1838 that the inherent tensions between settler aspirations and those of the Zulu kings first became apparent; at Blood River, later that same year, they could hardly have been more obvious. The emergence of European influence as a factor in the politics of the Royal House helped unsettle an already unstable dynastic situation, and had a significant influence on the civil war of 1856. The struggles of the 1879 Anglo–Zulu War represent this conflict of interests in its most naked form, while the battles of the post-war years – oNdini and Tshaneni – contain all the same elements, but were waged by proxy.

By 1906, the military power of the Royal House had been broken, but its emotional pull among many African groups – who may never have been part of the original kingdom – served as a focus for profound discontent with an unsympathetic new order. The rebels drew on the symbols and mythology of the old Zulu kingdom, even though its contemporary representative, Dinuzulu kaCetshwayo, was powerless to give them practical help.

A cornerstone of the power of the Royal House – and therefore of British suspicion and mistrust of the Zulu kingdom – was the Zulu military system. To the British, the Zulu army was a highly disciplined, aggressive and unnatural institution: unnatural because the warriors were refused permission to marry until the king granted them the right, supposedly as a reward for success in battle. In British minds, this conjured up a terrifying image of hordes of ferocious warriors, their sexual frustration somehow transmuted to blood-lust, desperate to sink their broad-bladed stabbing spears into the body of a white man – or worse, woman! – as part of their rites of passage. In fact, this image is grotesquely distorted, a heady combination of misinformation and half-knowledge, fuelled by the same frustrated European sexual psychology that had given Freud so much food for thought.

The Zulu army was certainly a very different institution from its British counterpart. It was not a full-time professional body, governed by its own rules and a self-contained culture which set it apart from civilian society; it was instead a part-time citizen soldiery. Once they reached the age of about eighteen, Zulu youths were banded together into an *ibutho* (pl. *amabutho*), which the British characterised as regiments. Each *ibutho* therefore consisted of men of the same age group, and it was given a distinctive name, and a ceremonial costume consisting of a particular combination of feathers and furs. War shields were also of a uniform size and colour – at least in the early days of the kingdom – and were also granted by the king.

When mustered, the *amabutho* were housed at large royal homesteads, often consisting of several hundred huts, called *amakhanda*, literally 'heads'. The *amakhanda* were situated around the country, serving as centres of royal authority. Indeed, one of the most important functions of the *amabutho* system was that it focused the most obvious form of power within the kingdom – the service of young, fit men – upon the person of the king. Because the *amabutho* were raised according to their age, rather than geographical region, the warriors came from all over the country, regardless of their clan origins, and their loyalty was directed away from their local chiefs and towards the sovereign. In a conglomerate kingdom like that of the Zulus, the *amabutho* served as a powerful centralising force.

The warriors did not spend all their time in the service of the king; nor, indeed, was that service solely military. The king would call up particular *amabutho* when he had a specific task to perform; this might entail repairing his homesteads, hoeing his fields, or organising a hunt. When the task was complete, the warriors returned to live with their families in their ordinary homesteads. Only for the great national ceremonies, such as the annual *umKhosi*, or harvest festival, or for a full-scale war, were the *amabutho* likely to be mustered in their entirety. Moreover, the king was only entitled to first call on the young men's service as long as they were unmarried.

Marriage was an important rite of passage in Zulu society, and it marked the point at which young men left their father's homestead, and established a new one of their own. By this means they passed finally from youth to manhood, and in doing so their first responsibility reverted to their immediate family, and by extension to their local chief. Thus, when the men married, their period of service ended, and they were effectively lost as a direct resource to the king. It was for this reason that the Zulu kings prolonged their bachelor state for as long as possible. This was not as uncomfortable as it sounds, for Zulu moral codes allowed a certain amount of sexual freedom before marriage, provided pregnancy did not result.

In the early days of the kingdom, it was unusual for *amabutho* to be allowed to marry much before the men had reached their late thirties, although by the 1860s the age began to drop, simply because migration to Natal offered the possibility of quicker access to cattle and wives for those warriors who were too impatient to wait. It was not unusual for the king to insist that an *ibutho* performed a last task before it was allowed to marry; on occasion this task was military, and this gave rise to the idea among whites that a regiment needed to 'wash its spears' in the blood of an enemy before permission was granted. Once an *ibutho* had been allowed to marry, it effectively passed onto a reserve list; the warriors continued to acknowledge their ties to their *ibutho*, but were only mustered for the great ceremonies, or to fight in time of serious crisis. The young men of the kingdom remained the first line of defence.

In demanding that the Zulu king disband the *amabutho* as part of their ultimatum in December 1878, the British showed their superficial understanding of the system, yet wholly misunderstood the true nature of the king's relationship with his *amabutho*. For them, it was simply a question of freeing the young men from their servitude, and allowing them to marry at will. In British eyes the army would simply cease to exist, and the Zulus would be nothing more than a nation of pastoralists; if that happened, of course, the Zulus would have no means of self-defence, and British political aims would have been fulfilled without bloodshed. The British, however, assumed that King Cetshwayo would refuse the ultimatum, and indeed he had little choice; not because, as the British believed, he was a bloodthirsty tyrant at the head of a nation of savages, but simply because the *amabutho* system was one of the fundamental strands which bound the nation together. Without it, royal power collapsed. Either way, the British intended to prise those strands apart, and the grim methods by which this was ultimately achieved form the backdrop to this book.

The ten featured battles also reflect something of the experience of the Zulu army over the kingdom's history. Thukela, in 1838, of all the battles of the colonial period, represents perhaps the army in its purest form. Scarcely touched by European technology, commanded by men who had distinguished themselves under Shaka, buoyed up by a successful reputation, not yet tainted by defeat at the white man's hands, this was in many ways the battle that Shaka never fought, in which courage and technical skill won the day over superior weapon technology. Similarly, 'Ndondakusuka was the last great pre-colonial battle, which, despite the presence of a handful of whites, was fought out along traditional lines. Even by 1879, the balance had shifted, for the Zulu army was not quite so cohesive as it had been a generation before, and it had already been influenced by European technology. Sadly, not enough; the Zulus still relied on their stabbing spears as their main weapon, but where raw courage had triumphed over heavy losses in early 1838, European weapons now proved ultimately too powerful. In the post-war years the ghost of the *amabutho* system lingered alongside the emergence of a new, more flexible approach, which understood the lessons of 1879. Yet, during the post-war period, even when the Zulu army was no more, its spirit survived; ironically, the terrible catalogue of bloodshed which marked the period between 1880 and 1906 is testimony to the success of the British attempt to turn that spirit against itself.

ACKNOWLEDGEMENTS

Many people have assisted my explorations of Zulu history and culture over the years. Perhaps my greatest debt remains to *Makhandakhanda*; 'SB' Bourquin, who first made the ghosts of the past come alive for me among the green hills of Zululand. Over the years, Ian Castle has proved a steadfast travelling companion, and has given invaluable advice; he also contributed the maps to the present volume. Professor John Laband has been unfailingly generous, both as a host, and with his deep knowledge; our conversations in cyberspace have proved very helpful when picking over various details of the battles herein. Graeme and Cynthia Smythe have also suffered my sudden descents on Rorke's Drift and Dundee with rare good humour, while Gillian Berning has provided a tranquil refuge from all the mayhem in Durban. Dr Ian Player and Barry Leitch have earned lasting gratitude by introducing me to a number of traditional Zulu historians, including Prince Gilenja Biyela, and Mdiceni Gumede. Rai England can always be relied upon to provide some fresh images from his comprehensive collection of contemporary newspapers, and has not failed me now. My greatest thanks are due, however, to my wife Carolyn, who, while in the advanced stages of pregnancy, had to endure a grumpy and irritable husband, struggling to meet his deadline.

THE BATTLE OF THE THUKELA
17 April 1838
'The Great Elephant will trample you'

The area known as Zululand is spectacularly beautiful. Situated on the eastern seaboard of southern Africa, it falls in a series of terraces from the Kahlamba Mountains – known to the first white explorers as the Drakensberg, or Dragon Mountains – to the subtropical coast of the Indian Ocean. The inland heights almost cut Zululand off from the plains of the interior, and rain-bearing winds blowing off the sea deposit their load on the escarpment in the summer months, giving rise to a series of major river systems, which have cut spectacular valleys on their way back down to the coast. It is a land of contrasts: the steep, rugged mountain foothills are bleak and windy, and snow on the berg is not unusual in winter. In the middle reaches, the hills seem to fold over on one another, stretching off towards the hazy blue horizon. The coast is almost as impenetrable as the mountains, as the surf crashes with dramatic fury on a hundred miles of bush-covered sand-dunes. In summer the humidity of the subtropical coastal belt is stifling.

Before human habitation made too much mark on the landscape, the terrain was largely open grassland, broken here and there by patches of dark primordial forest, and thick bush which nestled in hollows or along the valley floors. It teemed with all the rich variety of the wildlife of the African bush – lion, rhino, buffalo, elephant, and countless species of buck. The origin of human habitation in the region is not known, but archaeologists have found traces of settlement which date back a thousand years, while the groups from among whom the Zulus of today have emerged were undoubtedly in place by the fifteenth century.

Politically, it is difficult to define the limits of Zululand. Broadly, the term describes the country between the Thukela river – which lies about 60 miles north of present-day Durban – in the south, and the Mozambique and Swaziland borders in the north. Certainly, this was the extent of the Zulu kingdom during its most static phase, although at times the Zulu kings exercised authority over country considerably further south, while their hold over the northern borders was always tenuous. In fact, the kings defined their boundaries in terms of the people who gave them allegiance, rather than by geographical features, and the idea of a single Zulu identity is largely mythical.

By the fifteenth century, the area between the Phongolo River in the north and the Mzimkhulu in the south was settled by independent African chiefdoms, who spoke broadly the same language and followed broadly the same customs. By the middle of the eighteenth century, many of the chiefdoms in the northern part of this district had been drawn into conflict with one another by forces which, even today, remain mysterious; and historical accident, combined with the military and political skills of King Shaka, ensured that the original Zulu chiefdom came to dominate most of its neighbours. The original Zulu heartland was just a few square miles of strikingly beautiful country, situated along the valley of the Mkhumbane stream, south of the White Mfolozi. Here Shaka's forebears are buried, stretching back into antiquity, and even today the area is known as emaKhosini – 'the place of the kings'.

King Shaka's reign was characterised by a prolonged struggle with local rivals, notably the Ndwandwe chiefdom of Zwide kaLanga, which lay to the north of Shaka's territory, around modern Nongoma. By about 1818 Shaka had defeated the Ndwandwe, and driven a section of the chiefdom out, incorporating the rest. In 1826 the Ndwandwe attempted to return, only to be defeated decisively by Shaka at the battle of Ndolowane. Although Shaka's kingdom was never as large, secure or monolithic as it has sometimes been painted, his triumph over the Ndwandwe effectively marks the Zulu transition from chiefdom to kingdom.

The state-building process required extraordinary energy and foresight, and the kingdom remained a conglomerate of local chiefdoms, with a sophisticated state apparatus overlaid on top. Through an extension of the traditional *amabutho* system – the brigading of young men of a similar age together for a period of national service – Shaka was able to take control of the most powerful resource in the country out of the hands of local chiefs, and vest it in the monarchy. The *amabutho* were quartered at large royal homesteads, *amakhanda*, which were sited strategically about the country, to guard against both outside attack and internal dissension.

Yet Shaka had probably not succeeded in establishing effective control over his new kingdom by the time he was assassinated in September 1828. Many chiefdoms within the kingdom were still unreconciled to Zulu rule, while Zulu influence south of the Thukela river was patchy. Shaka's successor – one of his assassins, his brother, Dingane kaSenzangakhona – faced a painful period of adjustment, eliminating steadfast supporters of the old regime while trying not to alienate the important regional chiefs. Whereas Shaka had shifted the focus of the kingdom southward – his last royal homestead, Dukuza, was built south of the Thukela River – Dingane preferred to move north, building a new homestead, eMgungundlovu, 'The Place Surrounding the Elephant', in the heart of the emaKhosini valley.

One reason for this withdrawal was the growing influence of a white community at Port Natal. The south-eastern seaboard had remained unknown to the European world until Christmas Day 1497, when the Portuguese explorer, Vasco da Gama, had noted its existence in his log as he sailed around the Cape and up the east coast of Africa, searching for a route to the Indies. He christened it *Terra Natalis*, in honour of the birth of Christ, and for centuries the name Natal was used to describe the country to the south of the Thukela. This was a forbidding and wild coast, a land of hidden reefs and dangerous shoals, and open, surf-swept beaches. Only one landfall was thought to be viable, a protected bay known to Portuguese seafarers as *Rio da Natal*, and to the British as Port Natal. A few ships called here over the years, but it was hardly welcoming, the beautiful, calm inland lagoon almost cut off by two jaws of land, the channel in between blocked for most of the year by a dangerous sand-bar, just a few feet below the surface. Mostly, it was a refuge only to handfuls of pathetic survivors from ships wrecked up and down the coast. Many of these either tried to make the perilous overland journey to the nearest European settlement – the Portuguese enclave at Mozambique in the north – or married into the local African population, and soon forgot all traces of their original language and culture. The Africans called them *abelungu* – pallid sea-creatures, washed up like flotsam on the beach.

The first *abelungu* came to stay in Zululand in 1824, when King Shaka was at the height of his power. At that time, the British empire was awash with adventurous young officers, whose promising careers had been cut short by the imprisonment of Napoleon, and the end of decades of war in Europe. Many were keen to use their professional skills to push out the boundaries of the empire, and to make themselves rich in the process. One such was an ex-Royal Navy lieutenant, Francis George Farewell, who secured the backing of wealthy Cape Town merchants to equip an expedition to make contact with the Zulu kingdom. The British were keen to set up a rival trading base to siphon off the lucrative Lourenço Marques trade. Garbled stories of Shaka's rise had filtered down to British garrisons on the eastern Cape frontier, and they conjured up an alluring image of a kingdom wealthy beyond feasibility in cattle and ivory. Ironically, it was Shaka's very success, therefore, which helped sow the seeds of his nation's destruction.

Farewell and his party, just six strong, braved the bar and set up a makeshift camp at Port Natal. At that time, Shaka had recently attacked the Thuli chiefdom, which lived in the vicinity of the bay, and had largely broken it up, sending the survivors scattering into the bush. Shaka had installed his own representatives nearby, and the whites soon made contact with the king himself, who was then living at Dukuza. Shaka was pleased to see them; the Europeans offered all manner of exotic trade goods, which the king could distribute as a sign of royal favour, thus transforming them into a means of extending his own power and patronage. Moreover, the Port Natal settlement was directly and uniquely under his control, and far more accessible than the tenuous channel to the Portuguese in the north. Shaka paid for his goods in ivory, and gave Farewell's men permission to hunt in some of his territories. Zululand's wildlife, largely unaffected for centuries by inefficient African hunting methods, would be almost obliterated within a few short decades by the advent of the firearm.

Shaka established the whites as a client chiefdom, exactly as he did with many of the African groups who sought his protection. He gave them land to live on, and afforded them his protection; in return, he expected to be able to call upon their service. Now and then, he even recruited them to add their firepower to his military expeditions. Under his patronage the whites lived a gloriously free Robinson Crusoe existence, setting themselves up as African chiefs, building African homesteads, and taking African wives. They soon began to accumulate retainers from among the local groups fragmented by Shaka, who came to realise that they offered protection and security from further Zulu attacks. The white settlers were an individualistic, free-spirited bunch, who hunted, traded, quarrelled and schemed among themselves, interfered in Zulu politics, used their protected status to their own ends in outrageous ways, and soon came to try the patience of both Shaka and his successor. Indeed, through their diaries they contrived to blacken the reputation of their host in order to exaggerate their own courage and endeavour – an enduring piece of ingratitude that still shapes Western images of King Shaka. Moreover, they failed to appreciate that Zulu concepts of land ownership were communal, and that Shaka had not given them an inalienable right to Port Natal, but merely the right to live there so long as he saw fit. The settlers considered the port their own, and several times tried to pass over legal title to the British government. The Colonial Office persistently refused, on the not unreasonable grounds that Farewell's men were little better than pirates, but it was from this tenuous claim that all future British possessions in Natal nevertheless devolved.

The news of Shaka's death came as a shock to the tiny trader community, and indeed several of them promptly fled to the bush, fearing that without his support their behaviour would not be tolerated. In fact,

however, Dingane made every effort to reassure them. Like his prede-
cessor, he needed trade goods, and by this time, too, the Zulus were beginning to appreciate the importance of European firearms. Within a few
months of Shaka's death, Dingane had abandoned Dukuza, and established
himself at eMgungundlovu. This had the effect of reducing control over the
white community, who began to extend their hunting operations through
the length of Natal.

King Dingane has been perhaps the most maligned of the early Zulu
kings. Whereas Shaka was characterised as cruel and despotic in the
traders' accounts, he was at least regarded as brave and dynamic. One
single act of violence at the end of his career, however, has irredeemably
blackened King Dingane's reputation, however, and he has often been
described as possessing all of Shaka's vices and none of his virtues.
According to this view, Dingane was lazy, fat, capricious, treacherous and
bloodthirsty. Almost none of these accusations are true. While it is an
undeniable fact that violence was a feature of Zulu political life – every revo-
lution brings with it a purging of the old regime's supporters, and Dingane
was no different in that respect – there is nothing to suggest that he
personally enjoyed the infliction of suffering.

Like every other Zulu man, Dingane had been enrolled in an *ibutho*, and
had served on several campaigns, but he had none of the warrior spirit of
his elder brother. His first act was to allow many of Shaka's regiments to
stand down and marry, and his reign began on an optimistically peaceful
note. He wanted to throw away the stabbing spear, he claimed, and take up
the dancing stick. King Dingane had something of an artistic frame of mind,
and he enjoyed composing songs, choreographing dancing displays, and
creating spectacular costumes of bead-work for the women of his household. Unfortunately, circumstances contrived to thwart the fine intentions
with which he began his reign.

Across the next decade the relationship between the king and the
traders deteriorated, until it became so strained that it ultimately exploded
in violence. The main cause of tension was a growing flood of political
refugees trying to throw off Dingane's authority. Many chiefdoms and individuals had been reluctant to accept the authority of the Zulu royal house,
while others felt themselves bound to the Zulu kingdom by personal allegiance to King Shaka. With Shaka dead, and with little chance of ousting
Dingane, they preferred to remove themselves from the orbit of royal
influence.

The tone was set within a year of Shaka's death by the followers of the
powerful Qwabe chief, Nqetho kaKhondlo, who simply abandoned their

traditional lands in south-eastern Zululand, and crossed the Thukela into Natal. Carefully avoiding chiefdoms loyal to the king, they worked their way to southern Natal, where they tried to re-establish themselves. Coincidentally, this move brought to an end Lieutenant Farewell's adventurous career; in 1829 he was returning overland from a trip to the Cape, and stopped off to see Nqetho in his new homestead. Nqetho suspected him of being a Zulu spy, and that night Farewell's tent was surrounded, and the great pioneer of Natal stabbed to death through the canvas.

Dingane's reaction to the defection of the Qwabe was to intimidate dissidents at home, and begin a series of punitive campaigns against chiefdoms on the periphery of his control in Natal, whom he suspected of wavering. Each attack, however, merely led to a flood of refugees into Port Natal, where the survivors placed themselves under protection of the traders. The latter were happy to welcome this influx, since adherents were the basis of their power and prestige. Although several of the original group were no longer at the Port – having died, like Farewell, or wandered off restlessly, in pursuit of other dreams – they had been replaced by newcomers, many of whom had come out to South Africa under the British immigration scheme of 1820. Large numbers of settlers had been brought out and settled on the Eastern Cape frontier, only to find that the lands promised them were unworkable, and that they were exposed to raids by hostile Xhosa groups. Disillusioned, many spread across southern Africa, and a handful fetched up at Port Natal, where those with a taste for anarchy and adventure could still live like chiefs, marrying African wives, and accumulating cattle and followers. By the mid-1830s, there were about 30 whites at the Port, with over 2000 retainers. Realising that Dingane was reluctant to punish them directly, they were increasingly confident of their position, and flaunted the king's directive to refuse refugees or to trade directly with Zulu subjects.

In 1831, the first major rift occurred. One of the original settlers, a tall carpenter by the name of John Cane, was commissioned by Dingane to lead a Zulu envoy mission to the Cape. This was not a new idea; Shaka had also tried to open up a channel of communication with the British authorities, but without success. Cane's expedition fared no better; it was detained on the Cape frontier by suspicious border officials, and eventually refused permission to proceed. The envoys returned disillusioned with British attitudes.

Meanwhile, a war was brewing on the frontier – the sixth against the local Xhosa chiefdoms – and the Zulus were alarmed by the evidence of British aggression. Rumours began to circulate of an impending British invasion, and John Cane, embarrassed by his failure, avoided reporting to King Dingane face-to-face, and instead went hunting. Dingane lost patience, and sent an *impi* (armed group) under the command of a famous warrior, Zulu kaNogandaya, to destroy Cane's settlements, while at the same time apologising to the other traders, and explaining his actions. Cane fled before Zulu's force, and the *impi* destroyed his homestead and carried off his cattle. Within a few weeks Dingane let it be known that he considered this punishment enough, and Cane returned to rebuild his settlements.

Nevertheless, the incident destroyed forever the traders' confidence that they could behave as they liked and get away with it. Dingane still considered them tributaries, and he expected their respect in return for the considerable privileges they enjoyed. It brought home to them, too, the true state of their vulnerability, and this contributed to another incident, in 1833. A Zulu force, sent to attack a chiefdom in Natal, returned by a route close to the port. The traders, fuelled by rumours spread by the refugee community, were convinced it was set to attack them, and once more John Cane got himself into trouble. He ambushed the Zulu force with part of his retinue of trained hunters, and shot down over 200 unresisting warriors before he realised his mistake. Once again, fearing the royal wrath, the traders fled to the bush, and once again Dingane acted with remarkable restraint. Against the advice of some of his senior councillors, who were beginning to lose their patience, he accepted the incident as a genuine mistake, and allowed the settlers to return.

The situation, nevertheless, remained tense, despite the arrival of a new player in the game. Captain Allen Gardiner was another retired naval officer, but unlike Farewell he had turned to God rather than trade. He arrived at the Port with the intention of introducing both the Zulus and the godless traders to Christianity, and soon found himself embroiled in local politics. The settlers at first welcomed him as a figure of authority, and elected him their representative in their dealings with Dingane. Gardiner thrashed out a treaty with the Zulu king, in which Dingane agreed to guarantee the traders' safety against the return of any new refugees arriving at the port. Gardiner was put to the test almost immediately but, despite qualms of conscience, stuck to his word, only to find that his colleagues were conniving to break the treaty behind his back. Dingane promptly reacted by banning trade between Port Natal and the Zulu kingdom, and the settlers once again panicked, fearing an attack. The situation eased somewhat when John Cane agreed to lead some of his adherents in support of Dingane's campaign against the Swazi in 1837, but the fact remained that the traders could no longer rely in Dingane's goodwill to protect them.

Their initial reaction to their predicament was to appeal, through Gardiner, to the British for protection; but they were disappointed at the response, for although they were granted British legal jurisdiction, they were denied any other support. Instead, they fell back on their own resources.

A key figure in the growing belligerence of the Port Natal community was one Alexander Biggar. Biggar had been a professional soldier, who had served as paymaster in the 85th Regiment during the Peninsular and Anglo–American wars. He had been court-martialled for irregularities over regimental accounts in 1819 and cashiered, and had come to South Africa with the 1820 settlers. Like many of his companions, he found it impossible to survive on the land allocated to him. A restless character, with an apparent dislike of authority, he became a fierce critic of the colonial administration. He moved to a new farm outside Grahamstown, but when this was destroyed by the Xhosa in the Sixth Frontier War of 1834–5, he abandoned the Eastern Cape entirely, and opted to seek his fortune at Port Natal. He brought with him his sons George and Robert, and a number of mixed-race retainers, whom he had trained as hunters. Arriving during the latest scare with Dingane, he promptly undertook to organise the settlement's defence.

The result was the Port Natal Volunteers, which came into being between April and September 1837. Biggar himself was elected commandant, and was joined by about twenty traders and up to 300 mixed-race and African retainers. The latter were a formidable force, despite the fact that they were armed only with smooth-bore flintlock muskets of the old military Brown Bess pattern. Most had been trained by their white chiefs as elephant hunters, and they were good shots, self-reliant and well accustomed to living on their own resources. Despite Biggar's efforts, however, the anarchic community did not respond well to military discipline, and the major weakness of the newly recruited army would remain the individualistic and quarrelsome attitude of the traders themselves.

In fact, the Port Natal Volunteers would not be tested in action, because at this point history introduced a new element. Ever since the British had finally taken over control of the Cape in 1806, discontent with their administration had been growing among the original European settlers. These were predominantly Dutch, who had first established a way-station at the Cape as early as 1652, and whose population had been swollen over the years by a trickle of German and French refugees from Europe. In particular, the farming communities on the eastern frontier, who were tough, resilient and independent-minded, complained of British interference in their affairs and of their unsympathetic attitude towards disputes with local African groups. Many frontier farmers suffered considerable financial loss when the British outlawed slavery in their dominions in 1833, while others felt bitter that the British had done little to protect them in the Frontier War of 1834–5.

By 1835, many frontier families had come to accept that their only hope was to remove themselves from British authority altogether, and establish new settlements where they could live according to their own ideologies. This idea followed in the long-established tradition of the *trekboer*, the semi-nomadic frontier farmer who spent much of his time away from home each year, wandering with his flocks in search of grazing. The Great Trek, however, was certainly different in scale; over an eighteen-month period, beginning in early 1835, over 15,000 Boer men, women and children, with their retainers, abandoned the frontier districts and set off into the interior in search of a Promised Land.

This exodus still provokes strong emotions today, and it was undeniably an epic of human endurance, as the Trekkers braved harsh environments, wild animals and the hostility of the African groups into whose territories they trespassed along the way. Indeed, their progress was marked by a series of violent clashes with indigenous groups, and news of their coming had reached Natal long before an advance party under the leadership of Piet Retief, a one-time wine-farmer and border commandant, crossed the Kahlamba Mountains in October 1837.

Certainly, the Port Natal traders were not surprised to see them, as a scouting party – the *Kommissie* Trek – had already visited the settlement as early as 1834. In order to gauge the reaction of the trader community, Retief now visited the Port before paying his respects to King Dingane. He made no secret that he was looking for land to settle, and those parts of Natal which had been temporarily depopulated by Zulu punitive expeditions seemed ideal for his purpose. The traders enthusiastically offered Retief their allegiance. For them, the Boers offered a strong European alternative to King Dingane's rule, with all its restrictions and insecurities, but without the vacillation and bureaucracy of British domination from the distant Cape.

In this regard, however, the traders were to be spectacularly disillusioned, for instead of ushering in a new age of security and freedom, the arrival of the Boers provoked a confrontation with the Zulus which would bring tragedy to all concerned, and lead directly to the first military clash between English-speaking settlers and the Zulu kingdom.

After leaving Port Natal, Retief visited eMgungundlovu, and the evidence suggests that he bungled his mission badly. The Zulus were already suspicious of Boer intentions, and Retief's apparently high-handed manner merely made them more so. In return for considering Retief's request for land, Dingane set the Boers a task – to recover cattle stolen from Zulu outposts in the Kahlamba foothills by groups beyond the mountains. Retief was happy to comply, but achieved his aim by trickery, refusing to hand over a captured chief – and some of the recovered booty – to Dingane. Furthermore, his followers began to descend the Kahlamba passes before any agreement had been formally ratified. In Zulu eyes, his behaviour confirmed the prevailing opinion that the Trekkers were likely to be dangerous and arrogant neighbours. When Retief and 69 Boer men, with 30 coloured servants, visited eMgungundlovu in the middle of February 1838 to receive their reward, Dingane entertained them with a dance of his massed *amabutho*. At the height of the dance, he suddenly stood up and called on his warriors to seize the Boers, who were quickly overpowered, dragged off to the hill of execution and clubbed to death.

This terrible act was to scar the Afrikaner soul and poison relationships between them and the black population of southern Africa for more than a century. To Dingane, however, the Boers had shown criminal disrespect, proving that they were a danger to be eliminated by any means possible. In Zulu custom, the lives of the families of criminals were also forfeit, and shortly after the murder of Retief, Dingane sent his army to attack Boer settlements in Natal.

Word of the projected onslaught reached the Port Natal community, and Biggar sent his youngest son, George, to warn Retief's followers. Sadly, George Biggar arrived too late; the Zulus struck the Boer encampments on the Bushmans and Bloukrans Rivers at about midnight on 16–17 February. The Boers had scattered in family groups over a wide area, and those in the vanguard had no warning and were wiped out. Those further off heard the sound of distant gunfire and managed to organise some defence, but by the time the Zulus retired the following morning, 281 Boer men, women and children, and 250 mixed-race servants, had been killed. Thousands of head of cattle were carried away, leaving the Boer parties immobilised in their temporary camps. George Biggar, arriving in the aftermath of the attack, was mistaken for a Zulu in the confusion, and shot dead. The loss hardened the Biggar family's attitude towards King Dingane and the Zulu army.

In fact, the king had gone to great lengths to assure the British community that they were not under threat. Nevertheless, the sudden ferocious attack had heightened the settlers' fears, and hardened their determination to throw off Dingane's authority. Indeed, King Dingane's attempt to destroy the Boer threat in one blow must be considered a failure. Although his army had easily overcome unprepared encampments, it had been unable to overrun those parties who had managed to form a defensive circle of wagons – a laager – suggesting for the first time an ominous weakness that would hamper the attempts of the Zulu military to counter European encroachment time and again over the next fifty years; lacking firearms themselves, the Zulus were almost helpless in the face of a stout barricade resolutely defended with musketry.

Shocked, bereaved, leaderless, living in insanitary conditions, the Boer families in the Kahlamba foothills nevertheless held on, and in due course were reinforced by new leaders and fresh parties from beyond the mountains. By the middle of March, they were thirsting for revenge, and keen to recover their stolen cattle. The new Boer leaders, Hendrik Potgieter and Piet Uys, suggested a joint operation with the Port Natal traders, who readily agreed to the scheme.

The two armies set out at the beginning of April. The Boer party consisted of mounted men, and struck at the Zulu border from the west. The settler army consisted of about 30 traders, under the command of the last surviving members of Farewell's original party, John Cane and Henry Ogle, known to the Zulus respectively as Jana and Wohlo. The Boer party immediately ran into difficulties. On 10 April it caught sight of a herd of Zulu cattle grazing near a hill known as eThaleni, and gave chase, only to find that it had fallen into a trap carefully set by one of Dingane's senior military commanders, Nzobo kaSobadli. The Boers found themselves surrounded by several thousand Zulus, principally of the uMkhulutshane *ibutho*, who rose up in the long grass around them. The Boer forces scattered, and Piet Uys himself was killed in the rout. In the first open fight between Zulu and Boer forces, the Zulus proved themselves masters of the field.

The Port Natal expedition had more luck. Travelling inland from the coast at the end of March, it attacked several Zulu homesteads in Thukela valley, in the shadow of a distinctive rocky outcrop called Ntunjambili, or Kranzkop. These were homesteads belonging to Dingane's adherents who lived on the Natal side of the river, and they contained numerous royal cattle. Many of the cattle-guards were away, fighting with the army that Nzobo was commanding against Potgieter and Uys. There was virtually no opposition, and the only casualties suffered by the settler force were one auxiliary killed by a snake-bite, and another shot by John Cane for stealing.

The expedition returned with several hundred women and children as captives – a valuable addition to their growing chiefdoms – and as many as 6000 head of cattle. A missionary, the Reverend Hewitson, described Cane and his followers on the march, painting a vivid picture of a Zulu army in the field, with its support services, all under the command of a rugged frontiersman:

> About 400 Zulus came bellowing a war-song. It sounded exactly like the noise of angry bulls.No one could mistake its angry meaning; its tone was that of gloomy revenge. The words in English were: 'The wild beast has driven us from our homes, but we will catch him!' They were headed by a white man, who had an old straw at on, with an ostrich feather stuck in it. He had on his shoulder an elephant gun covered with panther's skin, and walked quite at ease at the head of his party, who went on with their dismal song, except that occasionally they all whistled the Zulu charge. They had flags flying, on one of which was written, 'Izin kumbi' (or the locust); on another 'For justice we fight.' They did not fatigue themselves with jumping or shouting, but the monotonous howl could be heard for at least two miles. In front they drove cattle for slaughter; in rear the degraded wives carried Indian corn, pumpkins, etc., all of which passed so quickly by me that it seemed like a frightful dream.

A significant rift, however, occurred during the expedition, which marred its success, and would have grim consequences in future operations. A quarrel broke out between Cane's and Ogle's followers, probably over the distribution of the spoils, which seems to have been resolved in the traditional Zulu manner, by a stick-fight. Ogle's men came off decidedly the worse, and relations between them were soured. Another missionary, the Reverend Owen, who secured permission to establish himself in Zululand just in time to witness Retief's massacre, saw the army return on 2 April, and was impressed with neither their motives nor their discipline. They were, he decided, motivated more by greed than anything else, and their unity was such that 'every man does what is right in his own eyes'.

Heartened by this success, the traders decided to make a second foray a fortnight later. They were probably encouraged in this by Robert Biggar. The Biggars had been away at the time of the first expedition, and Robert had returned before his father. Robert was undoubtedly motivated by the death of his brother, for which he blamed the Zulus, but there was another factor, for, as one of John Cane's sons remarked wryly years later, the

Biggars were newcomers to the area and could not match the impressive herds of cattle owned by the more established settlers. The quickest way to build up a fortune was to raid the Zulus.

In the middle of April, the settlers therefore reassembled their forces, which they optimistically dubbed The Grand Army of Natal. The principal commanders seem to have been Robert Biggar, John Cane and a trader named John Stubbs. None of these had any military background, although Biggar, of course, knew something of military ways from his father, and Cane – the former carpenter – was both an experienced hunter and had commanded his own retainers in action on several occasions. He had fought both with and against King Dingane's forces and could be reckoned to have a good understanding of the Zulu military outlook.

Only one man in the Grand Army seemed to have any genuine military experience – a settler by the name of Robert Joyce, who was a deserter from the British 72nd Regiment. Most of the traders, however, were armed to the teeth with heavy-calibre hunting weapons, pistols, cutlasses and knives. In all, the Grand Army consisted of a total of eighteen settlers, with 400 auxiliaries drawn from their hunting retinues. These men were armed with muskets, and knew how to use them.

Significantly, almost half the white community of Port Natal declined to support the expedition, and this included Henry Ogle. Still smarting from his quarrel with Cane, he refused to go himself, but did authorise his retainers to join the party. This effective core of the army was supported by between 2000 and 3000 auxiliaries, drawn from the refugee community at the port who had sought the traders' protection. They were armed with their traditional weapons – cow-hide shields, spears and knobkerries – but their morale was unpredictable. Some were said to be enthusiastic, while others would only accompany the expedition under threat, a fact that is probably explained by the internal rivalries within the force.

It is not clear whether the settlers knew of the defeat of Uys's commando before they set out. In any event, the expedition left the port on about 14 April, intending this time to march not inland, but northward, striking up the coast. The missionary community, who since the attack on Retief had fled Zululand and were sheltering at the port, tried to dissuade them, and presented a picture of a ramshackle army divided among itself, with no very clear objectives. According to one missionary, some of the African auxiliaries were so old that they could only walk with the aid of a stick. Probably learning a lesson from the previous foray, the auxiliaries were identified by a strip of white calico cloth which they wound around their heads.

The coastal strip south of the Thukela River was not occupied by any groups that offered allegiance to Dingane, and the army struck the lower reaches of the river late on the afternoon of the 16th without opposition. The Thukela is one of the great rivers of KwaZulu/Natal, and its lower reaches, not far from the mouth and within sight of the sea, formed a natural physical barrier. The country on either side was open and undulating, rising up within a few miles on the Zulu bank into a series of hilly terraces. The river was perhaps 150 yards wide, a solid sheet of brown water in the rainy season, but reduced to a few deep channels flowing between large sandbanks in the dry winter months. There are few clues as to its state in April 1838, but it may well have been reasonably full with late spring rains.

The army had probably reached the Lower Drift, one of the best crossing points along the entire stretch of the river, which had already become acknowledged as the main traders' route into Zululand. The main force, however, made no immediate attempt to cross; instead, a party of musketeers in Cane's service, under the command of a minor chief of the Luthuli people named Funwayo kaMpopoma, were sent across as scouts. Most of the country on the opposite bank was deserted, but in the abandoned homestead of a Zulu named Kude they captured two warriors who turned out to be scouts attached to a Zulu army. Funwayo had the men interrogated, then shot, and his patrol returned across the river to report.

The encounter was an ominous one. The emptiness of the country on the Zulu bank suggested that civilians had been withdrawn ahead of the settlers' attack. Not only did the Zulus know they were coming, but the presence of the two scouts suggested an army was near by. Indeed, the scouts had probably admitted as much, since an earnest discussion now broke out among the settlers, as to whether they should cross the river themselves, and seize the initiative before any Zulu force arrived, or await developments. Biggar and his men were keen to advance without delay, while the more experienced Cane urged them to take up a defensive position on the knolls on the south bank of the river – much the same spot, incidentally, that the British chose as one of the permanent bases for their invasion of Zululand in 1879. In the end, Biggar's enthusiasm seems to have infected most of the settlers, and Cane was overruled. The commanders decided to cross the river before dawn the following morning, and to advance and attack 'in the horns of the morning' – first light, when the horns of cattle can first be seen against the lightening sky, the traditional Zulu time of attack. This decision indicates the extent to which the settlers had absorbed the military practices of the people among whom they lived.

Their immediate target was a wealthy Zulu homestead on the hills oppo-site, known as 'Ndondakusuka.

In fact, as they must have known, the country ahead was perhaps the area best prepared against attack. Precisely because it was a main entry and exit point, Dingane had established a number of royal homesteads in the region. The area immediately beyond the river was known as the Hlomendlini district – the district of the 'troops raised at home' - so named after two *amakhanda*, the Hlomendlini mhlope ('white Hlomendlini') and Hlomendlini mnyama ('black Hlomendlini'). These housed a number of regiments, and had been placed there to guard the southern border of the kingdom against potential white encroachment, and also to stem the flow of refugees out of the country from that quarter. The term 'white' was usually applied to senior *amabutho*, and certainly the Hlomendlini mhlope was regarded as the senior of the two settlements, falling under the command of one of Dingane's senior military officials, Nongalaza kaNon-dela, whose personal homestead was close by.

Situated between the Hlomendlini settlements and the site of modern-day Eshowe was the kwaNjanduna royal homestead, which had been taken over by Shaka from the Cele clan, and moved from its original location south of the Thukela by Dingane. This, too, had a garrison attached. And further inland, on the heights beyond the Mhlatuze River, lay kwaKhangela, one of the oldest and most important royal settlements in the kingdom.

Much of the south-eastern corner of Zululand was ruled in the king's name by his younger brother, Mpande kaSenzangakhona. Most histories have portrayed Mpande as a simpleton, but beneath a carefully cultivated air of indolence he possessed the shrewd intellect of a political survivor. Mpande's own homesteads were in the coastal sector, and he maintained close ties both with the commanders of the kwaKhangela homestead and with Nongalaza.

Moreover, the 'Ndondakusuka homestead itself was the personal resi-dence of one of the most respected warriors in the kingdom, Zulu kaNogandaya. Many of the heroes of the early period of Zulu history survive as little more than bold stereotypes remembered in oral tradition, but a good deal of information has come down to us concerning this man Zulu. His given name was Komfiya, and he was the head of a junior lineage of the Qwabe people, over whose traditional lands Mpande now ruled. Before the Zulus had absorbed the Qwabe, Komfiya had fallen out with the chief, Khondlo, and had left to *konza* (give allegiance to) the rising young star, Shaka. Shaka had been impressed by Komfiya's courage and willing-ness to embrace the Zulu cause, which was not impaired even when Shaka attacked the Qwabe. During the great Zulu/Ndwandwe campaigns of 1818–19, Komfiya had established himself as a royal favourite. Addressing his troops before the climactic battle of Mhlatuze, Shaka had challenged any of his warriors to excel his own reputation in battle, promising to honour them if they did by granting them the right to use two lines from his personal *izimbongi*, the praise-poem which recorded his great deeds. In the following fight, Komfiya threw himself into the thick of the action, striking down enemies all around him, and afterwards Shaka duly referred to him as 'the Heavens that Thundered in the Open, When no-one was Near' – a pun on his own family name, Zulu, which means 'the heavens'. Thereafter, Komfiya was known by the name Zulu.

By 1838 he was a married man, wearing the headring, of middle-height, with a stocky, powerful build, a Roman nose and prominent eyebrows. He carried his reputation in his intimidating manner, and most warriors were in awe of him. He had risen to the command of the *amabutho* stationed at Hlomendlini mnyama, and in battle he habitually carried the shield – white with dark smudged markings – of the regiment in which he had been enrolled, the uMwanqa. Furthermore, Zulu was one of only a handful of Dingane's *izinduna* (officers) already to have led troops against the whites; he had been in command of the force which had destroyed John Cane's homestead in 1831. He was certain to be involved in any coming confrontation, and one wonders what John Cane might have made of the reckoning.

The Grand Army of Natal crossed the Thukela early on the morning of 17 April. If it crossed at the Lower Drift, it had perhaps two miles to cover before it reached the 'Ndondakusuka homestead; and it must have marched in good order, for it apparently took up a position close to the homestead without being detected. Given the limitations of the firearms of the day, it was probably no more than a hundred yards from the fence of palings which would, typically, have surrounded the huts. Cane himself seems to have been in the middle, with Biggar on the right, and the other settlers in the front rank, mingling with their trained musketeers. The auxiliaries armed only with shields and spears stood behind. As the first hint of dawn rose in the sky, the traders opened a heavy volume of fire into the huts.

There are no reports of Zulu civilians living in the huts – a sure sign that they were expecting an attack – and in fact the homestead was probably occupied by the vanguard of the Zulu force lying near by. It was customary for a Zulu army to advance screened by a thin line of scouts, thrown out well ahead of a body of skirmishers, who remained between them and the main columns. Cane, at least, would have known this, and the scouts they had captured the night before might well have told them that the skirmishers following them had arrived at 'Ndondakusuka.

Without issuing any warning, the settlers directed a fierce fusillade into the huts. As the bullets whipped and crackled through the thatch, somebody noticed one of the huts collapse, apparently pulled down from within. The warriors inside the huts were trying to escape the hail of fire by climbing up the poles that supported the roofs and clinging to the framework supporting the thatch. The musketeers were directed to redirect their aim, and fired instead into the top of the huts. It is not clear how long this fire went on, but even if it lasted only a few minutes it must have caused great execution, since the Zulus had no escape route open to them, nor any means of retaliating.

On the command to cease firing, men were sent forward to set fire to the huts. One wounded Zulu was dragged out of the blazing wreckage, and defiantly said to his capturers: 'Kill me right now, but the Great Elephant is coming, and will soon trample you under foot.'

The Great Elephant was a praise-name for the king and his army, and the dying warrior was quite right. A Zulu army had indeed been approaching the river from the direction of the Eshowe heights, and had spent the night in the valleys a few miles beyond 'Ndondakusuka. The composition of this force remains uncertain, but the names of its commanders have survived in Zulu oral tradition, and this gives some clue. Prince Mpande himself was said to have gathered the army and to have supervised the rituals that were necessary to bind it together and ensure supernatural superiority in the coming fight – a factor which, in Zulu eyes, was almost as crucial an ingredient of victory as command decisions in battle itself. It is not clear, however, whether Mpande accompanied the army to the front; he had no great reputation as a warrior, and most accounts agree that Nongalaza kaNondela held the senior field command. Almost certainly, therefore, the main part of the army consisted of the Hlomendlini mhlope *amabutho*; and since Zulu kaNogandaya was also present as a general, the Hlomendlini mnyama regiments probably made up the rest of the army. Also in attendance was the *ibutho* associated with the Njanduna homestead.

The army had probably roused itself early, before the settlers had attacked 'Ndondakusuka, and the sound of the firing brought them forward at a run. Zulu sources suggest that the army was extremely angry at the settlers for breaking their allegiance to Dingane in their earlier foray, and was burning for vengeance. The formidable Zulu kaNogandaya can hardly have been pleased, either, at the destruction of his homestead.

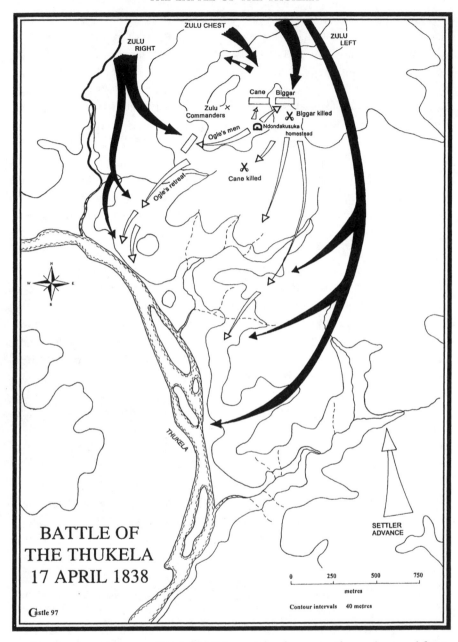

ZULU CHEST

ZULU
RIGHT

ZULU
LEFT

Cane Biggar

Zulu ✕
Commanders

✗ Biggar killed

Ogle's men Ndondakusuka
homestead

Ogle's retreat

✗
Cane killed

N
W — E
S

THUKELA

BATTLE OF
THE THUKELA
17 APRIL 1838

SETTLER
ADVANCE

0   250   500   750

metres

Contour intervals   40 metres

Castle 97

By the time they caught sight of the settler forces as they advanced from
the hill behind 'Ndondakusuka, the Zulus had taken up their traditional
attack formation, *izimpondo zankomo* ('horns of the beast'). The
Hlomendlini mhlope regiments, which probably made up the central body
– the *isifuba* ('chest') – took advantage of valleys and broken ground to the

30

north of the hill to swing around from that direction, apparently in advance of the flanking parties, or 'horns'. At about the same time, a group of Zulu commanders, including Nongalaza and Zulu kaNogandaya, appeared near the top of the hill, above the burning homestead. By this time the main settler force had taken up a position a little to one side of the homestead, perhaps to be clear of any smoke, and to give a better view of the northern approaches. As the chest ran forward to attack, the settlers opened up a heavy fire, and the attack stalled, going to ground in the broken terrain. Robert Joyce, the army deserter, apparently directed the fire of about ten of the settlers and some of the auxiliaries to such good effect that the chest was driven back, and retired out of sight behind the hill.

Under normal circumstances, the chest usually attacks only after the horns have begun to deploy to encircle the enemy, and it may well be that as the result of the army's hurried deployment, its advance had been premature. Certainly, it allowed the settlers a breathing space to predict the Zulus' next move. Expecting an attack by the horns, Cane divided his forces in two, sending Ogle's contingent off to his left, in anticipation of an attack by the Zulu right, while he and Biggar led the remainder to their right, to counter the Zulu left. Sure enough, the Zulu horns soon came into view, the left horn swinging to the north of the chest's line of advance, the right appearing from round the western side of the hill.

As the Zulus advanced to within 100 yards, the settler forces opened up a murderous fire, mowing the enemy down until their attacks stalled. Nevertheless, the Zulus seemed determined to carry on the fight and, according to one Zulu source, even the wounded 'crawled forward with their spears, to throw them lying down in an effort to kill'. It is worth noting that this was the first time that a Zulu army had faced an infantry force trained along European lines, and armed with firearms. The settler army, deployed on foot, was using very different tactics from the mounted skirmishing and defensive wagon-laagers of the Boers, and the sheer volume of fire they were producing exceeded anything the Trekkers had hitherto brought to bear. Nevertheless, the Zulu army showed not the slightest sign of being unnerved by this new and awesome experience. The commanders merely sought to manoeuvre their men to afford them some protection, and take advantage of any weaknesses among the settlers.

The Zulu breakthrough came on their right. Here the horn had been driven back out of range of the withering fire, but instead of following up their advantage, Ogle's men retired to their left, towards the river. Probably they were feeling isolated, separated from the main settler force, and their own commander was not present to keep them in hand. Possibly, too, they recalled their earlier quarrel with Cane's men, and were not confident that the rest of the army would protect their line of retreat.

In any event, the movement was not lost on the Zulu commanders, who immediately signalled to their men to resume the attack. The right horn, rushing forward once more, managed to charge home, driving Ogle's force in some confusion towards the river. In classic Zulu style, some elements extended further to their right, slipping between the struggling mêlée and the river, separating Ogle's men from an easy crossing place below the hill. Streaming away with the Zulus in pursuit, they found themselves forced downstream, where a line of cliffs cut them off from the river. Their only chance of escaping the Zulus, who were right in among them, stabbing them as they ran, was to leap down the cliffs and into the water.

The collapse of Ogle's contingent spurred the Zulu left into renewed effort. Here, resistance was heavier, for Cane and Biggar were keeping their men under firm control, and directing a withering fire on the regiments facing them. In some accounts, the Zulu front ranks melted away under this fire, the bodies piling up on one another as the warriors behind pressed forward. The pressure was so intense that the remaining settler forces were driven back, below the 'Ndondakusuka homestead, towards the river. By this time, however, the Zulu left had extended beyond the settler flank, and was swinging round to cut off their line of retreat. Sheer weight of numbers began to tell, and the Zulus managed to press home their attack. Since their weapons were designed for use at close quarters, where the settlers could hardly use their muskets to good effect, the tide now swung overwhelmingly in favour of the Zulus.

Robert Biggar was surrounded and killed on the settler right, and fighting raged all around Cane. On horseback, with a clay pipe clenched between his teeth, he continued to fire until struck both in the chest and back by hurled spears. Nestling his musket in the crook of his arm, he tried to escape, but fell off his horse from loss of blood. His last act was to shoot one of his own followers who was coming to help him, believing him to be a Zulu. John Stubbs, too, fell under the spear of a young warrior, exclaiming indignantly: 'Am I to be killed by a boy like you?'

By now, the tips of the Zulu horns had almost completely surrounded the surviving settlers, whose Grand Army of Natal suddenly disintegrated. Many of the auxiliaries tore off their distinguishing headbands in the hope of passing themselves off as Zulus, only to be shot in the confusion by men on their own side who were still fighting. The survivors broke, and tried to slip between the horns, but the Zulus pursued them down the length of the river, flushing out those who tried to hide in the undergrowth on its banks. Many of those who did make it into the water were drowned.

The defeat of the Grand Army of Natal was complete. Of the eighteen settlers who accompanied the force, only four survived, while only a handful of their mixed-race adherents got away. As many as half the auxiliaries were killed, and the battlefield was marked for a decade afterwards with the bones and skulls of the slain. Zulu losses are impossible to calculate, but were undoubtedly heavy. Some contemporary accounts put them as high as 2000 men.

The political consequences of the Zulu victory were enormous. Their victory dispelled any illusions the settlers might have harboured that Africans went in awe of their white skins or weapons; the Zulus had proved themselves more than capable of defending themselves against a European attack. Moreover, the battle, and particularly Cane's death, marked the final rift of the goodwill which had been established between King Shaka and Farewell's party fourteen years before. There would never again be an occasion when settlers in Natal accepted the authority of a black king, and the battle marked the first stage of a struggle for supremacy which would end only with the destruction of Zulu royal authority 50 years later.

The first survivors trickled back to the port over the next 24 hours. The black community promptly scattered into the bush, while the white settlers took refuge on a boat which happened to be in the harbour, or on one of the islands in the bay. They feared that the Zulus would follow up their victory with an attack on the port, and they were proved correct. For a day or two the victorious *impi* was preoccupied with the post-combat purification rituals which were essential after every action, but on 24 April it suddenly came into sight on the outskirts of the settlement. For several days the settlers watched from their refuges as the Zulus ransacked the settlement, setting fire to their wattle-and-daub shacks, looting their property, and carrying off any valuables they had left behind. Then, at last, the Zulus withdrew, and the hardiest among the traders returned to pick up the pieces.

The defeat at the Thukela ended the British settlers as an important factor in the war. Attention instead turned to the Boers and, in the end, the issue was decided by a combination of Boer determination and division within the Zulu Royal House. A few individuals continued the struggle; Alexander Biggar returned to Natal to find his two sons dead, and sought revenge for his bereavement by joining the Boer forces. Biggar was present at the battle of Blood River in December, but was killed in a running fight on the banks of the White Mfolozi a week later. Ironically, in the aftermath of Blood River, Mpande defected to the Boers, bringing with him the military establishment of the district over which he ruled. It was Mpande's troops, led by the same Nongalaza who had triumphed at the Thukela, who finally defeated Dingane's supporters at the battle of the Maqongqo Hills in 1840. Dingane fled, and the Boers gave their support to Mpande as his successor.

On his return to Zululand, Mpande left behind a number of his retainers who preferred to seek sanctuary in Natal rather than live again under the Royal House. One of these was none other than Zulu kaNogandaya, who had made no secret of the fact that he despised Mpande for a coward, and who had taken as wife a woman Mpande had admired. Fearing for his life under the new regime, Zulu had sought refuge with, of all people, Henry Ogle; it had been the collapse of Ogle's followers at the battle of the Thukela which had given Zulu his most memorable victory.

— 2 —
THE BATTLE OF BLOOD RIVER
16 December 1838
'All were killed, that not one escaped'

By the middle of 1838, it seemed that King Dingane kaSenzangakhona was winning his struggle against European encroachment. Only too aware of the devastating effect of the awesome weapons carried by the whites, he had attempted to deal with the threat posed by the Boers through stratagem, rather then open confrontation. In Zulu eyes, Retief and his followers had marked themselves as enemies of the state by their profound disrespect for royal authority and the mystique of kingship; and their lives, and those of their followers, had been forfeit as a result. The attack on the Boer encampments in Natal had caused heavy casualties and effectively immobilised the Trekkers by driving off their livestock, while the treacherous action of the British settlers at Port Natal, in turning against their host and protector, had been suitably punished by the crushing defeat at the Thukela, and by the sacking of their settlement. Indeed, even those twin military assets by which the Europeans had set so much store, and of which the Zulus themselves had been wary – the gun and the horse – had been proved in a series of reverses to be greatly overrated. By the end of April 1838, the first round in the enduring struggle between white interlopers and the Zulu army had gone decidedly in the latter's favour; the army had not suffered a single significant defeat, while none of the king's royal homesteads had been threatened, let alone attacked.

Yet this apparent state of affairs was fundamentally misleading. True, whenever the Zulus had caught the whites in an even fight in the open, they had been able to scatter them; but the successful defence of some of the laagers further up the reaches of the Bushmans and Bloukrans Rivers had hinted at a greater truth, that the Zulus were powerless in the face of secure defensive positions – and this lesson was not lost on the whites. Furthermore, traumatised though they were, the spirit of the Trekkers was not broken. After a few weeks their grief gave way to a fierce desire for revenge which was not dampened by the defeat of the Uys–Potgieter commando at eThaleni, nor the bitter recriminations that followed it. Trekker groups in the Transvaal high veld rallied to their aid, despite being preoccupied with their own successful campaign against the Ndebele kingdom of Mzilikazi kaMashobane. A steady trickle of fighting men crossed the Kahlamba passes and offered their support to those leaders who were emerging from among the ranks of the survivors.

The true state of the balance of power was revealed by a further round of fighting in August 1838. The refusal of Retief's original group to abandon Natal, and their subsequent reinforcement, presented a clear challenge to King Dingane. The whole point of his attack on Retief had been to kill the Trekker snake by cutting off its head; now the body seemed to have sprung fresh heads, and still to be slithering inexorably into his territory. After the activity of April, the Zulu army had dispersed to allow the warriors to perform the necessary post-combat rituals, to recover, and to catch up with their domestic duties at home. By the first week of August, however, the king, urged on by his senior military advisers, who were wholly committed to resolving the conflict by force, reassembled part of the army, and doctored it for a fresh campaign. The Port Natal community appeared utterly cowed, and there seemed little need to waste further effort on them. Instead, the king sent about 10,000 men, senior *amabutho* associated with eMgungundlovu itself, to finish what they had started in February, and destroy the remaining Boer settlements.

By this time, however, the Boers had taken steps to protect themselves against surprise attacks. The scattered camps of February had come together to form a single laager on a low ridge, known as Gatsrand, in the Bushmans River valley. Some 290 wagons were arranged in a double line along the contour of the ridge, forming an elongated triangle, with the base running parallel to the river. A light ship's cannon was positioned to cover the apex, and the field of fire was generally open, though here and there dongas running down to the river afforded a little dead ground. In some places on the gentle slope, the Trekkers had dug pits to hamper the enemy advance, and delay them where they were most exposed to Boer fire. Because of the casualty rate among Retief's party and in the subsequent fights, the laager was defended by only 75 able-bodied men, under the command of Hans Dons de Lange and J. Potgieter. There were many more women and children in the laager, and spear-proof shelters of planking and hides had been built to protect them, but some preferred in any case to help their men in battle by loading their muskets. Despite their careful preparations, however, the Trekkers had not been able to resolve the crucial question of what to do with their livestock; since there was no room for them inside the laager, they had to be left grazing outside, and were effectively abandoned to the enemy.

The Zulu force, commanded by Ndlela kaSompisi, reached the vicinity of the Gatsrand early on the morning of 13 August, and advanced up the river valley towards the laager. They had hoped to take the Boers by surprise, but were thwarted by some of Potgieter's herdboys, who spotted them in the distance, and raised the alarm. De Lange and Potgieter rode out to confirm the report, and then placed the laager in readiness. The Zulus came within sight at about 10 a.m., still arrayed in marching columns. They halted, and began to deploy in attack formation, throwing out the right horn which swung about beyond range of the apex of the laager to surround it on the far side. Another detachment made a difficult crossing of the river, which was full, and completed the encirclement.

By about midday they were in position, and launched the first of a series of attacks against the wagons. At close range, they were met by a hail of musketry-fire, augmented by home-made canister fired from the cannon. For a while they persisted in the assault, supports rushing up from the rear to fill the gaps as the front rank was mown down. Even when they reached the wagons, however, they could not find a way in, and after several unsuccessful forays they withdrew to the cover of the dead ground. Seeing them retreat, De Lange decided to risk a sortie, and a party of men rode out to harry the enemy from horseback. The Zulus must have been exhausted by their efforts, because, instead of mounting a counter-attack while the Boers were vulnerable, they retired out of range into the sheltered country downstream. Unwilling to risk themselves too much in the open, the Boers returned to the laager, and spent an uncomfortable night watching their enemies slaughter some of the cattle which had been left outside.

At first light, De Lange sortied out again, trying to provoke the Zulus to attack, and falling back inside the laager as they did so. This time the Zulus attempted to drive out the Trekkers with fire, rushing up to the laager carrying spears tied round with blazing bundles of grass. Once again they were shot down, however, mostly before they could charge to within throwing range. Here and there, where the spears struck home, the flames were easily doused. After several unsuccessful attacks, the Zulus drew off again, some elements being detached to round up and drive off the Trekkers' cattle. To mask their retreat, and to prevent the Trekkers from pursuing them, the Zulus set fire to the grass. Most of the army remained camped in the vicinity overnight, but they were clearly discouraged by their inability to break through the Trekker defences, and on the third morning – 15 August – they were content to perform a war-dance and withdraw. The Boers once again rode after them, but their horses were tired and hungry after their confinement in the laager, and they were unable to prevent the Zulus retreating in good order.

The battle of Veglaer – 'fight laager' – as the Boers called it, or emGabeni, the 'battle of the pits', as the Zulus remembered it, had been a stalemate; but given their objectives, it must be considered a Zulu defeat. It was unusual for a Zulu army to continue a fight for more than a day's duration, and now, despite attacking for two days, and remaining in the vicinity for part of the third, they had failed to inflict any significant damage on the Boer position, or to tempt them into the open. Their use of fire and dead ground had shown a sound tactical appreciation of the situation, but ultimately had provided no answers. By reason of their offensive military outlook, their preference for a decisive clash, and the difficulties of supply which Zulu armies traditionally endured when camped in one place for any length of time, it had proved impractical for them to lay siege any longer to the Boer position. Only by capturing Trekker livestock, which not only impoverished the farmers but immobilised their transport, could they make any claim to victory. When the army returned to eMgungundlovu, all the evidence suggests that the king and his councillors were at a loss as to what other methods they could try, and the initiative in the war passed over to the Voortrekkers.

The Trekkers, however, could find little means of ending the stalemate by their own efforts, and in September they sent a deputation to appeal for help from one of the most dynamic Trek leaders. Andries Pretorius, at the age of 39, was younger than most Boer patriarchs, and had already established a reputation as a tough and resourceful commander. A native of Graaf-Reinet in the Eastern Cape, he had proven his mettle when leading a large commando in the Sixth Frontier War of 1834–5. He had taken part in the final stages of the war against Mzilikazi's Ndebele kingdom on the high veld, and had joined Retief's party in Natal. Shortly before Retief's death, he had bought a farm from a British settler, and had returned to Graaf-Reinet to make his final arrangements to leave the colony for good. Physically, he was a tall man, with powerful arms, and in the words of an oft-quoted observer, 'he had a belly on him like a brass drum'. He was confident of his ability as a commander, and the French traveller and naturalist, Adulphe Delagorgue, was amused to note that Pretorius thought himself in the same mould as Napoleon.

Certainly, when Pretorius crossed the mountain passes in November 1837, he transmitted a much-needed air of military briskness to revitalise the demoralised laagers. He was accompanied by 60 armed and mounted men, whose families were following behind with their wagons. He also brought with him a small ship's cannon, mounted on an improvised carriage. He immediately began to make plans to carry the war into the very heart of Zululand.

The lessons of the recent fighting were not lost on Pretorius. It had been mounted commandos who had broken up the Ndebele kingdom, but they had achieved their victories largely through surprise, and the disaster at eThaleni proved that, when operating on Zulu soil, the Natal Trekkers were unlikely to achieve that. At both eThaleni and the Thukela, the Zulus had shown themselves more than capable of withstanding even heavy musketry, and of charging home to overcome scattered formations. Veglaer, by contrast, suggested just how helpless the Zulus were against defences which kept out of range of their stabbing spears, while at the same time exposing them to an efficient killing zone.

Pretorius determined to use the best of both techniques. He assembled 64 wagons, which were loaded only with provisions and ammunition, so as to remain light and manoeuvrable, and to reduce the number of oxen required to pull them – each had a span of just ten oxen, rather than the minimum of sixteen normally needed. Since this was a fighting commando, only men were included, and the women and children were left in the camps below the Kahlamba foothills. Including Pretorius and his deputies, the commando consisted of 472 men, one of the largest forces fielded by the Boers during the Trek. The Boers were accustomed to riding and shooting in their everyday lives, and Pretorius expected them to fight from horseback if necessary. Since each man habitually rode one horse, and employed an *agterryer*, or groom, to look after a spare, there were over 700 horses with the commando; and 200 mixed-race grooms and 130 wagon-drivers were needed to ensure that the column remained mobile.

The commando set out in the first week of December, skirting through the northern reaches of Natal, heading towards the open grassy country which gave access to Zululand along the upper reaches of the Ncome and Mzinyathi Rivers. This terrain was less steep than the broken, rugged country downstream, easier for wagon transport, and less likely to afford the Zulu concealment. At some point along the way, the commando was joined by four settlers from Port Natal, including Alexander Biggar, who was seeking revenge for the death of his sons. Biggar brought with him 120 of his retainers from Port Natal, all of whom were probably trained hunters, armed with muskets, and possibly even experienced in the basics of European military discipline.

In retrospect, it is obvious that the odds, from the start, were stacked in Pretorius's favour, although it can hardly have seemed so to his men. The country through which they moved was only lightly populated, and the commando must have appeared small and vulnerable in the rolling African landscape, framed by the distant blue line of the Berg. The Trekkers were painfully aware that they were outnumbered many times over by Dingane's warriors, and the horrors of Bloukrans and Weenen must have been fresh in their minds. They were individualistic frontiersmen, not professional soldiers, and were not bound by the ties of shared experience, discipline and patriotism that played so important a role in the morale of European armies. They did, however, share a common Calvinistic faith and it required all their reserves of religious conviction to hold them true to their purpose. Pretorius understood this, for he was from the same stock, and every morning and evening he organised services in which his minister, Sarel Celliers, led the commando in prayers and hymns, and instilled in them a sense of righteous purpose.

On 9 December, at a place called Danskraal – where a local chief, hedging his bets against Dingane's defeat, greeted them with a dance of welcome – Celliers for the first time introduced into these services a vow, whereby the Trekkers promised to honour divine help should God grant them a victory. This vow was repeated at each service along the line of advance and over the next few days achieved all the weight of a solemn covenant of faith.

On 15 December, the commando reached the western bank of the Ncome River, whose name, ironically, means 'the pleasant one'. Scouts were sent across the river in advance of the wagons, and rode back to report that they had spotted a Zulu army in the hills a few miles beyond the river. Pretorius himself rode out to confirm the truth of this report, but resisted the suggestions of some of his more aggressive commandants that he should attack immediately. It was already afternoon, and he had no wish to repeat the mistakes of eThaleni. Instead, he decided to take up a defensive position on the western bank of the river, and one or two wagons which had already started to cross were ordered to return.

The Ncome at this point flows through an undulating valley, framed by a saddle-backed hill on the Boer side – later known, inevitably, as Vegkop ('fight hill') – and by ridges two or three miles away on the Zulu side. December is the wet season in southern Africa, and the river was full: a sluggish brown sheet of water several feet deep. It was fordable at two distinct drifts, but in between it flowed through a deep, wide pool, which the Boers described as a *zeekoegat*, or 'hippo-pool'. Here and there the flats on either side were waterlogged and marshy, while reeds grew thickly along the banks. A narrow donga, about eight feet deep – part of a drainage system which carried water away from Vegkop – flowed into the river at the bottom end of the pool.

Pretorius at once saw the defensive possibilities of the spot, and ordered his men to build a laager in the angle between the donga and the river. The Ncome itself would restrict the Zulu approach to the two drifts, making it difficult for them to use their encircling tactics effectively. The donga would protect the laager on one side, while the area immediately around the laager was otherwise flat and open, without a trace of cover. There is an extraordinary monument on the spot today: 64 life-sized wagons, plated with bronze, erected in the 1960s, intended to symbolise the permanence of Afrikaner rule. The modern laager lies about 200 yards from the river and, since it was built more than 120 years after the battle, there must be some question as to the accuracy of its location. Be that as it may, Pretorius might well have placed the laager further back from the river bank than many accounts have suggested, since such a position would have had the advantage of exploiting the river as a barrier, while at the same time depriving the Zulus of its value as potential cover.

The laager itself was roughly circular, with the side facing the donga perhaps straightened to run parallel to it. The disselboom (shaft) of each wagon was run under the one in front, and they were tied together with leather ropes to prevent the Zulus dragging them out of place. Two or three were left free, so that the defenders could pull them out of the line should they wish to make a sortie. Pretorius had taken the precaution of having *vegbekke* (wooden gates or hurdles) prepared as the commando advanced through areas where bush was plentiful, and these were now unloaded and tied into place, so as to block the gaps between and under the wagons.

Contemporary accounts disagree as to the number of cannon with the party, but most probably there were two, placed so as to cover the river on one side, and the open country, to the north and west, on the other. Pretorius had no intention of leaving his livestock outside the laager to be carried away, and plans were made to ensure that all animals could be safely secured inside. Considering that the combined total of horses and oxen was over 1500, this was no easy task; the grooms were instructed to hold four horses each, while the wagon-drivers and voorloopers prepared to tie each span of oxen head-to-head. They then tethered them to the ground, to avoid the risk of their stampeding in panic once the noise of battle had begun.

The Zulus made no attempt to approach the laager that afternoon, and Pretorius had plenty of time to complete his arrangements in peace. That night, the Trekkers kept up their courage by repeating the Vow, and singing hymns. To guard against a surprise attack in darkness, they tied lanterns to their long whip-stocks, and hung them out over the wagons, so that they cast a thin light for a few yards over the surrounding grass.

That the coming clash was likely to be significant was equally apparent to the Zulus. King Dingane had assembled most of the *amabutho* from the heart of the kingdom, although apparently the Hlomendlini regiments had still been left to guard against a sudden attack by the Port Natal settlers. The army which bivouacked that night in the hills beyond the river numbered between 12,000 and 16,000 men, and was led by Dingane's most senior commander, Ndlela kaSompisi. Details of the composition of the force remain sketchy, but its core seems to have consisted of the senior men of the uDlangezwa and iziNyosi *amabutho*, together with the slightly younger uMkhulutshane, all of whom were based at eMgungundlovu itself. A number of subordinate regiments, also associated with eMgungundlovu, were probably attached to them. The uDlambedlu, and the uKhokhoti – a regiment of cadets, not yet properly enrolled, who carried only knobbed sticks instead of spears – made up the younger element.

The Zulu army began its approach before dawn on the 16th. Their scouts had identified the Boer position, which could, in any case, be clearly seen, a flickering circle of light glowing eerily in the pre-dawn mist. Approaching from the south-east, with the younger regiments in advance on either side, ready to throw out horns, the Zulu force hit the river at an angle, with the left horn ahead of the rest. It was still dark when the left horn – principally the uDlambedlu regiment – forded the river at the drift below the hippo-pool, swinging round to cross the donga well clear of the laager, and moving into position to the north-west. Inside the laager, the Trekkers were already awake, and the Port Natal men, who had faced the Zulu army previously, could hear the ominous sound of several thousand feet swishing through the grass, and knew what it portended.

When the sun came up, the sight was awesome. Ndlela had probably intended to be fully deployed by that time, but the river may have delayed him, and only the left horn was actually across the water on the Boer side. The warriors were sitting in neat rows, ten ranks deep, scarcely 200 yards from the north-western face of the laager. The remainder of Ndlela's force could be seen forming up on the hills opposite, a mile away. To one Boer in the laager it seemed that 'all Zululand was out there'. If any of the Trekkers were tempted to run, however, it soon became apparent that there was nowhere to go, since the Zulus surrounded them on every side.

Visitors to the site today are struck by the extent of the area encompassed by 64 wagons, but to the original defenders it must have seemed a

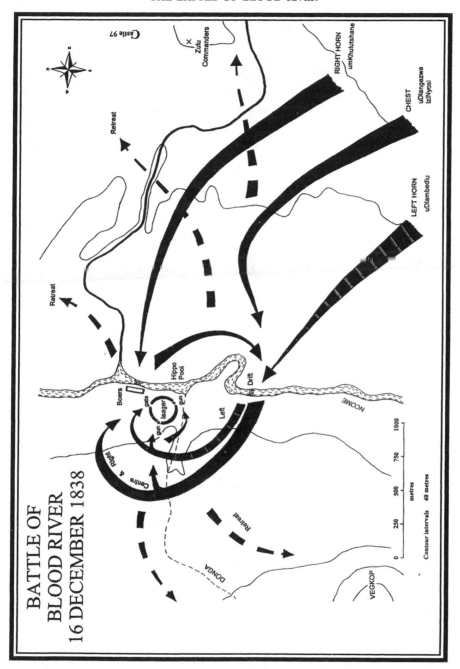

BATTLE OF
BLOOD RIVER
16 DECEMBER 1838

very small island of security indeed. Furthermore, that space was seething with agitated livestock, which probably presented as much of a risk to the laager from the inside as the Zulus did on the outside. The crucial role

43

played by the grooms and drivers in the coming fight should not be over-looked.

Under ideal circumstances, it was customary for a Zulu army to deploy one horn in order to threaten the enemy's line of retreat, but to delay its attack until the remainder of the army was ready to launch a coordinated assault. In practice, this move was always vulnerable, because the encircling horn could often be provoked into launching a premature attack, without support. It was a fundamental weakness of the Zulu military outlook that the warriors, having endured several days of heightened emotional intensity, induced by their pre-combat rituals, could seldom be restrained once they had sighted the enemy. This was particularly true of the younger, less experienced warriors who traditionally made up the horns, and who lacked the reserves of experience and discipline possessed by the older men. This is almost certainly what happened now; no sooner was the sun up than the left horn rose, the warriors drummed their spears on their shields, and without waiting for the rest of the army to come up, they charged.

This initial attack played right into Pretorius's hands. As the left horn rushed forward, their front became constricted, and they inevitably bunched together. Pretorius had placed his men evenly along the *veghekke* and between the wagons, and they opened fire in groups, each man firing after his neighbour, so that by the time a group of eight or ten had fired, the first man had reloaded. The crackle of musketry was therefore continuous; it was a clear, windless day, and a pall of black-powder smoke erupted from the curved wall of the laager, and rose straight up into the sky.

Most of the Boers were armed with ordinary flintlock muskets, but some carried heavy-calibre double-barrelled hunting pieces, called *roers*. The range of even these was limited – most smooth-bore muskets were really only effective at ranges of 80 yards or less – but because the Zulu line of attack was squeezed together, as if through a funnel, the Trekkers could hardly miss. Many, in any case, were firing *loopers* – small canvas bags of shot which disintegrated in flight, spraying across a wide area like a large shotgun. The small ship's cannon were also loaded with canister shot, improvised from musket-balls, stones and pieces of jagged iron.

The sudden fusillade blew great gaps in the Zulu ranks; although they pushed their attack to within a few yards of the wagons, the uDlambedlu could not stand before the terrible fire, and retired out of range. Having regrouped, however, they came forward again, but with the same result. Several times they courageously attempted to brave the fire, but after half-a-dozen attacks it became clear that they had no hope of forcing an entry. Instead, some elements veered to their right, and poured down into the donga which ran along the southern face of the laager. This afforded them some protection from the relentless fusillade, but the warriors were still packed so close that they could scarcely move. Some, indeed, were lying or crouching down, sheltering with their shields on their backs, reluctant to climb the banks to attempt to cross the few feet of open ground that separated them from the laager.

Pretorius, seeing his chance, called for some of his men to ride out and attack the Zulus. The Boers lined the lip of the donga and fired down at point-blank range into the mass of cowering warriors who, unable to move, suffered fearful casualties. Those uDlambedlu who survived began to lose heart and retired from the field in confusion. The Boers rode after them, firing at any groups who tried to rally, and scattering the Zulus towards Vegkop or the river.

By this time, the remainder of the army was manoeuvring into position. The main body had come to a halt on the hills across the river, and the Zulu commanders had taken up a position on a nearby knoll which gave a good view of the battlefield. The right horn, the uMkhulutshane and associated units from eMgungundlovu, was advancing rapidly towards the second drift upstream, above the hippo-pool. As it advanced across the flats and marshy hollows, it was lost to sight to the laager, and was in any case too far away for the Trekkers to fire upon. Instead, Pretorius ordered some of the mounted men – who were probably still wandering the field hunting down members of the uDlambedlu – to move out and line the bank above the drift before the Zulus could reach it. As the uMkhulutshane rose from cover, therefore, and prepared to enter the water, they encountered a sudden heavy fire from the opposite bank.

Any attempt to cross the river under such circumstances was clearly impossible. Instead, they retired out of range once more, and moved southwards, heading towards the drift by which the left horn had crossed before dawn. By the time they reached it, the chest – the uDlangezwa and iziNyosi – had also advanced, and were close behind them. The *amabutho* waded through the drift in densely packed masses. Only the young cadets, the uKhokhoti, were kept back with the commanders as a reserve. Pretorius took advantage of the lull to turn one of his cannon on the Zulu command group, and a shell arced across the river to explode close to the Zulu generals. The Boers took consolation in the fact that several men appeared to be hit.

Once across the drift, the right horn spread out to launch its attack over the same ground covered so unsuccessfully by the left horn an hour or so previously. There can be no doubting Pretorius's judgement in his selection of the site; try as they might, the Zulu *amabutho* could neither find room to manoeuvre properly, nor to attack on all sides at once. The attacks of the uMkhulutshane were no more successful than those of the uDlambedlu; they rushed forward over the corpses of their comrades, only to be driven back by the same heavy fire. There was scarcely time for the Boers to load and aim; they simply poured powder down the barrels, slipped in the ball, thumped the butt hard on the ground instead of ramming, then pointed the muzzle over the barricade. The excitement, noise and fury of battle must have been intense – the boom of the guns, the war-cries of the Zulus, the screams and shouts of the wounded, all mingling with the lowing of the terrified cattle inside the laager, and heightened by the acrid smell of powder, blood, and dung. The assault on the senses was so overwhelming that one Boer veteran recalled, 'of that fight nothing remains in my memory except shouting and tumult and lamentation, and a sea of black faces; and a dense smoke that rose straight as a plumb line upwards from the ground'.

After several attempts, the right horn gave up its assaults. There was some confusion and congestion as the older men of the chest pushed forward through them to take up the front line, making disparaging remarks about the courage of the lads who comprised the horns. In fact, however, the Zulu forces were becoming badly disorganised, and the attacks launched by the chest were just as uncoordinated, and no more successful, than those of their predecessors. By late morning, the warriors were showing a marked reluctance to respond to the shouts of their commanders, and Pretorius judged the moment right to make a counter-attack.

Those wagons which had been left to serve as gates were rolled aside, and most of the Boer force rode out on horseback. As they saw them coming, the Zulus began to rise up and drift away, and the Boers rode in among them in groups, shooting them down from the saddle. Now the Zulu resolve collapsed completely, and the warriors, exhausted by several hours of pointless and costly actions, began to abandon the field. Many fled towards Vegkop, with the Boers in pursuit, while a dense mob plunged into the river to escape to the opposite bank. Here, however, they were desperately vulnerable to Boer fire, and parties of Trekkers lined the bank and mowed them down as they struggled helplessly in the water. According to Sarel Celliers:

> When they saw that there would be no escape, as we were driving them towards the sea-cow hole, they jumped into the water and

were among the rushes at the river's edge. I believe that all were killed, that not one escaped. I was witness to the fact that the water looked like a pool of blood; whence came the name of Blood River.

Many warriors tried to hide in the shallows, cowering among the reeds, or submerging themselves in the water, with only their nostrils exposed in order to breathe. Once the Boers realised what was happening, they searched them out, firing into the water where any obstruction broke the surface. Visiting the site two years later, the traveller Delagorgue was shocked by the sight of 'a large number of whitened bones and many [Zulu] skulls lying scattered in the long grass', and by the casual way the Boers talked of 'the sport of picking off their helpless prey'. Yet all their terrible sufferings of the past year must have come to mind in the final moments of the battle, and few of the Trekkers thought of anything but vengeance.

The pursuit did not stop once the Zulus had crossed the river. The Trekkers chased them relentlessly, even shooting at wounded men and corpses to ensure that they were not shamming. Probably, this stage of the fighting accounted for the heaviest casualties, as exhausted men wounded in earlier attacks were shot down without offering resistance. After the battle was over, the laager was surrounded by so many dead that, in Sarel Celliers's words, they lay 'thick on the ground as pumpkins on a fertile piece of garden soil'.

It is impossible to say how many Zulus died; according to Boer accounts as many as 1000 were killed around the laager, and 2000 more on the plain opposite. This does seem an extremely high figure, and probably the numbers seemed greater than they actually were to men who were not professional soldiers, and were unaccustomed to the aftermath of battle. Nevertheless, there is no doubt that the Zulu losses were heavy, if only because the Boers allowed few of the wounded to escape, and the survivors fled the field in something very close to a rout.

On the Boer side, only three men had been injured. One of them was Pretorius himself, who had dismounted to shoot a Zulu during the pursuit, only to be attacked by the man he was trying to kill. Pretorius's strength saved him, for he grabbed the stabbing spear by the blade, and wrestled the man to the ground, suffering a nasty cut to his right hand, until another Boer came up and shot the Zulu dead.

To the Boers, the victory seemed nothing short of miraculous, in which they clearly saw the hand of God. True to their word, they celebrated the anniversary of the battle each year with a religious service, and 16

December still has a special significance among many sectors of the Afrikaner community.

Once the Boers had recovered from the fight, they broke up the laager and, leaving the Zulu dead where they lay, advanced on eMgungundlovu in the hope of capturing King Dingane. They knew they were to be disappointed, however, long before they reached the royal homestead on 20 December, once their scouts spotted a huge pall of smoke rising up from the emaKhosini valley. The king had abandoned eMgungundlovu, and set it on fire. The Trekkers poked about in the ruins and looted what souvenirs they could. On the following day they made the melancholy discovery of the bones of Retief's party on the hill of execution. After burying them, they moved up onto the Mthonjaneni ridge.

The expedition, while undoubtedly a military success, so far bore very few tangible fruits of victory, and this probably explains the laxness which now almost led to disaster. On 27 December a mounted commando rode out with a Zulu deserter to round up cattle which were said to be lurking in the uPathe valley, near its junction with the White Mfolozi. It was a trap. The deserter, Bhongoza kaMefu, led the Boers into broken ground where they were suddenly attacked. Only luck and hard riding enabled them to slip through the Zulu cordon, but five whites and several of their retainers were killed. Among those who died was Alexander Biggar, who had refused to desert his retainers, who were on foot; his family had paid the final price for its adventuring in the Zulu kingdom.

Despite this narrow escape, the commando retired from Zululand confident of its success. Zulu sources point out, however, that it hardly lingered on its way back to the camps along the Kahlamba foothills, and claim some credit for cutting short the Boer expedition. Nevertheless, Pretorius and his men were greeted enthusiastically, and christened the *Wencommando* – the Victory Commando – a stark contrast to the ignominious *Vlugcommando* of eThaleni – the commando that ran away.

How decisive an event was the battle of Blood River? Perhaps rather less so than has often been claimed. No attempt was made to occupy Zulu territory, the Zulu army was not dispersed, and the Boers had failed to depose Dingane. Indeed, the king merely responded to the setback by building a new eMgungundlovu on the northern bank of the Black Mfolozi, a few miles beyond the Boer reach. In fact, the two sides had fought each other to a standstill, yet the Zulu kingdom remained intact, and the Boers lacked the resources to exploit their advantage. The true state of affairs is suggested by the peace accord which the Trekkers struck with Dingane in March the following year; Dingane allowed the Boers to remain unmolested in Natal, provided they made no further attacks on his territory. He agreed to pay a large fine in cattle to recompense the Trekkers for livestock taken in the attacks on the Kahlamba encampments but, significantly, he felt confident enough to ignore most of his obligations. Instead, Dingane tried – unsuccessfully, as it turned out – to counter the threat of increasing European encroachment by opening up lands north of the Phongolo River for Zulu settlement. This plan was frustrated when a major campaign to subdue the area was defeated by Swazi resistance in 1839.

The final resolution of the Zulu–Trekker conflict, when it came, was rich in ironies. For one thing, the peace accord of 1839 had been arranged through the medium of the one group the Trekkers feared most – the British. News of the slaughter in Natal had succeeded where the scheming of a generation of British settlers had failed, and it had attracted the attention of the authorities in distant Cape Town. Early in 1838 a small detachment of British troops was sent to occupy Port Natal, to establish a British claim to the area, and to try to prevent further fighting. In this last respect, arriving as it did shortly before Blood River, it was ineffectual, but the officer in charge did succeed in brokering the initial peace treaty between the warring parties once the fighting was over. Although this force, which was far too small to exert any direct control over the Trekkers, was soon withdrawn, it remained an indication of heightened British awareness of the region.

Shortly afterwards, however, the dispute was brought to a conclusion by a split in the Zulu Royal House. Prince Mpande kaSenzangakhona – the same man who had been nominally in charge of the forces which had routed John Cane at the Thukela river – took advantage of Dingane's preoccupation with northern Zululand to defect across the Thukela. This was hardly a new phenomenon – disaffected chiefs had been doing it since Dingane's succession – but what was staggering was the extent of Mpande's support. He took with him no less than 17,000 followers and 25,000 head of cattle, and many of the important chiefs and state officials on the coastal sector, including Nongalaza kaNondela and Zulu kaNogandaya, went with him. This was nothing less than a split in the kingdom, and it reflected the extent to which many Zulus were disillusioned with Dingane's rule. Even today, Mpande's flight is remembered as 'breaking the rope that held the nation together'.

At first the Trekkers regarded Mpande with some suspicion, but once convinced of his genuine intentions, they realised that they could use him to their advantage. Mpande offered to field an army and, with Boer support, finally to drive out Dingane. In the event, it was Mpande's forces, led by Nongalaza, who defeated Zulu loyalists at the battle of the

Magqongqo Hills in January 1840. The battle was over before Pretorius's commando reached the front, although their imminent arrival undoubtedly played an important part by serving to unnerve Dingane's forces.

The Maqongqo Hills finally broke Dingane's power. He retired to the foothills of the northern Lebombo Mountains and tried to rebuild his kingdom with those loyal followers who clung to him. But his prestige had been destroyed, and – an unwelcome guest – he was assassinated a few months later by members of the Nyawo chiefdom, whose lands he had occupied. By that time, the Boers had already given their support to Mpande, who was installed as king: the third of Senzangakhona's sons to rule the great kingdom.

In fact, the practical role played by the Trekkers in Dingane's final defeat had been limited, but the price they demanded for it was high, and Mpande knew he dare not provoke them. The Trekkers appropriated thousands of head of cattle, and grandly extended their claims to Zulu territory up to the Mfolozi River, annexing nearly half the kingdom – far more land, in fact, than there were farmers to occupy it. In the event, however, in the final ironic twist to the story, they had little enough time to enjoy their victory.

In 1842, disturbed by the unsettling effect Trekker policies were having on the region as a whole, British troops returned to Port Natal. Pretorius refused to accept their authority, and fighting broke out on the fringe of the great lagoon. More troops were rushed up from the Cape, and Trekker resistance collapsed. Natal became a British colony, and many Boers, disgusted by the prospect of living under British rule once more, trekked back across the mountains and into the interior.

In two decades of struggle, Natal had passed from the nominal control of the Zulu kings to that of the Boers, and finally to the British. In due course, the logic of that shift would bring all three groups into further conflict. In the meantime, King Mpande agreed to fix the southern boundaries of the kingdom for the first time. An Anglo–Zulu accord specified the Natal–Zulu border as the line of the Mzinyathi and Thukela rivers – an agreement which allowed Mpande quietly to recover all the territory the Boers had extracted from him.

— 3 —

THE BATTLE OF 'NDONDAKUSUKA
2 December 1856
'...the place of bones'

Until quite recently, it has been accepted wisdom that King Mpande was a weak and ineffectual leader. He was, it was said, so physically lazy that he became obese and in later life had to be pushed around in a small cart by his attendants; he was a simpleton, who survived only because his subjects had so little respect for him that they could afford to ignore his authority. He possessed none of his elder brothers' attributes, for he was neither strong, like Shaka, nor subtle, like Dingane.

An idle, fat, ineffectual fool. If ever a man successfully obscured his true nature, then, it was Mpande. The more astute whites who spent time in his company were shocked and surprised to find that there was far more to the new king than his public reputation suggested. The Frenchman, Delagorgue, who met him at the time of his defection to the Boers in 1839, found far more to admire in him than in the Trekkers, and was moved to compare him to a Roman emperor:

> The large, well-shaped, brilliant black eyes were overshadowed by a jutting brow, surmounted by a high, square forehead on which a few early wrinkles were beginning to show; the nose was not unusual, except for the flaring well-defined nostrils, the mouth was wide with a ready smile expressive of quick comprehension, and the square chin indicative of strength; in all it was a well-shaped head borne upon a superb body, shining and stout.

The missionary, William Colenso, on a visit to Zululand in the 1860s, commented that 'his appearance and acts were very unlike those of the "bloated, sensual, peevish, stupid old man", which common reports describe him to be'. And indeed, the bare facts of Mpande's reign give the lie to his ineffectual reputation. The third of Senzangakhona's sons to rule the kingdom, he also ruled it the longest, for over 30 years. Almost alone among his father's extensive progeny, he died peacefully, on his own sleeping mat.

He had inherited a kingdom split down the middle by civil war; patiently and carefully, he rebuilt it, facing a host of internal and external threats the likes of which his brothers had never dreamed. He manipulated and controlled the great chiefs within the kingdom, restored royal authority and revitalised the *amabutho* system, despite the growing European encroachment on his borders and the corrosive effects of white economic penetration. On his death in 1872, he passed over to his heir a kingdom which was not perhaps as robust as it had been in the golden days before 1838, but which had survived as a vibrant political and economic entity. Judged by that yardstick, Mpande was perhaps the most successful king of all.

When Mpande succeeded to the throne in February 1840, it was to a kingdom split and devastated by war. Although Dingane was defeated, many Zulus had remained loyal to him until the moment of his death, and only then returned from the northern borders to offer their allegiance to his successor. Such were the divisions within the kingdom that Dingane's followers were derisively nicknamed 'the rectum of Ndlela' – after their master's great supporter – by those who had had the wit to change sides earlier. Mpande received them with typical statesmanship, welcoming them back into the kingdom, and banning the use of such provocative talk. Yet it would take much more to bind the kingdom together than a policy of forgiveness. Both sides in the recent civil war had courted the great chiefly lines of Zululand – the so-called *izikhulu*, or great ones of the nation – and the price of success for either would involve allowing the chiefs a measure of independence that would have been unthinkable a decade earlier. The 'breaking of the rope' marked the point at which the *izikhulu* realised for the first time the extent to which royal power rested on their support, and it was a lesson they never forgot again. The reigns of both Mpande and his successor, Cetshwayo, were marked by a distinct tension between the power of the state at the centre and those who exercised it at regional levels.

Nevertheless, Mpande faced this problem with characteristic pragmatism. Important supporters such as Nongalaza kaNondela were rewarded, while supporters of the old regime were marginalised or killed off on pretext of practising witchcraft. Whole sections of the community, like the Mandlakazi of chief Maphitha kaSojiyisa, whose ruling lineage were descended from the family of Senzangakhona, Mpande's father, and who were therefore a subordinate section of the Royal House itself, were allowed to govern themselves with only nominal interference by the king. The Mandlakazi, in any case, lived north of the Black Mfolozi, a long way from the new centres of royal authority. Mpande built his new royal homestead, kwaNodwengu, on the Mahlabathini plain, across the White Mfolozi from eMgungundlovu. He was content to let Maphitha govern almost as an ally rather than a subject, and such was Maphitha's influence that the king was reluctant to make important decisions of state unless he was present at the royal councils. Although this, and similar, concessions undoubtedly helped the kingdom to survive at the time, the long-term repercussions would be serious.

To offset the growing power of the regional chiefs, Mpande tried to revitalise the army, despite powerful forces working against him. As Dingane had done with Shaka's regiments before him, Mpande, on his accession, allowed several of Dingane's regiments to marry and disperse. He continued to enrol new regiments, although he waged a constant battle with the regional chiefs, who made excuses to hold back their young men whenever a new regiment was formed. Moreover, the existence of colonial Natal on the borders, with its settler-driven economy which the Zulu kings could no longer pretend to control, offered a tempting alternative to service in the *amabutho* to many young men who were only too aware that life in the colony carried fewer obligations, and that brides there were easier to come by, than in Zululand. Natal's relatively open policy towards immigration from Zululand meant that hundreds of Zulus slipped across the borders each year.

To make service in the Zulu state more attractive, Mpande lessened the more irksome restraints on the *amabutho*, and lowered the age at which the men were permitted to marry. The flood of refugees only really dwindled to a trickle, however, once Natal became worried about the rise in its African population, and took action to slow it down; and many Africans came to realise that life under white rule, too, had its price.

In other respects, the population growth in colonial Natal – nearly 5000 immigrants from Britain flooded into the region between 1849 and 1852 – threatened to undermine the authority of the Zulu monarchy. Not only had the king to abandon his claim to the allegiance of those groups living south of the Thukela, but he found his foreign policy restricted by the need to maintain a good relationship with the British. Instead, Mpande looked to the north, and in the 1850s mounted a series of expeditions into southern Swaziland which, for a while, brought the area north of the Phongolo River under Zulu control, and offered the possibility of extending royal authority into new areas, hitherto untouched by European penetration.

Zululand, in contrast, was increasingly open to a flood of white hunters and traders, despite the king's attempts to limit them to specific areas. It became almost impossible for him to maintain his monopoly over European trade goods, and his economic position was undermined as traders sold openly to the regional chiefs, who grew rich at the royal expense. Furthermore, since the traders chiefly sold beads and blankets in exchange for cattle, many thousands of head were driven out of the kingdom each year, to the nation's impoverishment. White hunters, too, began the systematic onslaught on Zululand's wildlife, which only halted in the 1930s, when there was precious little left to shoot. Ironically, Mpande at least tried to turn the activities of the whites to some advantage, demanding a gift of firearms as the price for operating in his territory. Thus, from the late 1840s, the Zulu army had access for the first time to small quantities of Western weapons.

Despite these very real threats, Mpande had restored the kingdom to some sort of equilibrium by the 1850s. Then, tragically, it was to be torn apart in a way that was almost as dramatic as 'the breaking of the rope', and decidedly more bloody. And the cause of this disaster lay with Mpande himself.

The question of legitimate succession to the Zulu throne was always a complex one. Despite persistent rumours to the contrary, neither Shaka nor Dingane had fathered children. Those closest to the line of succession, therefore, were their brothers, and it is no coincidence that both ultimately fell victim to their father's sons; although the realities of Zulu politics were such that the stabbing spear was most often the means of ushering in a new regime, this was nonetheless only regarded as legitimate if the new claimant was of royal blood. Mpande, by contrast, had many children by his various wives, no less than 29 boys and 23 girls, according to one recent study. As children of the Royal House, their prestige within the kingdom was immense, and tension regarding the question of succession was, perhaps, inevitable.

In Zulu custom, the issue was not a new one and in a polygamous society there were specific rules that addressed it. Each married man nominated a Great Wife from among his household; she was seldom his first wife, and was usually a woman of considerable rank and influence in her own right. It was the first son of the Great Wife who was regarded as his father's legitimate heir. In households where the patriarch was inclined to blur the rules, however, it was not unknown for other sons to be favoured, while the sons of the first wife had to accept that boys born after them might succeed to their father's estate.

Mpande's Great Wife was Ngqumbazi, who was a member of the leading lineage of the influential Zungu people. Mpande had married Ngqumbazi in Shaka's time, and Shaka himself had paid *ilobolo* – the transfer of cattle to the bride's family which underpinned the marriage contract – on his younger brother's behalf. About 1832, Ngqumbazi had borne Mpande a son, ironically named Cetshwayo – 'the slandered one'. When Mpande 'broke the rope' in 1839, he had presented Cetshwayo to the Boer leadership as his heir, and the Boers, worried that their new ally might be killed by Dingane and his obligations forgotten in any ensuing confusion, clipped a piece out of Cetshwayo's ear, marking him as if he were a cow.

As Cetshwayo grew up, however, Mpande began to reconsider the question of the succession. There were several reasons for this; for one thing, the young Cetshwayo was a handsome, confident youth who carried his royal bearing in his manner, and Mpande began to feel uneasy that his own position might one day be threatened. For another, Mpande's relationship with Cetshwayo and his mother was not close; he preferred the company of another wife, Monase, and her son, Mbuyazi. Monase had been one of King Shaka's *isigodlo* girls (handmaidens) and had been given in marriage to Mpande by the founder of the nation himself, so that Mpande could raise a son who was regarded, according to the complicated Zulu laws of genealogy, as the son and heir of Shaka himself. Mpande therefore began to speak of Mbuyazi as Shaka's son, a sure hint that he was favouring him for the succession. Mbuyazi was only a few months younger than his brother, and when the royal princes became teenagers, tension began to build between them, and Mpande deliberately seemed to play one off against the other, tormenting Cetshwayo with the thought that his succession was by no means inevitable. When pressed by his councillors to avoid trouble and settle the issue, Mpande replied fatalistically, 'I won my kingship by force of arms, so must others do likewise ... Our house did not gain the kingship by being appointed to sit on a mat [i.e. by peaceful succession] ... Our house gained the kingship by stabbing with the assegai.'

That his sons might do the same was becoming apparent by the early 1850s. Mpande had attempted to keep trouble at bay by preventing them from establishing a power base in any particular region. In this he was completely unsuccessful. He placed Cetshwayo under the watchful eye of his relatives at the emLambongwenya royal homestead near modern Eshowe, while his mother, Ngqumbazi, had been set to rule over the kwaGqikazi *ikhanda*, north of the Black Mfolozi, at the other end of the country. As Cetshwayo grew up, however, it proved impossible to prevent him visiting his mother for long periods. This brought the prince into contact with the cadets who reported to kwaGqikazi at the start of their national service, and with the *amabutho* which represented their nominal headquarters. It was among these young men that Cetshwayo first started to court a following, and by the 1850s he had also established links with the powerful northern chiefdoms, including the Mandlakazi, to the west of kwaGqikazi, and the Buthelezi chiefdom to the south.

In this respect Cetshwayo seems to have had one advantage over Mbuyazi; a big man with a broad chest and a handsome, open face, Cetshwayo presented a friendly manner, despite occasional bouts of moodiness or temper. He talked freely to anyone, but was not above treating elders and chiefs with the respect their age and rank required. Mbuyazi, however, who was tall, with a light complexion and hooded eyes, and a distinctive tuft of hair on the nape of his neck, had a tendency to arrogance which offended the *izikhulu* and intimidated commoners.

Like every other Zulu male, the princes were enrolled in *amabutho*; and being of a similar age both became members of the uThulwana, which Mpande raised about 1850. Indeed, so many sons of Mpande, as well as sons of regional chiefs, were in the uThulwana that it was considered a cut above other regiments, assuming airs of privilege which only Mnyamana kaNgqengele, the strong-willed and astute chief of the Buthelezi and one of Mpande's closest advisers, could control. In 1852, the uThulwana were employed in one of Mpande's Swazi expeditions, and according to one story the young Cetshwayo distinguished himself by scattering an enemy patrol in hand-to-hand combat. Certainly the campaign did not do his reputation any harm, and he emerged from it with his personal prestige considerably enhanced. His followers were already beginning to think of themselves as a distinct grouping, and took to referring to themselves as uSuthu. This was an allusion to one of Mpande's expeditions; in 1851 he had raided the Pedi chiefdom in the north-eastern Transvaal. The Pedi had retired to natural strongholds rather than fight, but had to abandon their cattle. Mpande's *impi* returned home driving thousands of head of distinctive long-horned Sotho cattle. By calling themselves uSuthu, Cetshwayo's young followers were drawing on the image of these seemingly limitless herds, and the overtones of Zulu military superiority that the incident implied. In response, Mbuyazi's followers began to call themselves iziGqoza, from a verb meaning 'to drop down like drops of water', a reference to the steady trickle of supporters joining their cause. It did not escape Mpande's notice, however, that Cetshwayo's popularity was far greater than that of his favourite, Mbuyazi.

The king's response to the growing tension was once again to try to avoid a confrontation. To cut Cetshwayo off from his power-base in the north, he built a new royal homestead, oNdini, near Eshowe, in the south-eastern part of the country, and placed him there. Mbuyazi was ordered to establish his homesteads along the upper reaches of the White Mfolozi; the king's own favourite residence, kwaNodwengu, lay square between them. Nevertheless, this compromise, too, was a failure. For one thing, the king himself could not resist indicating where his support lay, presumably in the hope of persuading more of his subjects to join Mbuyazi. On one occasion, still remembered in Zulu folklore, the king presented war-shields to both sons at the head of their regiment. Both were cut from the same hide, and Cetshwayo, as the senior, was entitled to the shield taken from the side which bore the spear-mark that had killed the beast, since this was believed to have particular properties. At the last minute, however, Mpande took up both shields and crossed them over, tossing the senior one at Mbuyazi's feet. This was a public insult which many Zulus believed marked the start of open hostilities between the two princes. On another occasion, the king called up parties of both the uSuthu and iziGqoza to dance before him, and while heaping praise on the iziGqoza, was dismissive of the uSuthu.

If Mpande hoped to force Cetshwayo to back down, however, he had seriously misjudged the situation. In 1855 or early 1856, the two princes asked permission to conduct a hunt in the sparsely populated bush-country at the confluence of the Black and White Mfolozi Rivers – the traditional hunting ground of the Zulu kings since Shaka's time, and today, incidentally, part of the Mfolozi game reserve. They had clearly resolved to decide the issue, since both sides turned out carrying war-shields rather than the smaller *amahawu* shields usually used in hunting. The iziGqoza planned to reached the appointed rendezvous first, and to lie in wait for Cetshwayo's party; but they were unnerved to find that the uSuthu were already in position before them, and in large numbers. The iziGqoza backed out of an armed confrontation, but nevertheless marched home singing a chant that was heavily suggestive of their true intentions. 'We almost got the buck,' they sang. 'We almost stabbed it.'

Realising that an armed clash was imminent, Mpande tried to push Mbuyazi along a similar route to the one by which he had himself seized power. In November 1856 he gave permission for the iziGqoza to move from the White Mfolozi, and occupy instead a tract of land just north of the Thukela. This was the same area he had occupied as a prince under Dingane, and it offered Mbuyazi the chance either to flee into Natal or secure the support of the Natal authorities. The threat to Cetshwayo, however, whose own oNdini homestead was close by, was obvious. No sooner had Mbuyazi arrived in his new territory than Cetshwayo, urged on by some of his more powerful friends, who feared that Mbuyazi might yet outwit them, began to muster his allies. Even Maphitha kaSojiyisa despatched a large force of Mandlakazi down from the north to support him. This was not lost on Mbuyazi, who by the end of November, was gathering his own adherents and their cattle, and making preparations to decamp across the Thukela. At the same time, following his father's example, he made a serious effort to secure the support of the settler community in Natal.

It is an interesting comment on the extent of white penetration of Zululand at this time that at least one settler, a trader named Rathbone, had a house on the northern bank of the Thukela, while despite the obvious imminence of civil war, a number of traders had been operating freely in the country. Most tried to leave the country at the last moment, driving huge herds of cattle with them, only to find that Mbuyazi was moving in the same direction, and that the war was likely to break out around them. The traders and their wives had congregated on the northern bank of the Thukela River, in the vicinity of the Lower Drift, but early summer rains had swollen the river, and it was impossible to get their wagons safely across into Natal. Mbuyazi appealed for help to Rathbone, who directed him to Captain Joshua Walmesley, the colonial border agent on the Natal bank, opposite the drift. Walmesley quite rightly refused to intervene without official sanction, and sent off to Pietermaritzburg for advice. Meanwhile, however, he gave permission to his assistant, a young hunter and adventurer by the name of John Dunn, to cross into Zululand with about 30 of Walmesley's African police, ostensibly to try to head off a confrontation.

John Dunn was an interesting character who was to have a considerable impact on the history of the old Zulu kingdom, so it is worth pausing to consider his background. His father, Robert Dunn, was born in Scotland and came to South Africa as an 1820 settler. He married the daughter of Alexander Biggar, and in 1834 moved to Natal. John Dunn was born that same year. When Biggar moved to Natal, Robert Dunn continued to associate with him, and prospered as a hunter and trader. He escaped the war with Dingane that devastated the Biggar family, but the hazards of frontier life caught up with him, and in 1847 he was trampled to death by an elephant. John Dunn struck out on his own after his father's death, and worked as a transport rider. When, however, he was cheated of his wages by an unscrupulous employer, he turned his back on settler society, and crossed the Thukela to adopt a semi-nomadic lifestyle, abandoning the European ways and becoming, instead, a 'white Zulu'.

In 1854, a hunting party that included Joshua Walmesley came across John Dunn living near the amaTigulu River. Walmesley persuaded Dunn to return to Natal and work with him as his assistant. Dunn was an expert horseman and a crack shot, but throughout his life he remained more at home in Zulu society than among Europeans. Despite Walmesley's instructions, it seems that Dunn agreed to cross the Thukela in 1856 not so much to make peace, but in search of adventure, and in the hope of a reward should the iziGqoza prove victorious.

By the end of November, it was clear that a clash was imminent. Hundreds of iziGqoza non-combatants, with all their cattle and possessions, were sheltered in the valleys among the hills running down to the northern bank of the river. In all, there were, perhaps, 20,000 iziGqoza, although Mbuyazi's fighting men, deployed beyond the civilians in the direction of Cetshwayo's approach, numbered only about 7000 of these. Many of the white traders had temporarily abandoned their wagons on the Zulu bank, but had driven their cattle across to a large sandbank which was only a few yards from the Natal side. Sadly, the water, while only four feet deep across most of the drift, flowed through a narrow channel fifteen feet deep between the sand-bar and the safety of the Natal bank. A number of the men decided to take their chances with John Dunn's group, but most were determined to remain neutral, and clustered on the sandbank with their cattle.

Prince Cetshwayo's army, steadily approaching from the north, was between 15,000 and 20,000 strong, nearly three times that of Mbuyazi. Moreover, Cetshwayo brought only his fighting men and a few young mat-carriers with him, and so was not hampered by huge numbers of non-combatants. By the evening of 30 November, the uSuthu had reached the valley of the Mandeni stream, only a few miles from Mbuyazi's position. Both armies were preparing for a fight, and if Dunn had ever hoped to avert a collision, it must have been apparent even to him that this was now impossible.

The impending battle was to prove one of the most destructive in Zulu history, and it was to be fought out by armies which represented both the strength of the *amabutho* system, and its limitations as a means of overcoming regional tensions. Because this was a civil war, many of King Mpande's *amabutho* had split along local lines, men from an area loyal to Mbuyazi deserting their regiment to serve instead with their chosen master, and vice versa. In some areas, where regional chiefs were particularly strong, and their influence overreached that of the king, warriors had turned out to fight specifically with their chiefs, rather than with their regiments. Both armies therefore consisted of a mixed bag of *amabutho* and local troops.

Perhaps because the uSuthu forces were much larger, and because they survived to tell the tale, the names of the *amabutho* fighting for Cetshwayo are better remembered than those who fought for Mbuyazi. The uSuthu forces consisted of the uDlambedlu, iSangqu, uThulwana, iNdlondlo, iNdabakawombe, uDloko and izinGulube *amabutho*. Few of these regiments were complete, however, and a number of individuals from each were on the other side. The uSuthu were supported by the abaQulusi (descendants of an *ikhanda* founded by Shaka in northern Zululand, who fought as a regional rather than an age-grade regiment), by the Mandlakazi (Chief Maphitha's people) and by members of the Zungu, Mdlalose and Cube chiefdoms.

There is evidence to suggest that many of Cetshwayo's followers had brought with them their splendid ceremonial costumes, normally reserved for great national gatherings, and would wear them in action. Although Mbuyazi had divided his forces into *amaviyo* (companies), it would appear that none of his father's *amabutho* had given him unqualified support, and that his troops were therefore much less organised. Mbuyazi's followers, lacking established uniforms, had sought a sense of common identity by adopting a particular war-badge, which consisted of two strips of cowhide worn upright at the centre of their headdress, with bushy cow-tails attached to the tips. Both sides had armed themselves with a new type of war-shield, the *umbhumbulozu*, which was perhaps a foot shorter than the *isihlangu* – the great shield of Shaka's day – and was easier to wield in combat.

Dunn's followers, constituting the one essentially European element on either side, numbered perhaps 200 men, most of them trained African hunters, and were led by a handful of whites. They, too, had found a common sense of identity, and called themselves iziNqobo, 'the crushers'. The conflict had split the royal family down the middle, too; Mbuyazi had at least five of Mpande's sons with him, while Cetshwayo counted on the allegiance of six more. Significantly, few of the great notables of the kingdom supported Mbuyazi, but accompanying his troops was Nongalaza kaNondela, Mpande's faithful general, whose personal homestead lay near by. Nogalaza's participation was probably an attempt by the king to lend his favourite some much-needed practical experience.

On 1 December, Cetshwayo called his warriors into a circle to receive the final preparations for war. They were sprinkled with magical medicines which were supposed to ensure their superiority in the coming fight. Such was the prestige of Cetshwayo's war-doctor, Manembe kaGagamela, that many believed he had secured victory for the uSuthu even before the battle began. John Dunn, watching the proceedings through a telescope from a distance, urged Mbuyazi to try to hurry his men across the river, but his suggestion was turned down by some of Mbuyazi's brothers, who scoffed at Dunn for wanting to run away. The best Dunn could do was try to persuade Mbuyazi to attack instead, reducing the risk that the iziGqoza would be pinned against the river. His warriors were also prepared for war, and the two armies gingerly moved forward to probe each other. It was by now late afternoon, however, and apart from a few shots fired by Dunn at the uSuthu scouts, both sides were reluctant to commit themselves, with evening drawing on, and retired to their respective camping grounds. That night, both armies were drenched by a thunderstorm which seemed particularly to discourage the iziGqoza, who were convinced that it had been conjured up by Manembe.

When dawn broke on 2 December the sun rose on a damp, miserable day. The uSuthu broke camp and advanced down the Mandeni stream, taking up a position on the hills to the west, known as Masomongca. Below them, across the valley, the ground rose beyond the stream towards another ridge, and it was here that the iziGqoza deployed. From their respective positions, the two brothers faced each other for the last time across a few hundred yards of undulating country, lightly scattered with bush. Most of Mbuyazi's non-combatants had hidden in the valleys behind him, down towards the Thukela. Ironically, between Mbuyazi's position and the river lay the distinctive hill where Zulu kaNogandaya's 'Ndondakusuka homestead had once stood; the sons of Mpande were about to fight to the death on precisely the same ground where their father had won his greatest victory, eighteen years before.

Mbuyazi's warriors were drawn up in companies, with their left flank resting above a stream called Nkwaku, which flowed down to join the Mandeni. Along this ridge some of his men set fire to the grass behind them, marking the point beyond which, they said, they would not retreat. Despite this defiant gesture, however, a chill ran through the iziGqoza ranks when a puff of wind lifted an ostrich feather out of Mbuyazi's headdress, and cast it at his feet; an omen whose meaning was only too clear.

On the opposite ridge, the uSuthu, by contrast, faced battle confident of victory, for Cetshwayo had taken the trouble to secure a war-shield which had once belonged to Mbuyazi, and in front of his men had tossed it on the ground and knelt on it. In his followers' eyes, this assured him of invincible *itonya* – the mystical force by which one side in battle secured supernatural ascendancy over the other. Details of the exact uSuthu deployment are sketchy, but Cetshwayo seems to have positioned his organised *amabutho* on the right; the uDlambedlu, iSangqu, uThulwana and iNdlondo comprised the right horn, while the uDloko, izinGulube and iNdabakawombe formed the right-hand division of the chest. The retainers of the more important chiefs who supported him made up the left; the Mdlalose, Cube and abaQulusi completed the chest, while the left horn was made up of the Mandlakazi and Zungu. Almost certainly, Cetshwayo had chosen this formation because the warriors contributed by the various chiefdoms were long-standing supporters of the uSuthu, and could be relied upon in battle, while many of the *amabutho* had only declared for him at the last moment, and had yet to be tested. Cetshwayo himself commanded from a high-point on the ridge behind; he was carrying the shield of his regiment, the uThulwana, which at that time was black with one white spot on the lower half. He was wearing a headdress with a crane feather upright at the front, and may have been carrying a shotgun. Very few men on the uSuthu side had firearms, although Cetshwayo, too, had his own white mercenary, a young Boer by the name of Christian Groening, who held a command with one of the horns.

'Ndondakusuka was to prove one of the most destructive battles ever fought on Zulu soil, and it was one of the last waged in the classical manner of Shaka's day. Cetshwayo's plan was to throw out his right horn – the uDlambedlu, iSangqu, uThulwana and iNdlondlo *amabutho* – to surround the iziGqoza left, and cut between them and the river, threatening their line of retreat. According to John Dunn's own account, he had watched the uSuthu advance, and noticed that their right was apparently hidden. Suspecting their intention, he rode out ahead of his men, and found the horn already well advanced, moving up the valley of the Nkwaku. Calling out to them in Zulu, challenging them to wait and fight if they were not cowards, Dunn rode back to Mbuyazi's forces, collected his iziNqobo, and returned to intercept the uSuthu right. He was supported by a detachment of Mbuyazi's troops known as the iziMpisi, commanded by one of Mbuyazi's brothers, Prince Shonkweni kaMpande.

The two sides collided in the Nkwaku valley, and it was Dunn's men who opened fire and initiated the battle. The uSuthu rushed forward, shouting the name of their faction as a war-cry, while Shonkweni's iziMpisi sallied out to support Dunn, shouting the iziGqoza war-cry, 'Laba! Laba! Laba! Laba!' The iziGqoza were greatly encouraged by the firepower of Dunn's followers, and the uSuthu fell back. Seeing them retire, Cetshwayo sent forward the iNdabakawombe *ibutho* to support them, but although they attacked with considerable vigour, the assault crumpled once more in the face of Dunn's musketry. This caused the uSuthu commanders some concern, and they shouted down at their men, reminding them of what was at stake by calling out, 'Where will you take refuge?'

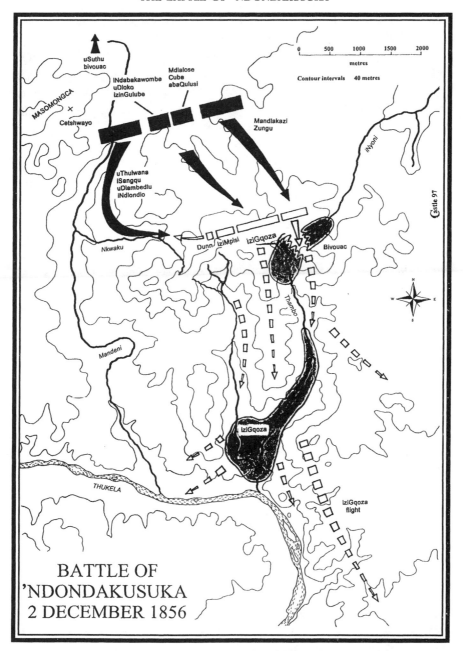

BATTLE OF 'NDONDAKUSUKA 2 DECEMBER 1856

The attack on the right having stalled, Cetshwayo directed his left horn to advance, keeping his chest uncommitted. The uSuthu left – the Mandlakazi and Zungu – broke out and struck at Mbuyazi's right, forcing it back from the ridge and down towards the iNyoni stream beyond.

According to most Zulu accounts, it was the Mandlakazi, led by two expe-rienced *izinduna*, Matsheni and Sikazana, and accompanied by two of Maphitha's sons, Hayiyana and Hlomuza, who turned the battle in favour of the uSuthu. The iziGqoza right abruptly collapsed, and began to retire down the iNyoni valley. This threatened the entire rear of Mbuyazi's line, and the left horn, hitherto so resolute, also suddenly gave way. The iziGqoza centre was now in an untenable position, and, despite its brave words earlier in the day, it turned and abandoned the ridge, crossing its own line in the grass without standing to fight. Seeing it retire, the uSuthu chest – the Mdlalose, Cube and abaQulusi contingents, and the iNdabakawombe uDloko and izinGulube *amabutho* – sounded the *ingomane*, an intimidating gesture of exultation and impending victory, lifting their shields and striking them with the butts of their spears, and moving forward to the attack. Cetshwayo himself, and his retinue of commanders and councillors, came down off the Masomongca ridge to join in the final assault.

At first, the iziGqoza retreat was orderly, and Dunn's followers, in particular, harried the uSuthu right horn to prevent it from cutting them off from the river. As the warriors fell back towards the Thukela, however, they ran into their civilian supporters hidden in the bush-covered valleys, and the latter, realising what was about to happen, stampeded towards the river. In the confusion, women, children and old men mingled with cattle and warriors, and all semblance of discipline fell apart. The uSuthu, following close behind, overwhelmed a half-hearted attempt at a rear-guard, and were soon attacking the civilians, herding a panic-stricken mob down towards the Thukela. Along the valley of one particular stream, they killed so many non-combatants that their skeletons lay visible for decades to come, and the stream is still known as Thambo ('bones').

In Zulu warfare, civilians were traditionally regarded as a legitimate target, if only because they were the support-base of enemy armies; the last stages of the battle at 'Ndondakusuka, however, defied rational explanation as exhilarated uSuthu struck out at the desperate fleeing figures all around them. In one expressive Zulu phrase, this was no longer fighting but 'mashing up porridge'. A hunter, William Baldwin, passing through the area a few days later, was shocked to hear victorious uSuthu boasting of the part they had played in the carnage:

> One man said he had killed six, another five, nine, or three; and one great warrior had killed twenty, and then he would count on his fingers so many young men, so many wives, and so many unmarried girls – *intombis* – and laugh over it immensely.

The iziGqoza rout streamed across the flats towards the river, exactly as the ill-fated Grand Army of Natal had done beforehand in 1838, heading towards the drift, the only possible escape route. Dunn kept up his fighting retreat until close to the river, when his small party of retainers was overwhelmed by a mob of terrified civilians. So many people tried to cling to his horse that Dunn was forced to abandon it, and plunged into the river, trying to swim across. The water was already full of a seething mass of humanity; many were swept away and drowned, while the uSuthu pursued them into the shallows, stabbing those who tried to hide along the banks. There were crocodiles in the river, too, and they added their share to the carnage.

Some elements of the uSuthu pressed on to the island where the white traders and their families were sheltering, rounded up their herds and drove them back to the Zulu bank. The whites, too, were terrified, but the trader Rathbone was astonished to notice that even at the height of the killing the uSuthu made no attempt to attack them, and a few warriors who recognised him even greeted him respectfully. The Zulus remembered this incident, too, in terms that imply some criticism of the role played by the traders; the first two lines of Cetshwayo's praises refer to himself as 'The Little Branch of Leaves which extinguished the Great Fire kindled by Mantshonga (Captain Walmesley) and Ngqelebane (Rathbone)'. This phrase was to recur in equally dramatic circumstances 23 years later, at the height of the battle of Isandlwana.

There was a flat-bottomed ferry which used to ply its trade across the Lower Drift, and the ferryman, with unusual courage and humanity, cast off to try to save some of the survivors in the water. He was almost capsized for his pains, but Dunn, at least, had cause to thank him, for he was among those fished out of the river. Most of his iziNqobo were killed, as indeed were the majority of the iziGqoza. Mbuyazi was apparently stabbed during the fighting, but his corpse was lost in the confusion, and rumours that he had survived continued to plague Cetshwayo for years afterwards. In all, six sons of Mpande were killed, including Shonkweni, who had emerged as a hero among the iziGqoza. The slaughter was immense; even the conservative figures compiled by official sources in Natal suggest that the iziGqoza lost as many as 5000 warriors, and two or three times that number of non-combatants. The hunter, Baldwin, returning from an expedition, left a graphic account of the aftermath twelve days later:

> The whole air was tainted with dead bodies for the last twelve miles, which I walked against a head wind. They were lying in every possible attitude along the road, men, women, and children of all

possible sizes and ages; the warriors untouched, with their war-dresses on, but all in a dreadful state of decomposition. I was never so glad of anything in my life as of getting the Tugela between me and the dead, as, what with the strong head wind and the horrible effluvia, it was quite overpowering ... as we neared the Tugela, the bodies lay so thick in the road and on each side that it was impossible to avoid them any longer ... I saw many instances of mothers with babies on their backs, with assegais through both, and children of all ages assegaid between the shoulder-blades.

Bodies carried out to sea by the river continued to wash up on beaches for miles along the coast for days afterwards.

It is impossible to assess the uSuthu losses. Baldwin encountered Cetshwayo and his advisers, proceeding slowly home in triumph. His attendants were holding branches over him, to keep off the sun, 'teaching him to be king', as they put it. Cetshwayo's attitude towards the whites was friendly enough, and he promised to return the cattle his men had seized from the river in the confusion. A missionary, S. M. Samuelson, whose station lay on the route of Cetshwayo's triumphant return, recalled the many wounded, 'who were following the cattle, with gaping wounds, groaning as they went along'.

The political consequences of the battle were enormous. The iziGqoza had ceased to exist as a military threat, and Cetshwayo had largely assured his succession. Nevertheless, Mpande – who was distraught at the loss of so many of his favourite sons – continued to torment Cetshwayo with the possibility of nominating an heir from among his sons who had not yet reached adulthood. In the aftermath of the battle, several of Mpande's minor sons, realising that their father's attitude placed them in some danger from Cetshwayo's jealousy, fled across the border into Natal or the Transvaal. Those who remained were staunchly loyal to Cetshwayo. In fact, however, there were few contenders left who might have wished to take up the challenge, and it is difficult to avoid the impression that throughout his later years Mpande was merely playing for time. He delayed giving the uThulwana permission to marry until the last possible moment – until he himself was married Cetshwayo could not be considered truly a man, and worthy of his inheritance – but in 1867 he finally gave way, and the uThulwana were allowed to don the headring. From that point few important decisions were taken within the kingdom without Cetshwayo's influence.

One curious side effect of the battle was the rise to prominence of John Dunn. Dunn had barely survived the battle but, nothing daunted, he accepted a commission from the traders who had lost cattle to go and beg their return from Cetshwayo. Under the circumstances this took some nerve, but Cetshwayo, impressed with Dunn's forthright manner, not only released the cattle into his care, but offered Dunn a role as adviser. Cetshwayo needed a white man to act as an intermediary in his political and financial dealings with the white world, and Dunn accepted. Cetshwayo established him as chief of the south-eastern part of the country – the gateway to Zululand – which included, ironically, the battlefield of 'Ndondakusuka. Here Dunn thrived, vetting white visitors on Cetshwayo's behalf, and importing European goods, including firearms, into the kingdom. Although he lived a Western lifestyle, after the manner of an English country gentleman, he maintained a Zulu household, which eventually included almost 50 wives, a matrimonial arrangement which effectively allied him to some of the most powerful chiefdoms in Zululand. He successfully straddled both the black and the white world, until the outbreak of the Anglo–Zulu War in 1879 left him with some stark choices.

Mpande finally died peacefully, of old age, towards the end of 1872. Even at that time Cetshwayo feared that some rival might emerge to challenge his succession, and he invited representatives of the colonial administration in Natal to attend his 'coronation' in September 1873. Ironically, the long-term effects of this piece of political manoeuvring were to prove far more destructive to the kingdom than might any internal rival.

4

THE BATTLE OF NYEZANE
22 January 1879
'Terribly earnest work'

The world in which Cetshwayo came to power in August 1873 was very different from the one that had greeted his father's accession 33 years earlier. The implicit shift in the balance of power between the Zulu kingdom and Natal, which Mpande had exploited to his advantage, had become a reality of daily life by 1873. The population of Natal, both black and white, had risen to exceed that of Zululand, and its economic power had grown proportionately. No Zulu king could now hope to monopolise the European trade in Zululand; the country teemed with white traders and hunters. Whites flooded the country with beads, blankets and metal wire, used to decorate spears and knobkerries, and in exchange carried away what remained of the country's ivory, and thousands of head of cattle. Moreover, cattle diseases introduced by contact with European herds, notably bovine pleuro-pneumonia ('lung-sickness') decimated those herds which remained. King Cetshwayo found it difficult to uniform his *amabutho* with shields of a similar colour, as Shaka had done; one probable reason was that the country no longer had access to a large enough cattle resource.

The competition that characterised the relationship between the Zulu kingdom and its neighbours in the 1860s and 1870s manifested itself most obviously in rivalry for grazing land. On the north-western borders of the kingdom, where Zulu territory abutted that of the Transvaal republic in the foothills of the Kahlamba mountains, the boundary ran along no fixed geographical feature, and tension had arisen since Mpande had allowed Boers living on the border to graze their cattle on the comparatively open grassland of his northern marches. The border line had become blurred, and the Boers had begun to encroach more and more on land claimed by the Zulus; in the words of a memorable Zulu simile, they were like toads, who hopped closer and closer, and were hardly noticed until they had hopped right up to the hearth of the king's royal homestead.

The existence of the fixed border to the south at least prevented friction over the question of land ownership, but it did limit the king's ability to control groups in Natal who remained part of the broader orbit of the kingdom. Indeed, because Natal offered such a secure refuge to those seeking to avoid the constraints of life under the royal family, Natal had, in effect, become a focus of opposition to the Royal House, and the danger posed by this opposition increased as Natal's influence grew.

King Cetshwayo was only too aware of the ambiguities of his position. He had grown to manhood in an air of insecurity, never quite certain of his birthright, always under threat of opposition, even of violence. It had made him both jealous both of his position and his power, sensitive to potential threats, yet vigorous and forthright in his solutions. He had little patience for the subtle methods of his father, and undoubtedly hoped to continue the restoration of royal prestige which had started under Mpande. Cetshwayo came to form new *amabutho* more regularly than his father had done, and tightened up the rules that governed their behaviour, which Mpande had sometimes allowed to slide. Cetshwayo was a traditionalist, who had a keen sense of the history and culture of his people, while at the same time possessing a far greater under-standing of the white world than his predecessors. He cultivated white friends like John Dunn, and actively sought to acquire firearms in large numbers, realising that his own armies were hopelessly outclassed without them.

As the great chiefs had once used the civil war between Mpande and Dingane as an opportunity to sell their support in return for greater autonomy, so the same happened in the civil war of 1856. Even after 'Ndondakusuka, Mpande manoeuvred to keep his own influence alive by keeping his son guessing, and encouraging internal groups who might counter his influence. When the old king died in late 1872, Cetshwayo still feared an opposition party might emerge to challenge him from within the country; his solution to this problem showed just how far the balance of power with Natal had shifted since Shaka's day, and, indeed, brought the logical conclusion of that shift a significant step nearer.

Cetshwayo appealed to the colonial administration in Natal to send representatives to the ceremonies which would install him as king. By showing that he had the support of the British, Cetshwayo hoped to intim-idate any potential rivals; and indeed, his plan worked to the extent that he was duly inaugurated, without any trouble, in several great ceremonies in August and September 1873. During the last of these, Natal's Secretary for Native Affairs, Theophilus Shepstone, signalled official British approval by placing a tinsel crown on Cetshwayo's head, and reading a stern lecture to the new king and his assembled chiefs on the virtues of civilised govern-ment. Cetshwayo is said to have been indignant at the tawdry finery and patronising words – as well he might have been.

Once installed, Cetshwayo built himself a new royal homestead, variously known as oNdini or uluNdi, from the common root *undi*, meaning 'the heights', a huge settlement of over 1200 huts, said to match Dingane's eMgungundlovu in its magnificence. It was situated on the Mahlabathini plain, north of the White Mfolozi, just a mile or two from his father's kwaNodwengu homestead. Mpande had been buried in state at Nodwengu, and the homestead allowed to fall into ruin, but his son kept the name alive and built a new *ikhanda*, also called kwaNodwengu, close by. Indeed, under Mpande and Cetshwayo, the Mahlabathini plain had become the hub of the Zulu kingdom, with no less than twelve large *amakhanda* clustered there or on the hills around. Once a year, at the time of the great umKhosi ceremony, which blessed the first fruits before the new harvest, they were the focus of a great gathering of the nation, when the *amabutho* were summoned before the king and a crowd of thousands of women and children, in a vibrant demonstration of the power and resilience of the Zulu way of life.

To the small settler communities scattered along the exposed border regions of Natal and the Transvaal, however, that power and resilience was decidedly unnerving. Only once in their mutual history had a Zulu king lifted his protection from the white community in Natal, when Dingane had attacked the Voortrekkers and then razed Port Natal. While it would be unfair to suggest that the whites had deserved their fate, it is at least true that the Zulu king had been provoked. Mpande had always taken great pains to remain on good terms with the British, and all the evidence suggests Cetshwayo intended to do the same. Nevertheless, isolation and vulnerability, stimulated by folk-memories of the terrible events of 1838, encouraged insecurity among the settlers, many of whom came to regard Cetshwayo as a despot, and his army as a naked threat. This growing feeling of unease in white Natal, articulated and exploited by men such as Shepstone, who had their own expansionist agenda, helped shape the attitudes which finally brought Natal and the Zulu kingdom into direct conflict.

In the 1870s, a new, more aggressive, spirit began to infect British policy-making in southern Africa. For two generations, South Africa had been both a political burden and a drain on the exchequer. Britain, like Holland before her, had wanted nothing from the Cape but a way-station on the long haul to India; but gradually the imperial boundaries had crept forward, often driven by the settlers' enduring need for fresh grazing land, and new territories were reluctantly paid for with the blood of the redcoat. Nevertheless the region remained a cockpit of rivalries: Anglo–Boer

resentment was never far below the surface, while increasingly beleaguered African groups often reacted violently to both nationalities.

In the 1860s, however, diamonds were discovered at Kimberley, north
of the Cape, and the situation changed dramatically. Hitherto of little
intrinsic value, southern Africa now offered a return on Britain's invest-
ment. To develop the country's natural resources, however, would
require the implementation of an infrastructure from scratch, and one,
moreover, in which the road and rail network did not grind to a halt at the
border of every impoverished Boer republic or destitute African
kingdom. British administrators began to think in terms of bringing the
entire region under some sort of overall British control. The scheme was,
rather grandly, called Confederation, and it was modelled on one which
had, apparently, proved successful in Canada. It did, of course, beg the
question of what would happen if any of the territories they had in mind
did not wish to be ruled by the British – an attitude that was not incon-
ceivable, given that many had been established in the first place as a
refuge against British authority.

The first victim of Confederation was the Transvaal Republic. The Transvaal had been established during the Great Trek, and its white population
was both physically scattered and, by history and temperament, disin-
clined to pay much heed to any form of authority. As a result, the affairs of
the Transvaal were chaotic, and British representatives conducted a highly
selective opinion survey before declaring that they had been invited to
take over the Transvaal for its own good. In April 1877, British troops
marched into Pretoria and raised the Union flag; hard-line republicans
were too stunned to object.

As it happened, the British mistook the deliberate cogitations of the
Boers for indifference, and under-estimated the extent of Boer opposition
– an error that would cost them dear in due course. In the meantime,
however, Britain settled down to govern her new territories – Theophilus
Shepstone was given the job of administrator – and promptly performed
an astonishing *volte face* over the question of the disputed border with
the Zulus. Shepstone, while employed in Natal, had hitherto always
favoured the Zulu claim, as part of his wider programme of limiting the
influence of the Boers. Now that they were in the British fold, he shifted
his support to the Boers. This was by no means inconsistent from his view-
point – his objective had all along been the extension of British influence
and the reduction of her rivals – but to the Zulus it seemed a personal
betrayal. The man who had given his support to Cetshwayo at the coronation was now defending Zululand's enemies. Consequently, the move

was greeted with great bitterness, and was regarded by many as the first step on the road to war.

It was against this background that a new British High Commissioner arrived in South Africa. Sir Henry Bartle Frere, an experienced proconsul with a long and distinguished record in India, was sent out by the Colonial Office with the express intention of pushing through the Confederation scheme. Within months of his arrival at the Cape, Frere had come to share the opinions of men like Shepstone who argued that the Transvaal border dispute proved that the Zulu kingdom was fundamentally opposed to British interests in southern Africa, and must ultimately be broken up if such interests were to prosper.

Some, indeed, went further, seeing Zulu influence behind a wave of unrest that swept through African groups south of the Limpopo in the 1870s. In truth, this was nothing but a common reaction to years of impoverishment and dispossession, but Frere began to wonder if a short, sharp and, above all, successful war against the Zulus might not, in any event, be extremely advantageous for Confederation. It would persuade African groups that they could not expect to oppose British expansionism indefinitely, it would show waverers to the Confederation cause that Britain was, if necessary, prepared to flex her military muscles, and it would demonstrate the advantages of British rule to groups who felt themselves threatened by the Zulu presence.

It was mainly Frere's decision to provoke a confrontation with King Cetshwayo, although it must be said that a degree of force was always implicit in the Confederation policy. Frere set up a boundary commission to look into the question of the disputed border with the Transvaal; he fully expected it to support the Transvaal claim, and hoped to use this as an excuse to present an ultimatum to the Zulus. Rather to his surprise, however, the commission decided in favour of the Zulus.

While Frere was pondering his next move, the sons of a border chieftain named Sihayo, who lived opposite the crossing at Rorke's Drift on the Mzinyathi, played into his hands. Two of Sihayo's wives had run away from their husband, and his outraged sons crossed the border to bring them back by force. Such incidents were by no means uncommon – hot pursuit actions from both sides had largely been tolerated in the past – but to Frere they were proof of the Zulus' hostile intent.

In December 1878 he invited King Cetshwayo's representatives to a meeting at the Lower Drift on the Thukela, ostensibly to hear the result of the boundary commission's findings. To this Frere had added an ultimatum; he demanded that Cetshwayo surrender Sihayo's sons, and, furthermore, that he should disband the *amabutho* system and accept a British resident at oNdini. The ultimatum effectively required Cetshwayo to renounce his nation's sovereignty; Frere did not expect him to accept but, if he did, the British objective was secured anyway. Failure to comply with the ultimatum would mean war; King Cetshwayo was neatly damned if he gave into British demands, and damned if he did not.

The British ultimatum was due to expire on 11 January 1879. While the Zulus considered their position, well aware that they had been forced into a corner by their former allies, but not really understanding why, Frere gave affairs into the hands of the senior British commander in southern Africa, Lieutenant General Lord Chelmsford. Chelmsford has sometimes been pilloried for his lack of imagination and incompetence, a superficial judgement which is largely unfair. He was in his early fifties, a professional soldier who had wide experience of colonial campaigning, and had served in India, Abyssinia and, most recently, had just brought a messy little war against the Xhosa people on the Cape frontier to a successful conclusion.

A tall, reserved and dignified man with a pleasant manner, Chelmsford was undoubtedly competent, but without that instinctive flair and inspiration which makes for truly great generals. He was also to a large extent deceived by his experiences on the Frontier, for he planned his war against the Zulus as if they were Xhosa; yet the Xhosa, who waged a guerrilla warfare from bush-covered mountain strongholds, fought in a very different way from the Zulus. Chelmsford believed that the Zulus, like the Xhosa, would avoid open battle, and such thinking shaped both his grand strategy and his battlefield tactics. This, as he would find out, was a mistake.

Chelmsford's initial plan was to invade Zululand from five separate points along the border, with each column converging on the great cluster of *amakhanda* on the Mahlabathini plain. Convinced that he would have to 'drive the Zulus into a corner and make them fight', he hoped to force the Zulu army into battle, while at the same time limiting its ability to make a counter-strike into Natal or the Transvaal. The strategy itself was not unsound; there was, however, an element of risk in that it would spread Chelmsford's troops very thinly on the ground, and dilute his greatest asset, the firepower of his regular infantry battalions.

Like most British commanders about to embark on a colonial campaign, Chelmsford had too few troops at hand to be sure of completing the job. The British military presence in South Africa had seldom been large, although Chelmsford did have available the seasoned troops who had just finished mopping up on the Cape Frontier. He requested reinforcements from home, but the British government, which was already facing a tense situation in Afghanistan, had no wish to become embroiled in another war in South Africa, and still hoped that Confederation might be pushed through without a resort to arms. Chelmsford was sent a mere handful of battalions from home, and had to make do. In the event, the forces available to him at the start of hostilities were just six battalions of infantry, two artillery batteries and no regular cavalry.

To make good the shortfall, Chelmsford had to rely on volunteer units – raised among the settler community in Natal for defence of the colony – and irregulars, who were recruited by the British authorities for a specific period. Most of these were mounted units. A further source of manpower was the black population of Natal, many of whom had a history of antagonism towards the Zulu Royal House. The colonial administration was reluctant to sanction the raising of black troops, both for fear of arming potential insurgents, and because of the risk of poisoning the relationship with Zululand for generations to come. In the event, Chelmsford outmanoeuvred the civilian opposition, and three regiments of the so-called Natal Native Contingent (NNC) were raised on the eve of war.

The 1st Regiment consisted of three battalions, each of a thousand men, and the 2nd and 3rd of two thousand each. Early plans to uniform and dress the men along British lines were abandoned for reasons of cost, and instead only one man in ten was issued with a firearm. These were usually obsolete patterns, and ammunition was limited. Most of the men carried their traditional weapons – shields and spears – and the only thing which distinguished them from their Zulu counterparts was a red rag wrapped around their heads. Officers were appointed from among the ranks of colonials or regular special service officers, but white NCOs were generally recruited from the unemployed adventurers recently demobilised on the Cape Frontier, most of whom could not speak Zulu, and had little respect for the men under their command.

The showing of the NNC would prove poor throughout the war, though the fault lay not so much in the poor fighting quality of Natal's Africans, as in the fact that promising material was squandered through parsimony and inadequate preparation. Nevertheless, it is interesting to reflect that by the end of the war, almost as many Africans had been under arms on the British side as on the Zulu. For many Africans, Great Britain's quarrel with King Cetshwayo was merely the latest incident in the long-running struggle for the Natal and Zululand region, which had its origins in the rise and history of the House of Senzangakhona.

Assembling his troops was only one part of Chelmsford's logistical challenge. Unlike its Zulu counterpart, which carried its food on the hoof and otherwise lived mainly off the land, the British army had to transport all its own supplies and impedimenta – tents, ammunition, medical and signalling equipment. There were far too few commissariat resources available, and Chelmsford was forced to buy or hire civilian transport wagons – and thousands of oxen – just to keep his army mobile.

It soon became clear that five offensive columns were beyond his capabilities, and the number was reduced to three. One would cross the Thukela and the best-known entry point into Zululand, the Lower Thukela Drift, another would cross at Rorke's Drift on the Mzinyathi – the best crossing on the central border, named after a trader, Jim Rorke – and the third would move down from Utrecht in the disputed territory along the Ncome (Blood) River. The other two columns were reduced in size and given a defensive role; they were situated at the Middle Drift on the Thukela, midway between the Lower and Rorke's Drifts, and further north on the Transvaal border, to keep an eye on both the Zulus and the disgruntled Boers.

Chelmsford picked his column commanders from among a number of officers who had served on the Cape Frontier with him; Colonel Charles Pearson would command the right-flank column, Colonel Richard Glyn the centre column, and Colonel Henry Evelyn Wood the left-flank column. Since Chelmsford expected the centre column to bear the brunt of any fighting, he opted to accompany that force, a decision which largely reduced Glyn to an administrative role.

While the British columns assembled threateningly on his borders, King Cetshwayo discussed the crisis with his assembled *ibandla*, the council consisting of the great chiefs of the nation. Opinion among the council was split; some argued that Sihayo's sons should take the consequences of their rash actions, and that the kingdom as a whole should not be made to suffer. Others realised that Sihayo's sons were not the real issue, and were paralysed by the suspicion that the British wanted nothing more than the break-up of the kingdom. Certainly, the demand that the *amabutho* be disbanded suggested exactly that, and none of the councillors could bring themselves to consider that option seriously. Instead, the great council preferred to play a waiting game; to call up the army, but refrain from taking any provocative action until the British intentions became clear.

That the British really meant business was all too apparent even before the ultimatum expired on 11 January 1879. As early as the 6th, some of Colonel Wood's mounted troops had crossed the Ncome into Zulu territory, and begun rounding up Zulu cattle. In many ways, this premature action set the tone for the coming conflict; to many Zulus it seemed that the war was not about politics but greed – the British and their colonial allies did not want political control of the kingdom so much as Zulu land and cattle. Certainly, the British would prove to be expert cattle raiders. Lord Chelmsford himself was more punctilious in respect of form; the Centre Column did not cross into Zululand until the 11th. He wasted no time in demonstrating his purpose, however, and on the 12th attacked and destroyed Chief Sihayo's homestead, which lay across his line of advance. The first shots of the war had been fired, and the great test for the Zulu kingdom and its army began.

News of the attack on Sihayo's homestead finally determined King Cetshwayo's reaction. Most of the army was already assembled, and over the next few days the remaining elements marched in from outlying *amakhanda*, and the great ceremonies necessary to prepare them for war began. The army was ritually purified, then doctored with medicine which was said to bind the warriors together, and give them supernatural ascendancy over the enemy. Selected regiments were called before the king, and warriors from each challenged one another, stoking up regimental rivalries that could be used to good effect once the fighting commenced. When these ceremonies were complete, the warriors were excluded from ordinary civilian life, their spirits focused on war, and they could only return to normality following the terrible release of battle, and the cleansing ceremonies that followed it.

The British dispositions posed some very real strategic problems for the Zulu high command. The presence of the three invading columns was only too obvious, but since the king was able to rely on intelligence reports filtered back from the borders by his civilian population, he knew, also, of the smaller columns poised menacingly between the main British thrusts. Furthermore, there was no reason to suppose that the British might not also take advantage of their complete mastery of the sea and attempt to land another column, perhaps on the northern beaches, at Lake St Lucia, or even through Portuguese Delagoa. Also to the north, inland, there was a distinct possibility that the British might persuade the Swazi kingdom, which had been largely hostile to the Zulus since King Dingane's time, to join the war. In the worst case, King Cetshwayo might find himself beset by enemies quite literally on all sides.

The resources available to meet these threats were limited. According to a careful count by Chelmsford's intelligence department before war began, the Zulu army consisted of a grand total of 40,000 men. In fact, this figure would prove a significant over-estimate, since it failed to take into account the fact that attendance among the more elderly *amabutho* was not compulsory. Many men would remain at home, in any case, either on the instruction of their chiefs, who needed some form of local protection, or to keep civilian life functioning. At best, King Cetshwayo's army numbered 29,000, and throughout the war he would prove unable to concentrate more than 25,000 for any single campaign. Furthermore, although the king had made a determined effort to obtain firearms since his victory at 'Ndondakusuka in 1856, and many thousands of guns had found their way into the country, they were mostly obsolete weapons in poor condition, and most of the warriors continued to rely on their traditional shields and spears. In that respect, they were likely to be considerably outclassed by the awesome technological sophistication of the British.

When the *ibandla* decided its strategy in the aftermath of Chelmsford's attack on Sihayo, it naturally concluded that the British Centre Column posed the most immediate threat. The main army, under the leadership of two of Cetshwayo's senior military advisers, Chief Ntshingwayo kaMahole and Chief Mavumengwana kaNdlela, was directed to check the column advancing from KwaJim – Jim Rorke's place. In the coastal sector, men who lived locally were ordered to gather at the local *amakhanda*, to harass Pearson's progress, and a small *impi* was despatched from oNdini to support them.

In the north, the situation was more fluid; this was the territory of the abaQulusi, who were not an age-based regiment, but a territorial one, being the descendants of an *ikhanda* established in the region by King Shaka. The abaQulusi were fiercely loyal to the Royal House, of which they considered themselves a section. In the same region, too, lived Mbilini waMswati, a Swazi prince who had fled his own country after a succession dispute, and given his allegiance to Cetshwayo. Mbilini was a resourceful guerrilla fighter, and Cetshwayo relied on his daring, and the vigour of the Qulusi, supported by a small contingent from oNdini, to check Wood's advance.

There were few enough warriors left to guard against the other threats, although local elements gathered on the Zulu bank at Middle Drift to watch Durnford's column, while cattle-guards were employed to keep an eye on Rowlands. The only answer the king had to any sudden strike from the north was to keep a body of warriors with him at oNdini, although, significantly, they were drawn largely from the iNdabakawombe *ibutho*, which was composed of men in their late fifties, and of limited military value.

Ironically, it was the least aggressive of the British columns which would feel the weight of the Zulu response first. The No. 1, or Right Flank Column, under Colonel Pearson, was not ready to enter Zululand when the ultimatum expired on the 11th, and the first troops did not cross the Thukela until the following day, despite the fact that the British had maintained a base in the area since the ultimatum, a month previously. Pearson's crossing point, the Lower Drift, lay directly beside the 'ultimatum tree', and an impressive earthwork, Fort Pearson, had been built on a steep knoll overlooking it on the Natal side.

Once again, an enemy army was entering Zululand by the coastal route; the site of the Thukela and 'Ndondakusuka battles lay close to Pearson's line of advance. Nevertheless, there were good practical reasons why Pearson had been delayed. For one thing, after several years of drought, the weather had broken, and hot, humid summer days gave way to fierce rain-storms in the evenings. Although the track from Durban to the Thukela was well established, the passage of so much military traffic soon destroyed it, and convoys of troops and supplies took a painfully long time to reach the border. Indeed, some men had just freshly arrived in South Africa: the 99th Regiment, one of only two battalions sent out by the home government in response to Chelmsford's requests for reinforcements, did not land in Durban until the first week of January, and did not reach the Thukela until the ultimatum expired. Furthermore, the crossing itself was not an easy one. The heavy rains had turned the river into a wide, sluggish sheet of brown water, which had risen to cover even those sandbanks where the traders had sheltered during the battle of 1856. Pearson's command included a contingent of sailors landed by HMS *Active*, and these had been put to good use manning a pont – a flat-bottomed ferry – which had been established on the river, tied to a hawser secured to a ship's anchor sunk in the Zulu bank. Nevertheless, heavy rain upstream had caused a sudden flood on one occasion, the anchor had been washed away, and one sailor had been drowned attempting to rescue it. Another was fastened in its place, but it was not until the 12th that Pearson was able to send his first detachments across. As elsewhere, the Zulus made no attempt to oppose the crossing, but groups of their scouts could be seen watching from the distant hills.

In many ways, the terrain through which Pearson was expected to advance was among the easiest facing the British column commanders. The high ridges and deep river gorges which characterised the inland districts had given way to an undulating landscape of rolling hills, carpeted with tall, wet grass after the rains. Indeed, the land gave the appearance of being waterlogged; the major rivers flowed across shallow sandy beds and through open valleys, while the country was criss-crossed by scores of narrow streams, full to bursting, as well as hundreds of dongas, with patches of low-lying marshy ground scattered in between. Most of the streams were fringed with bush, and where the ground level rose towards Eshowe, there were patches of dense forest on the hilltops. Several British observers were struck by the beauty of the landscape, but the wet weather would make it difficult country to cross, and the whereabouts of the Zulu army within it remained a mystery.

It took several days for Pearson to ferry his troops and supplies across the river, and a sprawling camp sprang up on the Zulu bank. For the most part, no attempt was made to protect the perimeter, but a new fort, Fort Tenedos, was built around an existing trading store, to protect the stockpile of supplies. Lord Chelmsford's initial instructions to Pearson were to advance to occupy the mission station at Eshowe, some 35 miles away by road, and from there to coordinate his advance with the other columns.

It is no coincidence that mission stations feature so heavily in the history of the Anglo–Zulu War; the British were desperately short of permanent structures to house their supplies, and mission stations were ideal for the purpose. Not that there were many in the Zulu kingdom itself; successive kings had resisted the pressure of various evangelical groups to be allowed to establish posts in Zulu territory, and when they had been sanctioned, they were usually sited well away from the main areas of settlement. The Eshowe station had been set up by the Norwegian mission society in 1860, but like others, had attracted few converts. The Zulus were deeply attached to their traditional beliefs, and were suspicious of the European values which underpinned most Christian endeavour. Most missionaries, as a result, saw the authority of the Zulu king as a block to their endeavours, and supported the British ultimatum in the hope that the destruction of the kingdom would open the road to enlightenment. The majority of them fled Zululand in the tense months before the ultimatum, and the empty cluster of church and outbuildings at Eshowe therefore presented the military with a golden opportunity.

It was not until the 17th – ironically, the very day that the great Zulu army moved out from oNdini – that Pearson completed the transfer of his command to Zulu soil. The composition of his force was typical of Lord Chelmsford's columns, and reflected the compromises that British commanders were often forced to make in the field during colonial campaigns. Inevitably, British successes were likely to be dependent on the massed firepower of the regular, imperial troops, but the practicalities of policing a large empire meant that there were seldom enough of these to do the job. The backbone of Pearson's column consisted of just two battalions of infantry – Pearson's old regiment, the 2/3rd (the Buffs), and the 99th, which consisted mainly of young short-service troops fresh out from England and was, moreover, under-strength. Additionally, he had one section from 11/7 Battery, RA, consisting of two light 7-pounder guns and a rocket trough, and a company of Royal Engineers.

To beef up the European contingent, the Navy had landed small detachments from HMS *Active* and *Tenedos*, with a hand-cranked Gatling machine-gun and two 24-pounder rocket tubes. Cavalry were in short supply – there were no regular British cavalry regiments in Zululand at the outbreak of the war – and Pearson's mounted contingent consisted of a squadron of regular Mounted Infantry, and a handful of the small Natal volunteer units – the Victoria, Stanger, Durban and Alexandra Mounted Rifles, and the Natal Hussars. These were part-time soldiers, who elected their own officers and provided their own uniforms, but who rode horses and carried carbines supplied by the colonial administration. Nevertheless, the European contingent in Pearson's command numbered scarcely more than 2000 men, and it was necessary to augment it with the two battalions of the 2nd Regiment of the Natal Native Contingent. A hundred of the best men had been drawn from the ranks of the NNC and formed into the Natal Native Pioneer Corps, who wore a uniform of sorts, and were all armed with firearms.

Pearson's column therefore came to a grand total of 4271 combat troops. To keep these in the field he needed no less than 384 wagons and 24 carts, manned by 622 civilian wagon-drivers and voorloopers. To draw this enormous baggage train, Pearson had over 3000 oxen, but even these were insufficient for the purpose, and he was able to put less than 200 wagons on the road at any given time.

Indeed, the lack of sufficient oxen was the largest single factor in determining Pearson's line of march when the column finally began its advance on 18 January. Worried that the boggy state of the ground and the sprawling nature of the wagon train might delay him, Pearson decided to advance in two divisions. The first, which he would command in person, would be a light flying column, and would consist of just 50 wagons, the Buffs, two guns, most of the mounted men and roughly half the NNC. This division would dash for Eshowe, with the second division, commanded by Colonel Welman of the 99th, 24 hours behind. By leaving such a gap between the two sections of his force, Pearson hoped to allow the road to dry out in between. Welman's column had 80 wagons but fewer troops, just two companies of the 99th, the Durban Mounted Rifles, Native Pioneers, and the remaining half of the NNC.

When Pearson's men finally began their advance in the dawn mist on the 18th, they had no more idea of the whereabouts of King Cetshwayo's forces than when they had crossed the river nearly a week before. A few scouts had been captured, but had given away little, beyond the vaguely menacing information that there were plenty more like them in the distant green hills. For all Pearson knew, his first division might be marching straight into the full weight of the Zulu army, but if the tiny convoy of 50 wagons and 2000 men felt at all vulnerable as they marched into the deserted, undulating landscape, their accounts do not reveal it. Most, it seemed, were only too delighted at being on the march at last, after the tedium and frustration of the previous few days.

From the beginning, however, the march proved a hard slog. Pearson's division had advanced scarcely six or seven miles from Fort Tenedos before it struck the iNyoni River, first of many natural obstacles which lay across its path. The river itself was not deep, but it was narrow and the banks were steep, and the wagons could only be dragged across by using double teams of oxen. It was late evening by the time the division had crossed, and Pearson wisely chose to camp close to the north bank. That night it rained, and there was a false alarm – the first of many – when an NNC piquet claimed to spot a Zulu force in the gloom, and the entire force stood to for several hours until it was clear that no attack was imminent. Nor was the following day's advance much better. Another stream, the mSundusi, lay just four miles ahead, and Pearson realised once again that much of the day's efforts would be taken up in crossing it. That morning, too, a report reached him from F. B. Fynney, a Natal Border Agent, that a Zulu force was heading in his direction. Pearson decided to wait for most of the day, until Welman's second division came slithering into sight along the muddy track, before detaching three companies of the Buffs to reinforce Welman, and pushing on to the far side of the mSundusi.

The Border Agent's report was interesting in a number of respects, not least because it showed that, from their remote posts on the frontier, the civil agents were better informed about the movements of the Zulu army, through their existing network of informers, than were the military, who were operating inside Zululand itself. Furthermore, Fynney's intelligence was substantially correct. Some 3500 warriors had indeed left oNdini two days before, and were already drawing close to Pearson's command. They were under the command of Godide kaNdlela, one of a tightly knit group of important individuals who served the Zulu king as a military high command.

Godide was chief of the Ntuli people, and his father, Ndlela kaSompisi, had been King Dingane's senior commander. Godide's younger brother, Mavumengwana, was acting as second-in-command to the main army, which was even then advancing on Lord Chelmsford's Centre Column. Godide's command consisted of some 40 *amaviyo*, or companies, of the uMxapho *ibutho*, men in their mid-thirties, and a further fifteen companies of older men of the uDlambedlu and izinGulube *amabutho*. His instructions were to rendezvous with local elements who had mustered at the *amakhanda* in the region – notably old oNdini (Hlalangubo) and kwaGingindlovu – and who had been monitoring Pearson's advance, and to try to check the British column. Almost certainly, the Zulu high command considered this a holding action, for the main weight of their counter-attack was intended to fall elsewhere.

On the whole, however, Pearson made few allowances for the possibility of attack at this stage. With the weather still poor, and another obstacle ahead – the amaTigulu River – he decided to remain camped on the mSundusi on the 20th, but sent his mounted men out to probe the line of advance, and his engineers to prepare a drift ready for the crossing. At 4.30 on the morning of the 21st, his division resumed its advance on the amaTigulu, only four miles away.

That morning Pearson received another report concerning the whereabouts of the Zulu force, this time suggesting that several thousand warriors had congregated at the kwaGingindlovu *ikhanda*, about five miles away on his right flank. This information was so specific that Pearson could scarcely afford to ignore it, and in any case his men were keen for a taste of action after the drudgery of the march. About midday, Pearson despatched two companies of the Buffs, the two RA guns, half the Naval Brigade with their 24-pounder rocket tube, two companies of the NNC, and a detachment of mounted men to investigate the report. Given that this force was only 600 strong, of whom 200 were poorly armed auxiliaries, he was taking something of a chance.

KwaGingindlovu – the name means 'swallower of the elephant' – had been built by the then Prince Cetshwayo in honour of his victory over Prince Mbuyazi at 'Ndondakusuka in 1856. It consisted of a circle of several hundred huts, surrounded by a palisade eight feet high. The troops approached with some caution, but to their disappointment the complex was deserted, apart from an elderly lady, who made a bid to escape. The troops good-naturedly detained her, and took her away with them; a missionary serving with the column was surprised to find that she was a sister of Dingiswayo kaJobe, a chief of the Mthethwa people who had been patron to the famous Shaka more than 50 years before. Before they left, the Naval Brigade fired one of their awesome 24-pounder rockets into the *ikhanda*, and the thatched huts exploded in a shower of sparks.

Pearson's foray marched back to join the rest of his command, disappointed that they had made no enemy contact. In fact, they had been much closer to the Zulus than they had realised. KwaGingindlovu had indeed served as a rallying point for warriors from various regiments who lived locally. In total, these consisted of about 2500 men, chiefly from the iNsukamngeni, iQwa, uDududu and iNdabakawombe *amabutho*, who had gathered both at kwaGingindlovu and Hlalangubo, further north. When Godide's contingent from oNdini reached the area about the 18th, however, the local elements had abandoned their barracks and gone north to meet it, effecting a junction in the region of Hlalangubo on the 20th, while Pearson waited in his camp on the mSundusi.

Godide resumed his march southwards on the 21st, but for once the Zulu intelligence system seems to have been faulty, and he expected to find the British closer to the Thukela. When the Zulu advance guard reached kwaGingindlovu late that afternoon, they were surprised to find that the British had set it on fire only a few hours earlier. Scouts were hurriedly sent out to ascertain the whereabouts of Pearson's command, and Godide shifted the line of his advance to intercept them.

The Zulu force caught up with Pearson's command shortly after dark that same evening. His force reunited, Pearson had camped on a grassy rise known as KwaSamabela, which overlooked the valley of the Nyezane River ahead, and the hills rising towards Eshowe beyond. Pearson seems to have made no particular attempt to secure this camp against attack, but the rumours of the Zulu approach may have made his piquets particularly alert. Godide's warriors completely surrounded the camp in the darkness, and the British might have been extremely vulnerable to a night attack. Yet the Zulus preferred to attack 'in the horns of the morning' rather than in the dark, for at night-time there were practical problems of command and control, as well as the risk of dark spirits interfering with the efficiency of their pre-combat rituals, tipping the balance of psychic power against them. On this occasion, the shouts of the piquets, calling out to one another, convinced Godide that the British were waiting for him, and led him to abandon the idea of an attack. As silently as they had come, the Zulu army slipped away, and it was only the following morning, when British patrols found huge swathes of grass around the camp trampled down by the *amabutho*, that they realised how close they had come.

The following day, 22 January, was to prove a fateful one for both the British army and the Zulu kingdom. Curiously enough, it was not a day that the Zulus would have chosen for fighting; the following night (22nd/23rd) was the night of the new moon, a time of ill-omen, when dark spiritual forces, known simply as *umnyama* ('blackness') were unleashed, and liable to wreak havoc in the undertakings of men. Ironically, circumstances would compel them to fight on all three fronts that same day.

Reveille sounded for Pearson's column at 4 a.m., as usual, half an hour before dawn. The mounted men rode out to scout down the road, while the infantry made coffee and packed their kit. At 4.30, the advance began. As the sun came up and the mist burned off the Nyezane valley, the British could see that the track dropped gently to the river, about four miles away. If the Zulu movements during the night were widely known, neither Pearson nor his commanders took any special precautions to counter the possibility of attack. The Nyezane River itself was narrow and the water waist-deep, flowing between banks fringed on either side with lush bush. On the far side there was a patch of open ground, scattered with bush, before the ground rose steeply in the first of a series of terraces which led up to the Eshowe heights. This rising ground consisted of a number of spurs sloping down towards the river, separated from one another by hollows and gullies, filled with bush. The track, such as it was, wound up one of these spurs, flanked on either side by gullies which gave way to further ridges on either side. Both the flanking ridges were higher than the centre one, up which ran the track, and the right-hand ridge was topped by a high grassy headland, known to the Zulus as Wombane Hill.

As he approached the Nyezane, Pearson ordered his mounted men – who were under the overall command of a Hussar officer, Major Percy Barrow – to cross the river and scout out the heights. Barrow returned to report that the hills appeared free of Zulus, and suggested that Pearson should allow the column to halt on the flat ground on the far side of the river. Pearson himself rode forward to inspect it. It was not ideal, since the bush would offer considerable cover to the enemy, but on the other hand it would take time to get the wagons across the river, and the men were unlikely to find a fresh supply of water once they began to ascend the heights. Pearson agreed to allow the men to breakfast on the flats while the wagons crossed. The mounted men were allowed to relax; some stripped off to enjoy an impromptu bathe in the river, while others began a breakfast of bully-beef and biscuits. The first of the wagons came up and crossed the river.

It was then, at about 8 a.m., that someone first spotted a group of Zulus further up the slope, close by the road. They appeared to be scouts, and were watching Pearson's actions intently. When told this, Pearson ordered a company of the 1/2nd NNC, under the command of the regiment's staff officer, Captain Fitzroy Hart, to advance up the track and clear the Zulus away. As the NNC began their probe, the Zulus moved down into the gully to the British right, were lost in the bush for a few moments, then reappeared some minutes later on the slope of Wombane. Hart led his men into the bush, where they became somewhat disorganised. They halted for a few moments on the far side to reform, and by this time the Zulu party had apparently disappeared somewhere over the crest of the hill. Nothing daunted, the NNC pushed up the slope to find them. As they advanced, a number of them began to feel distinctly uneasy. They tried to attract the attention of their white officers and NCOs, but these either would not listen, or could not understand. This was a grave mistake, for the NNC, with their hearing more attuned to the natural sounds of the bush, had detected something unusual in the swish of the grass and the whirring of insects. Several thought they had caught the faint sound of men whispering excitedly in the long grass ahead of them.

Suddenly, the position became chillingly clear. Scarcely a hundred yards ahead of the toiling NNC company, there rose from the grass not a small party of Zulu scouts, but several hundred fully armed warriors. The Zulus gave a shout of their war-cry, 'uSuthu!', then fired a ragged volley. In the first few seconds of that encounter, there was a moment of pure tragic farce. The officers of the NNC had been issued a small handbook, which included useful phrases of command. One of the white officers dramatically drew his sword, flourished it, and called out steadfastly, 'Baleka!' He was apparently under the impression that the word meant 'Charge!', but his imperfect understanding of Zulu was to cost him his life; 'baleka' means 'run'. The NNC needed no further bidding, and turned towards the safety of the bush-choked gully behind them.

Stunned by the sudden desertion of their command, a few of the officers and NCOs tried to make a stand, firing into the Zulus who had thrown down their firearms and were now rushing down towards them with stabbing spears drawn back. There was a brief flurry of fighting, and Lieutenant Raines, three white NCOs and three privates were killed, while the rest fled down the hill as fast as they could. As the Zulus passed over the bodies, they snatched up the fallen Martini-Henrys, and jabbed their spears into the corpses. This was a ritual which had its origins in the hunt, when all the men present in a hunting party claimed to themselves some of the honour of a dangerous kill by stabbing the carcass. It was a macabre testimony to the fighting qualities of the white soldiers, but it left the bodies a terrible spectacle; after the battle, one observer claimed that Lieutenant Raines was 'so riddled with assegai wounds that it would have been impossible to place your hand anywhere on his body without covering one'.

In fact, the NNC's encounter had triggered the collision which had been brewing for the past two days. After calling off the encirclement of the camp at kwaSamabela, Godide had withdrawn his army behind the heights overlooking the Nyezane crossing. Most of it lay just beyond the summit of Wombane, concealed from the flats below, but an advanced party, probably of the younger uMxapho *ibutho*, had concealed itself on the forward slopes, with scouts thrown out to watch the British approach. It had been Godide's intention to attack Pearson as his column struggled up the road, a tactic which might well have been successful, given that most British commanders feared an attack on the march, because of the difficulties of protecting their wagon-train. The chance encounter had spoiled any hope of a coordinated trap, however, and the sound of shots from the front brought the uMxapho rushing forward from beyond the brow of the hill.

Down at the river, Pearson's men, too, were alerted to the danger by the sudden sound of firing. The mounted troops were the quickest to react. The Natal Hussars and men of the Mounted Infantry had been deployed as vedettes to cover the crossing, and were spread out across the road half-way up the slope. Moving to their right, they took up a position beside the road, facing towards Wombane across the gully in between. There was a moment of confusion as the NNC, survivors of Hart's command who had fled the initial clash, suddenly emerged from the bush in front of them, and were mistaken for Zulus. Several of the mounted men opened fire on them before realising their mistake, and it is not known if there were any casualties.

Down at the river, meanwhile, the men of the Victoria and Stanger Rifles, whose breakfast had been rudely interrupted, quickly saddled-up and rode up the spur, before dismounting and taking up a position on the other side of the road from the Hussars and MI, effectively screening the head of the column. Here they found a slight rise, which gave them a good all-round view of the Zulu attack, which was developing rapidly to their right and rear.

By this time, a large number of warriors had streamed very rapidly round from behind Wombane, and were racing down the slope. Some rushed into the gully and took cover in the bush, creeping forward to within a hundred yards of the Hussars and MI, and opening a heavy fire on them. Others sprinted down towards the river in a great swinging arc that would have brought them out close to the drift. One British officer, beside the crossing, discerned their objective, and left a vivid impression of the attack. 'I looked round and saw the Zulus on our right, running like deer, in a long semicircle; this was the horn of their army, trying to surround the first part of the column and cut the line of wagons'. That the Zulus were attempting to deploy in their traditional 'beast's horns' formation became evident when another body, the chest, came into view at the head of the ridge above the road. At this stage, there was no sign of the right horn.

Pearson had managed to move perhaps half his division across the Nyezane when the first shots rang out. His engineers were still working on the drift, and the process of dragging the wagons across would continue throughout the fight. In standing orders drawn up just before the outbreak of war, Lord Chelmsford had instructed his commanders to fight in a formation which had proved very successful in the few pitched battles on the Cape Frontier. Here he had learned that it was British firepower which had won the day, and the preferred tactic was to form the infantry into an extended line, with guns in the centre, and auxiliaries and mounted volunteers on either flank. The Xhosa had seldom been able to sustain the casualties necessary to close with such a formation, and Chelmsford – and most of the officers under his command – hardly expected the Zulus to behave differently. Caught on the hop though he was, Pearson seems to have tried to deploy in such a pattern, even as the Zulu attack developed.

The Naval Brigade, two artillery 7-pounders, and two companies of the Buffs, under Captain Jackson and Lieutenant Martin, were already across the river, and Pearson ordered them to double up the slope and form up just beyond the mounted men. There was a low grassy knoll just to the right of the road, which, although overlooked by Wombane, nevertheless gave a slightly elevated view of both the track ahead and the gully to the right. Here the guns unlimbered, directed to the right, towards the slopes of Wombane, and Jackson's and Martin's companies fell in on either side of them. The Naval Brigade formed up on the left of the infantry, facing up the track.

Pearson himself rode up to the knoll to take command of the battle as it developed. Given the speed of the Zulu advance, the British deployment must have been very rapid, since the guns were in place before the Zulus in the gully could press forward far enough to threaten them. Once in position, the guns showered the slopes opposite them with shrapnel, forcing the Zulus to take advantage of the cover afforded by the grass and bush. Nevertheless, as one Engineer officer recalled, 'I didn't like the look of things. Nothing seemed to stop the Zulus. They slithered through the long grass, and although they suffered greatly, they came nearer.'

The knoll, however, offered Pearson a good anchor for his defence. The two Buffs companies had now uncased and unfurled their Colours, and were heavily engaged; and a third company, under Captain Foster, came up from the rear, and fell in below the knoll, bridging the gap between it and the Natal Hussars and Mounted Infantry. Pearson was, in effect, forming a line along the road, facing his right, with his left flank curled round, up the road, to deny it to the Zulu chest, which was edging cautiously down the slopes above.

By this time, the Zulu advance in the direction of the knoll had stalled. Hundreds of warriors were clustered in the gully, masked to some extent by the thick bush, but to progress from there, and close with the enemy, they had to charge uphill across a hundred yards of open country, exposed to a murderous fire. Most were content to engage in a spirited fire-fight with the redcoats in front of them. In this the British had the advantage, since the Zulu guns were obsolete patterns, 20 or 30 years old, often relying on poor-quality powder to propel home-made projectiles. Furthermore, much of the Zulu fire was high, because many warriors believed that by setting the rear sights at maximum elevation, they were increasing the velocity of the projectile. As a result, the air above the British line hummed and whistled with shot – a disconcerting experience for mounted officers, in particular – but casualties were surprisingly few. Pearson's horse was hit, and had to be put out of its misery, while one especially skilled Zulu sniper achieved a number of near misses from the cover of a tree at the foot of Wombane. A great deal of fire was directed at the trunk, behind which he was thought to be hiding, but to no effect, until a stray bullet clipped through the leaves, and knocked him out of his hiding place in the branches.

Indeed, the return fire was devastating. In addition to the thudding guns and the steady drum-roll of musketry, the British had one 9-pounder rocket trough and two 24-pounder rocket tubes at their disposal. Rockets were not particularly effective weapons since they were little more than giant fireworks, and the shells had neither sticks nor fins to stabilise them in flight, nor detonators to set off their explosive charge. The lighter trough was an artillery weapon, and was notoriously unreliable; the apparatus itself required to be erected on even ground to give any hope of accuracy, and the rockets themselves were unstable. It was not unknown for them to explode prematurely on leaving the trough, and they were at the mercy of cross-winds and any obstacle they encountered along the way. If they struck a tree or glanced off a rock, they might ricochet off at bizarre angles, and if the propellant burnt at an uneven rate they might twist in mid-air and even turn back towards their crew. The 24-pounder variant, carried by the Naval Brigade, was more reliable if only because a tube was a more secure launcher, and the heavier rocket more stable in flight.

Nevertheless, although neither could be relied upon for accuracy, they were valued by the British as terror weapons. All rockets spewed out an intimidating spray of smoke and sparks, and streaked through the air with an unnerving howl. It was widely believed that unsophisticated enemies – such as the British naively believed the Zulus to be – would be overawed by this demonstration of the white man's terrible magic, and would lose the will to fight at a stroke. In fact, although the Zulus were facing rockets for the first time at Nyezane, they do not seem to have been intimidated by them in the least. Their descriptions of them were both practical and poetic; they called them variously 'paraffin', after the combustible liquid that white traders had sold among them, or, with a touch more symbolism, *imbane weZulu* – 'the lightning of heaven'.

This is not to say, however, that rockets did not cause damage. Fifty years after the war, Chief Zimema, a warrior of the uMxapho *ibutho*, gave a chilling description of just what it was like to be on the receiving end of so much imperial military hardware:

> They brought out their 'by-and-by' [artillery] and we heard what we thought was a long pipe coming through the air toward us.... We never got nearer than 50 paces to the English, and although we tried to climb over our fallen brothers, we could not get very far ahead because the white men were firing heavily closer to the ground while the 'by-and-by' was firing over our heads into the regiments behind us ... The battle was so fierce that we had to wipe the blood and brains of the killed and wounded from our heads, faces, arms, legs and shields after the fighting.

Such a storm of fire kept the warriors pinned down in the gully below the knoll, but further to the Zulu left, the tip of the horn had continued to advance. Captain Warren Wynne of the Engineers had been supervising his men, who were keeping the drift clear for the passage of the wagons, when the battle had first begun. Hearing the firing, he had ridden up in time to see Pearson deploy on the knoll. The tip of the Zulu horn was already moving rapidly round to Pearson's right, however, threatening the wagons, and heading for the drift. Wynne returned to his men, and promptly ordered them to stop working and take up their rifles. He then formed them into line and advanced to the foot of the slope, deploying some way below Pearson's line, but effectively forming its right flank. The ground was covered with bush here, and Wynne carefully posted his men to take advantage of the cover, opening fire on the tip of the Zulu horn as it raced towards them 250 yards away. As two more companies of the Buffs crossed the river, under Captains Wyld and Harrison, they moved into a position on Wynne's right, effectively blocking any chance the Zulus might have had of completing the encircling movement.

Initially, Wyld and Harrison had been joined, too, by a detachment from HMS *Active*'s Naval Brigade, including the Gatling gun under the command of a popular young midshipman, Lewis Coker. The gunners had run the gun forward into the bush – and in doing so broken the limber-pole, much to Coker's disgust – in the hope of getting a clear line of fire, but in fact the low-lying ground made this impossible, and Coker decided instead to manhandle the gun up to the knoll.

The Gatling, invented by an American, Dr Richard Gatling, during the later stages of the Civil War, was the first of a number of multi-barrelled machine-guns adopted by the British Army and Navy. It consisted of ten heavy-calibre barrels arranged around a fixed axis; it was operated by cranking a handle, which rotated the barrels and fired each one in turn. Although Sir Garnet Wolseley had taken a Gatling on his expedition to Asante in West Africa in 1873, and had used it in a demonstration intended to overawe Asante envoys, it had not previously been fired by British troops in anger.

Once in position, Coker directed the gun towards the warriors sheltering in the bush at the foot of Wombane, and it opened up with a noisy clatter. Experience in Zululand would soon demonstrate that the weapon had its faults – the extractor claw had a tendency to tear the bases off the soft brass cartridges, leaving the rest stuck in the breech, while the bolts sometimes worked loose and fell out into the long grass – but when it worked, it spewed out rounds at the rate of 300 a minute, and could be devastatingly effective. The Zulu fire had been especially hot from one particular section of the bush, and Coker's crew directed their aim into it, suppressing the fire, and forcing the surviving Zulus to abandon their cover. As they scattered, the crew took up their rifles, to pick off individual targets.

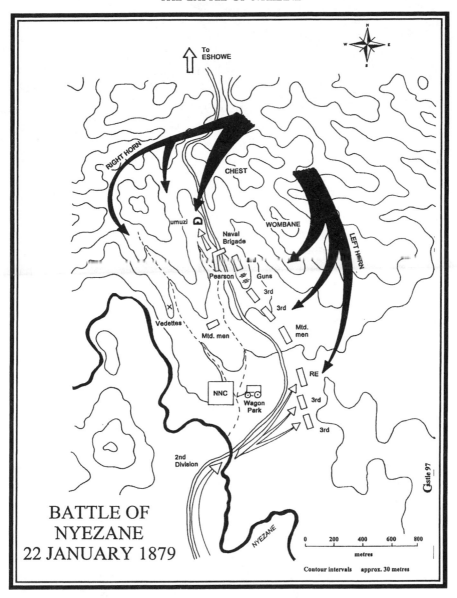

To
ESHOWE

RIGHT HORN

CHEST

WOMBANE

LEFT HORN

umuzi

Naval
Brigade

Pearson   Guns

3rd

3rd

Vedettes

Mtd. men

Mtd.
men

RE

NNC

3rd

Wagon
Park

3rd

2nd
Division

Castle 97

NYEZANE

BATTLE OF
NYEZANE
22 JANUARY 1879

0   200   400   600   800

metres

Contour intervals   approx. 30 metres

The Zulu left horn, which had attacked with such vigour, now seemed to have been checked, and Pearson's line was increasingly secure. The Zulus were not yet defeated, however, and another large body, the chest, had advanced cautiously down the spur from the head of the road, and had occupied a deserted homestead about three hundred yards from Pearson's left flank. Here they had opened a troublesome fire which struck down among the crowded British troops on the knoll. Furthermore, elements coming up from behind appeared to be preparing to extend as a right horn, with the intention of swinging out across the road and onto the next ridge across, effectively threatening Pearson's rear. As they did so, however, the Zulus came under fire from men of the Stanger and Victoria Mounted Rifles, who had been in position on the left of the road since the beginning of the fight. This appeared to discourage the Zulus, although a few companies attempted to extend still further to their right, masking their advance with the undulations of the ground, and hoping to slip round behind the Volunteers. Here, too, they were frustrated, for their move brought them out on the left-hand spur, directly in front of a small piquet of eight men of the Natal Hussars and Mounted Infantry, who had been placed as a vedette before the battle began. These men opened up a heavy fire, killing several of the leading Zulus, and causing the rest to fall back. After the battle, the failure of the right horn to launch any significant assault resulted in some recrimination among the Zulus. It seems likely, however, that the right horn mistook this vedette for a larger force, and was discouraged by the way the British were apparently protected on all sides.

At the head of the centre spur, meanwhile, the Zulus had been driven out of their secure position. HMS *Active*'s rocket tubes were under the command of Boatswain Cotter, who aimed them directly into the homestead up the slope ahead of him. This was exactly the work for which the rockets were best suited, and the first shell scorched straight through the homestead, setting several of the huts on fire. As the flames took hold, the Zulus reluctantly abandoned the position, and moved instead into the bush on either side of the track near by.

By this time, the Zulu attack had ground to a halt on all sides, and some groups along the length of the left horn were beginning to run the gauntlet of British fire, and retire back over the crest. Pearson's position had by now been reinforced by four half companies sent forward from Welman's Second Division; Welman had heard the firing ahead, and immediately despatched his men in support. With the Zulu attack checked, Commander Campbell, in charge of the *Active*'s Naval Brigade, suggested to Pearson that the time had come to make a foray, to drive the Zulu chest away from the vicinity of the burning homestead, and to clear the road ahead. Pearson agreed, and allowed Campbell to use his own men, sending for a company of the Buffs, under Captain Forster, and some NNC under Hart, to support him. The sailors received the order with delight, and set off up the slope with an undisciplined enthusiasm that amused the infantry officers:

The Jack Tars seemed mad for blood, for they charged up the hill in any formation banging away left and right, driving the Zulus before them. The company of the Buffs did their best to keep up with the sailors, but were not equal to the occasion, as they had been 'doubled' up from the rear in order to take part in the attack.

As the assault reached the top of the spur, however, it ran out of steam. The Zulus in front of them were secure in the bush, and stubbornly refused to give way, while the sailors were also exposed to fire from the higher ridges on either side. No less than seven sailors were hit, and the rest were forced to wait for the Buffs company coming up behind to reinforce them. The advance continued to within about 100 yards of the Zulu position, only to stall again. Two of the Buffs were killed, and Lieutenant Colonel Parnell, who had come forward himself to urge the men on, had his horse shot under him. Campbell sent orders to bring up a detachment of Royal Marines, who had been left guarding the Gatling, to come forward, but before they arrived, he had galvanised his own men once more. The sailors made a final rush forward, and this time the Zulu position collapsed. There was a brief flurry of hand-to-hand fighting, and the Zulus began to stream away up the track.

A prisoner taken in the battle later observed that the Zulus felt they were still holding their own until 'those horrible men in the white trousers rushed up and showered lead upon them'. Hart's NNC, coming up to the left of the sailors, flushed out the last Zulus lingering in the burning homestead, before Campbell and Parnell led their combined force further up the spur. Once they had reached the top, they gained sight of some of the rear slopes of Wombane, and directed their fire at several large bodies of the enemy who were reluctantly drifting away from the battlefield.

The success of Campbell's foray broke the last Zulu resistance. All along their line, the Zulus were now retiring. Many of them carried wounded colleagues, while others were so exhausted that they cast aside their shields and weapons and simply fled.

This was an ideal moment for Pearson to employ cavalry in pursuit, and turn the retreat into a rout. In fact, however, he had none apart from the Natal Volunteers and MI, and these he now ordered out of their various positions in the line, and to mount up and drive through the bush and long grass at the foot of Wombane. The last few Zulus scattered before them, but Pearson nonetheless recalled his men before they became too caught up in the chase, fearing that with their small numbers they might find themselves cut off.

At about 9.30 a.m., Pearson ordered the cease-fire to sound, and the battle was over. It had lasted little more than an hour and a half, and Pearson's casualties were surprisingly light, just twelve men killed and twenty more wounded, two of them mortally. The Zulu casualties were considerably higher, 300 dead by a conservative account, although the true figure was probably nearer 400, with hundreds more wounded.

The Natal Volunteers, recalled across the battlefield, were struck by the stoicism with which many of the Zulus suffered terrible injuries. Many were moved to compassion, and dismounted to offer their fallen enemies a drink, or try to drag them into the comfort of some shade. Here and there they came across clumps of seven or eight bodies, cut down by a volley, or horribly mangled by shellfire. The passage of the rockets was marked by a number of dead and wounded who bore hideous burn injuries from the flaming propellant.

On the whole, the battle had been a sobering experience. The regulars had behaved impeccably, the Natal Volunteers – most of whom were in action for the first time – had proved their worth, and even the NNC had shown themselves capable when they had been properly led. If the new weapon technology had not been entirely reliable, it had at least shown promise. The Gatling had easily suppressed enemy fire from the bush, and had chopped down knots of Zulus whenever they exposed themselves in the open. The rockets had been inaccurate – one artillery officer commented that the Naval Brigade's 24-pounders had scared their own side as much as the enemy – but had served their purpose as an incendiary device, and had undoubtedly inflicted casualties.

The British, nevertheless, were impressed with the Zulus, who had shown far more discipline, tactical instinct and sheer raw courage than ever they had expected. That in itself did not bode well for the future; Colour Sergeant Burnett of the 99th expressed the general mood when he wrote to colleagues at home: 'I tell you what it is: Our "school" at Chatham, over one hot whiskey, used to laugh about these niggers, but I assure you that fighting with them is terribly earnest work, and not child's play.'

Once the cease-fire had sounded, Pearson instructed the NNC to dig a pit beside the road, and the British casualties were buried there, under the shade of a large tree. A few of the Zulu bodies on the lower slopes of Nyezane were apparently gathered up and buried, but the rest were left where they lay. Nor was it possible to seek out and succour the Zulu wounded, since they were too scattered, and Pearson in any case had no facilities to care for large numbers of enemy wounded. Many lay out until they simply died of shock, loss of blood, or exposure; British convoys found wounded men still alive on the battlefield several days later. Others were lucky enough to have relatives and friends who lived close by, who came to seek them out once the *abelungu* had departed.

Pearson allowed his men to relax and recover for two hours, then they were ordered to fall in and resume the march. He was keen to demonstrate to the Zulus that their attack had not delayed him in the slightest, but there was a practical urgency, too; the sun had reached its height, and the unburied dead were already beginning to swell up and smell.

As the mounted men ahead of the column reached the top of the spur, they could see long lines of Zulus, retiring in good order to a flat-topped hill a few miles away to their right, where they were rallying. Further off, large numbers of non-combatants, old men, women, and boys, could also be seen, drifting disconsolately away; they had turned out to watch the *amabutho* destroy the invaders, and were stunned to see the flower of their youth defeated.

Nevertheless, although the Zulu army had been repulsed, it had by no means been destroyed. The effectiveness of the British firepower had come as a bitter shock to the regiment most exposed to it – the uMxapho – and the Zulus were also greatly disappointed in the performance of their own firearms, which seemed to have caused very few casualties in the British ranks. Yet the uMxapho were angry, too, at the performance of their colleagues in the chest and right horn, who were mostly older men, and who had appeared to them to hang back, and be reluctant to face the British fire. Indeed, King Cetshwayo, when he heard of the defeat, was said to have gone further, and blamed Chief Godide for not having exercised greater tactical control during the fight. There was some truth in this. The battle had begun with a spontaneous encounter and, typically, the younger uMxapho had rushed forward without waiting for the other regiments to be in position. If the attack had been better coordinated, the Zulus might still have benefited from the surprise, for Pearson, too, had been caught on the hop, and the column was dangerously exposed. In the final analysis, the British had won the battle not simply because of their firepower, but because their greater discipline had enabled them to regain the initiative first, and having gained it, to retain it.

For all that, Godide's force remained prepared to challenge Pearson once more, and rather than disperse immediately to undergo the necessary post-combat purification rituals, most of the warriors moved north into the Mhlatuze valley, which lay between Pearson and oNdini, assuming that the British would continue their advance in that direction.

If they expected another fight soon, however, they were to be disappointed. On the evening after the battle, Pearson halted his command on the windy ridge-tops not far from Eshowe, and on the following morning he occupied the deserted mission itself. The neat European church and dwellings, and the carefully tended orchard of fruit trees, struck many as a profound and peaceful contrast to their recent experience of battle in the heart of wildest Africa. Here Pearson unloaded his supplies, and set about establishing a temporary depot. He expected to receive orders from Lord Chelmsford soon, confirming the instructions for the next stage of his advance, but in the meantime the post was made secure. To the men's great regret, the fruit trees were cut down to clear a field of fire, the buildings were loopholed for defence, and Captain Wynne's Engineers began to trace out the lines of an earthwork enclosing the complex.

Yet when Pearson despatched a message to Chelmsford informing him of his victory, and that he had achieved his first objective, he received no immediate response. On the 26th, the first rumours reached the garrison that something was amiss. Some of the mounted men – Volunteers, who spoke Zulu – were out on vedette duty that morning, and heard Zulus shouting to one another across distant hilltops. They were spreading the news that they had won a great victory elsewhere in the kingdom. Later that day a runner brought a despatch from Pietermaritzburg, bearing the news that Colonel Durnford had been defeated and killed. As far as Pearson knew, Durnford's command was a small one, situated at Middle Drift along the central reaches of the Thukela. The news was worrying, but not disastrous, and Pearson ordered Wynne to redouble his efforts to secure the mission station. The blow fell the following day when a message arrived from Lord Chelmsford himself, baldly cancelling all his previous instructions, warning Pearson that he could expect to be attacked by the full weight of the Zulu army, and ordering him to act as he thought best.

It would be several days before the true situation became clear to Pearson's command. A disaster had befallen more than Durnford's command; early on the afternoon of the 22 January – the same day that Pearson had won his victory at Nyezane – almost half the troops of the Centre Column, reinforced by Durnford's men, had been wiped out when the main Zulu army had fallen on Chelmsford's camp at the foot of a distinctive rocky outcrop known as Isandlwana.

The implications for Pearson were devastating. His command was now unsupported, isolated some 35 miles from the border, deep inside enemy territory, and with every possibility that the Zulus would cut his line of communication. Reinforcements, and even fresh supplies, were unlikely to be forthcoming; indeed, he lacked even proper signalling equipment to open communications with the garrison on the Thukela. He was unable to advance, but reluctant to retreat; after a hurried council of war with his officers, he decided to lighten the burden on his supplies by sending the mounted men and NNC back to the river, but instructing the rest of his command to stay put.

Within a week, the Zulus had returned to throw a light cordon around the hills overlooking the mission station. Eshowe was effectively under siege; it would remain so for nearly three months, until the tide of war swung once more in Britain's favour.

5

THE BATTLE OF ISANDLWANA
22 January 1879
'Dead was everything'

In the final months before the outbreak of war in 1879, King Cetshwayo had summoned his *amabutho* several times to oNdini. Each time there had seemed to be the threat of immediate military action by the British, but each time the threat had subsided, and the warriors had been allowed to disperse. This had caused some resentment, for many of the men felt the British were teasing them, and grumbled that they would not answer the call again, unless hostilities were really imminent. Once the British had delivered their ultimatum, however, the mood within the country became belligerent. Members of the younger regiments were angry that the British were treating their king as if he were a naughty child, and the iNgoba-makhosi in particular refused to countenance any suggestion that the sons of Sihayo should be surrendered. The iNgobamakhosi were the king's favourite regiment, composed of young men in their mid-twenties, and its size reflected the king's success in his attempts to revitalise the *amabutho* system; moreover, Mehlokazulu, Sihayo's senior son and one of those on the British wanted list, commanded a section within the regiment.

Thus, when the king finally decided to face the inevitable and assembled the army once more in the second week of January 1879, there was little complaint from the *amabutho* as a whole. This was, in any case, the traditional time when the nation assembled to undergo the important rituals of the umKhosi ceremony, which ushered in the new harvest. The umKhosi was an annual celebration of the ties that bound king and nation together, and secured the blessing of the ancestral spirits of the Royal House over the ripening crops. Traditionally, the great chiefs from the outlying districts all came to pay their respects to the king, and the *amabutho* assembled in all their splendid accoutrements. In 1879, however, the great gathering had ominous overtones, for Cetshwayo ordered the regiments to leave much of their finery behind, and to come instead prepared for war.

In the event, many of the important umKhosi observances were abandoned in favour, specifically, of more military ceremonies. Over several days from about 13 January, the great army was ritually prepared for the coming fight. These ceremonies were designed to bind the army together, to urge them to set aside any internal divisions, and to commit themselves completely to the cause of the king and his ancestors. To prevent the enemy from working any supernatural influence over them, the warriors had first to be purified, and they were then given medicines to fortify them spiritually.

The men were led to a specially selected spot, where those *izinyanga* – doctors – who specialised in warfare had prepared a pit in the ground. The warriors queued to sip from a bowl of medicine given to them by the *izinyanga*, and then stepped forward to vomit in the pit. When the ceremony was complete, the *izinyanga* carefully filled in the pit and disguised the site, in case any of the vomit should fall into enemy hands; since it represented a powerful part of the collective spirit of the nation, it could be worked by an enemy to perform considerable damage.

A strand of grass, dipped in the vomit, was taken by the *izinyanga* and bound into the *inkatha yeswe ya'kwaZulu*, the sacred coil of the nation, which consisted of a grass rope, bound in python skin, incorporating elements that represented the psychic dimension of the great people and events who constituted the kingdom. The *inkatha* had been founded by Shaka, and was believed to be the spiritual lynchpin that bound the nation together. Curiously enough, Shaka's *inkatha* survived until the last days of the war, when it was destroyed unknowingly by British patrols burning Zulu homesteads; and within a few days of its destruction, the kingdom did indeed begin to unravel under British pressure.

Once the army had been purified, it had to be made ready for war. Traditionally, this involved the death of a wild black bull, which had to be wrestled to the ground, unarmed, by the youngest *ibutho* present. When the beast was dead, the *izinyanga* took charge of the carcass, roasting the meat, cutting it into strips, and smearing it with medicine. The great army was then assembled in a circle, and the *izinyanga* walked among them, tossing the strips into the crowd of excited warriors. Each man snatched a strip, and bit off a mouthful, before tossing it back into the air. In theory, the warriors were supposed to chew the meat, rather than swallow, and the ritual would infuse them with the courage and power of the bull.

After the bull ceremony, the warriors were summoned before the king, who had himself undergone various rituals to prevent both his person and the nation being weakened by spiritual pollution. The king called out regiments in pairs, choosing those who were of roughly the same age, and directing them to challenge one another. Warriors would leap out of the ranks, and *giya* – perform a solitary display of mock combat – calling out to rivals whom they recognised in the ranks of the opposite regiment, promising to excel them in the coming fight. In this way the king harnessed existing regimental rivalries, and directed them against the enemy. In January 1879, the king first set the iNgobamakhosi *ibutho* to challenge the uKhandempemvu, and a few days later the uMbonambi and the uNokhenke. It is no coincidence that all of these regiments would excel themselves over the coming months.

In 1879, the preparatory rituals included a new element, which was a reflection of the increased contact with the European world. Cetshwayo had secured the services of a Sotho *inyanga*, from beyond the Kahlamba Mountains. The BaSotho had a reputation for skill with firearms, and this doctor had brought special medicines, designed to make the guns carried by the Zulus fire straight and true. He burned this medicine on a potsherd, and those warriors who had guns were required to file past, holding their weapons muzzle-down, so that the smoke drifted up the barrel. Finally, the entire army was assembled once more, and the doctors walked among them, using wildebeest-tail switches to sprinkle the warriors with medicines from pots carried by their attendants. These medicines, *izintelezi*, would turn aside the weapons of the enemy.

Once the ceremonies were complete, the warriors were set apart from ordinary life. The ancestral spirits watched over them, and they were focused solely on war, protected against the harmful effects of shedding the blood of others, and prepared to some extent for their own suffering. They were required to abstain from all contact with their womenfolk, for fear of weakening themselves, and bringing disaster on the nation as a whole. They were possessed of an extraordinary collective tension, one which, moreover, would build steadily throughout the inevitable delays in reaching the front, and which could only find release in the adrenaline rush of combat.

King Cetshwayo did not accompany his army into the field in person. Instead, he gave command of the greater part of it to two of his most trusted generals, Ntshingwayo kaMahole and Mavumengwana kaNdlela. He had previously instructed them to lead the army towards Lord Chelmsford's incursion at Rorke's Drift, but to march slowly, so that the men were not exhausted when they reached the enemy. With the lesson of Blood River in mind, he strongly advised his generals not to attack defended positions, but to catch the British in the open. Nor, indeed, were they to ignore any opportunity, even at this late stage, to resolve the crisis by negotiation. Beyond that, he trusted them to use their own judgement. It was traditional, however, for the king to address the army as it set off on campaign, and once again the *amabutho* were formed up in a semicircle in the central enclosure of the kwaNodwengu *ikhanda*, close to oNdini. Cetshwayo spoke to them, pointing out that he had no quarrel with the British, and had not gone overseas to look for them, yet they had come into his lands to confront him. The young warriors were indignant. 'Give the matter to us,' they shouted, 'they will not take you while we are alive.' The king responded that he was sending them to attack the British, and that they should drive them back across the border, but on no account cross into Natal themselves. Then, late on the afternoon of 17 January, the largest army assembled in the kingdom's history marched out to face its greatest challenge.

Sure enough, the army did not proceed far that first night, crossing the White Mfolozi and bivouacking in the emaKhosini valley. Here were the graves of the nation's ancestors, and it was important that the army paid its respects to their shades before continuing. The following day, it contented itself with marching to the uSixepi *ikhanda*, on the slopes of the eMthonjaneni Heights overlooking the valley. Then Chief Godide's contingent separated from them, and departed for the coast.

The army now comprised some 24,000 men, mostly the younger *amabutho*, the pride of the nation. Youngest of all were the uVe, who had only recently been enrolled, and had been brigaded temporarily with the older iNgobamakhosi; then came the uKhandempemvu, the uNokhenke, the uMbonambi, iSangqu, uDududu, and iMbube, and a cluster of married, middle-aged regiments associated with the royal homestead at oNdini itself – the uThulwana, iNdluyengwe, iNdlondlo and uDloko.

Not all of these regiments were complete, however, as elements of each who lived in the coastal or northern districts had heeded the king's orders and had stayed behind there to watch the progress of the British flanking columns. Moreover, the *impi* also included a few companies of regiments such as the uMxapho, who had otherwise gone to reinforce the coastal sector, and a handful of men from older regiments who had still responded to the muster. A number of important individuals held regimental or company commands within the army, including Zibhebhu kaMaphitha, the shrewd and aggressive head of the Mandlakazi section of the royal house, who was senior *induna* of the uDloko, and had been appointed chief of scouts. Several of the king's brothers were present, although not always with specific appointments. Rather, they represented royal authority, and they included the princes Ndabuko kaMpande, Magwendu kaMpande, and Dabulamanzi kaMpande. Vumandaba kaNtati, one of the king's senior advisers, and one of the envoys who had received the British ultimatum, commanded the uKhandempemvu, and Sigcwelecwele kaMhlekehleke led the boisterous iNgobamakhosi. Chief Sihayo commanded a group of mounted men who acted as scouts, presumably because the army would be operating in his territory, while his son Mehlokazulu was present with his regiment.

Indeed, the Zulu intelligence system far outclassed that of its British counterpart. Because the Zulu army comprised the male portion of the nation under arms, there were always men present among its ranks who knew the terrain, when it was fighting on its own soil. Moreover, the civilian population constantly fed back information concerning the conspicuous movements of the redcoats. On the march, it was customary for scouts to be thrown out at least a day's march ahead of the army, while a vanguard of warriors, picked for their stamina and courage, served to screen the advance of the main body.

This was the system followed in 1879, and it could scarcely have been more effective. On 19 January, the army split into two columns as it climbed onto the great ridge which runs from Mthonjaneni towards Babanango Mountain. Ntshingwayo commanded the left column, and Mavumengwana the right, and the two columns advanced a few miles apart, but keeping within sight of each other. At this stage in the war, there seems to have been no shortage of provisions, and young lads not quite old enough to be enrolled drove slaughter cattle and carried mats and mealies for their fathers or brothers in the ranks. Many young girls also carried food for their kinsmen; after two or three days, once their load was exhausted, they would return to their homes, although many of the boys sought excuses to see something of the fighting.

It was customary for these non-combatants to march towards the rear of the columns, and to one side, so that they were unlikely to be caught in any surprise attack. Normally, when the army was moving rapidly, their provisions would last long enough to see the warriors beyond the kingdom's borders, and after that they would live by raiding their neighbours. In 1879, however, there are suggestions that the concentration of so many warriors actively fighting inside Zululand led to tensions with the civilian population, and many ordinary Zulus took the precaution of moving their grain supplies and livestock out of reach as the army passed by.

By the evening of the 19th, the army had reached Babanango Mountain, and on the 20th it advanced to Siphezi Mountain. It was, at that point, approaching to within striking distance of the British column, for that same day Lord Chelmsford advanced his camp to the foot of Isandlwana Hill, only about fifteen miles as the crow flies from Siphezi. The two armies were slowly feeling their way towards each other, waltzing grimly in a dance of death which would culminate in the most cataclysmic confrontation of the entire war.

In fact, Lord Chelmsford's progress had been slow since he had crossed the border at Rorke's Drift on the 11th. Like Pearson, his crossing had been unopposed, and he had established a large camp on the Zulu bank of the Mzinyathi. Like Pearson, too, he was following an established traders' track, which wound through the green hills towards oNdini. Directly ahead of Chelmsford lay the territory of Chief Sihayo, whose sons had been named in the British ultimatum.

Chelmsford was determined to prove that he meant business, and he could not afford, in any case, to advance while Sihayo remained potentially hostile. On the 12th, therefore, he had mounted a strong foray which had advanced into the Batshe Valley – Sihayo's heartland – and attacked his followers. As it happened, neither Sihayo himself, nor Mehlokazulu, were at home, both having gone to attend the king at oNdini. Sihayo, however, had left several hundred of his retainers under the command of another son, Mkhumbikazulu, to look after his cattle and property, and these had taken up a good defensive position in the boulders at the foot of a line of cliffs. In the event, they were easily dispersed after a short, sharp fight, during which Mkhumbikazulu was killed, and Chelmsford's victorious force advanced up the valley to Sihayo's homestead, kwaSoxhege. After looting it of curiosities, the British set it on fire, and retired to their camp at the river.

Chelmsford was well pleased with his initial encounter. The courage of the Zulus had not gone unremarked, but rather than persuade the British to reconsider their superior attitude towards their enemies, it merely encouraged a growing sense of complacency. Sihayo's followers may have fought well enough, but they were no match for the British, and both Chelmsford and most of the men under his command emerged from the incident more convinced than ever that they were equal to any challenge the Zulus might throw at them.

After the highpoint of the attack on Sihayo's homestead, however, Chelmsford became bogged down – quite literally – in the practical difficulties of his advance. From Rorke's Drift the track ran through the Batshe Valley before skirting a low range of hills, then dropped to cross the rocky bed of a stream known as the Manzimnyama. From here it rose again, passing across a nek between Isandlwana Hill and a koppie below it, before spilling out on an open plain which covered some twelve miles of open country. On the far side of the plain, in the direction of oNdini, the hills closed in once more in an arc which surrounded the spectacular head of the Mangeni Gorge to the south-east, running northwards in a series of inter-connected outcrops until they reached Siphezi. Chelmsford intended to make Isandlwana, just twelve miles away, his next temporary camp-site, but the road through the Batshe valley was in poor condition, and the regular nightly deluges of rain did not improve it. Rather than risk his column becoming bogged down, he opted instead to stay at Rorke's Drift, but to send his Engineers out under escort to prepare the road for his advance. It was not until the 20th that he was able to finally make the move.

In the light of subsequent events, Chelmsford was much criticised for the choice of camp-site at Isandlwana. The mountain itself still has a curious atmosphere, which is not just the result of the events that took place there. Isandlwana Hill, an isolated spur of the iNyoni ridge that frames it to the north, rises some 300 feet above the surrounding plain, and its sheer southern face reflects the shifting patterns of light, alternately dark and brooding, or mysterious, even remorseless, and enigmatic. It dominates the landscape for miles around, seeming to hang, on wet days, between the earth and the lowering cloud, while on bright days it is a dark smudge against the sunlit hills, its face largely in shadow. Certainly, many of those with Chelmsford's force felt its power, and noted that its curious outline bore a similarity to the sphinx – the regimental badge of the 24th Regiment, whose two battalions constituted the backbone of the column. Not everyone considered this to be a good omen.

Yet in fact, Isandlwana – the name means 'it looks just like a small hut', an obscure and typically Zulu reference to a fancied resemblance to a cow's internal organs – was as good a site for a camp as any. It offered a clear view of the enemy approach, and there was no shortage either of water or firewood. When No. 3 Column crossed the nek on the morning of the 20th, Chelmsford's staff marked out positions for the camp on a slope on the far side, facing towards the enemy, without giving too much thought to its defensibility. Despite the fact that Chelmsford's own Standing Orders, published before the war began, insisted that all permanent camps should be partially entrenched, no attempt was made to protect it. Chelmsford later argued that the camp was too large, and the ground too rocky, to dig trenches all round, and so it was; yet the real reason for this carelessness was that Chelmsford neither expected to remain at Isandlwana long, nor believed the Zulus would dare to attack him.

It is perhaps worth saying at this point that Lieutenant General Frederic Thesiger, Second Baron Chelmsford, was no fool. He was a career soldier, who had seen active service in a wide number of Victorian military expeditions, ranging in type from the post-Napoleonic formal fighting of the Crimea to the perfectly executed Abyssinian expedition of 1868. Chelmsford was a tall, bearded man with impeccable manners who was known for his politeness to everyone under his command; as he could afford to be, being assured of his place as an officer and a gentleman, a pillar of the Victorian establishment.

At a time when dissension was brewing in the British Army, when the ways of the great Duke himself, Wellington, and his admirers – who included the Duke of Cambridge, the Commander-in-Chief – were under attack from a school of younger, more radical reformers, Chelmsford conformed thoroughly to the old school, for he was in most things conservative. Yet if there was no obvious trace of dash or flair evident in his career, he was certainly competent, as his most recent service – bringing to a close the 9th Cape Frontier War – indicated. Chelmsford had been warned by a number of colonists not to underestimate the Zulus, but he could not quite bring himself to believe that they were in any important way different from the Xhosa. Ironically, given that the Victorian army was often criticised for not profiting by its own experience, Lord Chelmsford relied too heavily on his. In his mind, the concentrated modern firepower of the regular British infantry was inevitably superior to the wagon-laagers of the frontier farmers, which had not been tested since 1838, and he saw no reason to suppose that the Zulus could withstand its effects any more than the Xhosa had.

By the time Chelmsford arrived at Isandlwana, the first reports had reached him that the Zulu army had left oNdini three days before, and that a significant part of it was advancing in his direction. Quite correctly, he guessed that it was only a matter of time before he encountered it, and, indeed, that it might already be nearing the hills, twelve miles away, which impeded his view towards oNdini. The open plain in front of the camp would provide ample warning if the Zulus chose to mount a direct attack, but Chelmsford's flanks remained problematic. On his left, the iNyoni heights blocked his view only a mile from the camp, yet the surface of the heights was comparatively open, and Chelmsford was sceptical that the Zulus could, in any case, slip round him on that side, given that he was supported 30 miles away in that direction by Colonel Wood's Left-Flank Column.

More worrying was his right flank. Here, a high, rocky hill, Malakatha, cut off his view towards the Mzinyathi downstream, and a low plateau, Hlazakazi, ran away from him towards the head of the Mangeni Gorge. Beyond these hills Chelmsford knew that the country was wild and rugged, and it was possible that the Zulu army could slip into the Mangeni Gorge, then follow it down to the Mzinyathi, using the hills to mask a dangerous outflanking move. Even as his soldiers struggled to unpack their tents and equipment from their supply wagons, Chelmsford rode out with some of his staff, to view the Mangeni Gorge from the shoulder of Hlazakazi. His worries must have been confirmed by the undulating maze of blue hills which fold over one another to the horizon. From their vantage point Chelmsford's staff observed that the country below seemed deserted; it was on their minds, nevertheless, that an entire army might have lain hidden in this difficult terrain without them being able to spot a single warrior.

As soon as he returned to the camp, Chelmsford made preparations to scour thoroughly through the Malakatha and Hlazakazi complex. Like Pearson, he was dependent on a squadron of regular Mounted Infantry and a handful of Natal Volunteers for cavalry, but the men attached to his column included some of the most experienced volunteer troops in Natal, notably the quasi-military Natal Mounted Police and the Natal Carbineers. These were augmented by two smaller units, raised from among the farmers of the Mzinyathi border: the Newcastle Mounted Rifles and Buffalo Border Guard. Chelmsford instructed Major John Dartnell, an experienced soldier who had settled in Natal and commanded the Mounted Police, to lead a thorough reconnaissance of the heights. Dartnell would be supported by the 3rd Regiment, NNC, under the command of a Frontier War veteran, Commandant Rupert Lonsdale. The detachment was to set out at dawn the following morning, 21 January. While the mounted men were to search the summits of the range, the NNC would descend into the hot valleys beyond, work their way around the far side of Hlazakazi, and emerge via the Mangeni Gorge at the far end. They were to rendezvous with Dartnell's men at the head of the gorge. Chelmsford was quite specific that Dartnell's object was to look for signs of enemy activity in the hills, but that he was to return to Isandlwana before dark.

Dawn on the 21st was particularly striking, the rising sun catching on a distinctive cloud that hung over Isandlwana Hill. The NNC were excited at the possibility of action, while many of the regulars were disappointed to be left in camp, afraid that the colonials would snatch their share of the glory. In fact, both the NNC and the mounted men were in for a difficult day. The NNC faced a long march over very broken country, strewn with boulders and often covered in thick bush. To the rank and file, accustomed to moving in such terrain on foot, it was nothing out of the ordinary, but many of the white NCOs and officers began to suffer as the sun rose and the temperature climbed. Furthermore, the landscape seemed almost unnaturally empty, and the NNC were able to capture only a few herdboys and girls. There was no sign of the big *impi* that Lord Chelmsford was seeking.

No sign, that is, until the NNC made the difficult scramble out of the Mangeni Gorge late that afternoon. At the top they met up with Dartnell's mounted men, who had already tentatively scouted through the hills towards Siphezi, further towards oNdini. Here one group had run into a party of several hundred Zulus, who had retired rapidly, and been lost among the hills.

This encounter was a very real dilemma for Dartnell. While he had discovered no enemy presence on either side of the Malakatha–Hlazakazi range, he had now made contact with a force which might, indeed, have been moving towards the Mangeni Gorge, just as Lord Chelmsford predicted. If Dartnell were to be back at Isandlwana by nightfall, he would need to return soon; yet it was clearly unsatisfactory to leave without achieving some very clear idea of the enemy's whereabouts and intentions. He decided to order the NNC up onto a relatively secure position at the end of the Hlazakazi ridge, and to lead the mounted men into the hills at the head of the Mangeni Gorge.

It was a fateful decision; the horsemen had only ridden a few hundred yards when suddenly a Zulu force appeared over the skyline in front of them. The Zulus advanced rapidly, throwing out horns on either side, before halting, and retiring over the hill as quickly as they had appeared. It was an unnerving sight; it was difficult to tell how many warriors there had been, but there were certainly several hundred, and the mounted men were impressed by their order and discipline. Indeed, their sudden flight seemed all too convenient, and Dartnell resolved not to pursue them, suspecting that they were trying to lure him into a trap.

If Dartnell had been in a quandary before, he was doubly so now. He had indeed learned more about the Zulu whereabouts, but it had done him little good, except to give the impression that the surrounding hills were alive with the enemy. It was getting dark, and a march back to Isandlwana would not only break contact, it would expose his command to the possibility of an attack in the rear. The NNC on the heights were already getting jittery, and Dartnell decided instead to join them with the mounted men, and to send a message back to Chelmsford, informing him of what he had seen, and explaining that he would have to stay out overnight.

This message reached Chelmsford at about 1.30 in the morning, and it is crucial to understand his thinking when assessing his next actions. Everything that Dartnell told him confirmed his existing suspicions; the Zulus were exactly where he thought they would be, and, rather than risk a direct confrontation, they did indeed appear to be using the terrain to slip past his flank. This was just the sort of behaviour he had learned to expect of the Xhosa, who had become masters of the hit-and-run tactic. If he did nothing, it was highly likely that the Zulus would be gone by morning, probably lurking somewhere in his rear. Clearly, it would not be possible to advance his entire force to meet them in time; instead, he gave the order for roughly half his command to make ready to march out to confront them. He would take command of this party, to consist of most of the 2/24th, and four guns from N/5 Battery's complement of six. The baggage and camp equipment he would leave behind with a strong force to guard them; he would take along only ambulances, and with nothing to slow him down, he might be able to reach Dartnell at daybreak, in time to give the Zulus an unpleasant surprise.

Before Chelmsford departed, one of his staff reminded him that he did have further troops at his disposal. When planning the campaign, Chelmsford had stationed one of his defensive columns, under the command of Brevet Colonel Anthony Durnford, RE, on the high escarpment overlooking the Middle Drift and the Thukela, half-way between his own column and Pearson's. Durnford was an interesting character, and his role in the unfolding drama would be crucial. He had been Chief Military Engineer in Natal for a number of years, and in 1873 had been involved in an incident that had left a profound mark on him, both physically and psychologically.

In that year, a chieftain living in the Kahlamba foothills, Langalibalele kaMthimkhulu, had fallen foul of the Natal authorities over firearms which his young men had brought back as wages from working in the diamond fields. Langalibalele had tried to flee across the mountains into BaSotholand, and Durnford had been placed in charge of a group of colonial volunteers who had, quite literally, been ordered to cut Langalibalele off at the pass. The expedition had gone badly wrong, however, and several of the volunteers had been killed, while Durnford himself was badly injured by a spear-thrust through the his left elbow. Langalibalele, moreover, got away, though he was later betrayed by the BaSotho and arrested. Public opinion in Natal put the blame for the fiasco squarely on Durnford, and Durnford, too much of a gentleman to embroil himself in public wrangling, nursed a deep sense of injustice. Unlike many regular – and certainly colonial – officers, Durnford had come to like and respect the African people among whom he worked, and for this reason Chelmsford had placed him in charge of a column which consisted largely of black troops, both infantry and cavalry. Durnford undoubtedly saw the Zulu campaign as an opportunity to prove himself in action, and wipe out the stain of the Langalibalele affair. As a result, he was a little too keen, and Chelmsford had already had cause to rebuke him for acting too much on his own initiative. When Chelmsford moved forward to Isandlwana, he had ordered Durnford's column up from Middle Drift to Rorke's Drift, partly to have him available to support his own advance, but also very probably to have Durnford rather more firmly under his control.

Reminded of Durnford's presence, Chelmsford sent a rather casually worded order instructing him to move up to Isandlwana. By this time, the men of the 2/24th had been roused – silently, so as not to give the Zulus any clue as to what might be happening – and at about 2.30 on the morning of the 22nd, Lord Chelmsford marched out to do battle with the enemy. Behind him in the camp he left five companies of the 1/24th, one of the 2/24th, two guns under the command of Major Stuart Smith, about 130 mounted men, and several companies of the 3rd NNC, who had been kept back on piquet duty. These were all under the overall command of Lieutenant Colonel Henry Pulleine, 1/24th.

Pulleine was an experienced soldier who had served throughout much of the Cape Frontier War, but his great strength lay in administration, and he had never before commanded troops in action. Nor, indeed, did anyone suppose he was to do so now; clearly Chelmsford appointed Pulleine precisely because he wanted someone efficient to run the camp in his absence. No one, from Chelmsford down, thought the camp was in any danger, and, indeed, Chelmsford's instructions to Pulleine in the event of an attack had been to the point: he was told simply to 'defend the camp'.

In the event, Chelmsford's morning proved to be frustrating. He reached the Mangeni Valley just after dawn – although his artillery lagged behind, hampered by the many dongas that cut across the track – only to find that the Zulus had disappeared during the night. Small groups could be seen here and there, watching from the hilltops, while the rest seemed to have retired in the direction of Siphezi Mountain. This was a pattern of warfare all too familiar to Chelmsford, who resigned himself to the need to flush the enemy out. Dartnell's mounted men were brought down from their bivouac, and sent to search through the surrounding hills, while the NNC and 24th companies scattered in pursuit of the Zulu stragglers. Here and there, sporadic skirmishing broke out, but there seemed to be no prospect of a major engagement.

Back at the camp, the morning passed quietly, with the men going about their business. A convoy of thirty wagons was due to return to Rorke's Drift to collect a stockpile of supplies, but the order had been cancelled pending the result of Chelmsford's foray, and the wagons were parked on the nek, behind the camp. At about 6 a.m., a large body of Zulus suddenly appeared on the crest of the iNyoni ridge, to the immediate left of the camp. The warriors made no attempt to descend the escarpment to attack, and the movement seems to have provoked curiosity in the camp, rather than alarm. Many of those present had seen equally large bodies of the enemy on the Cape Frontier, and they had learned to regard an attack as unlikely. Nevertheless, Pulleine prudently ordered the 1/24th to stand to, the men forming up on their parade-grounds in front of their tents. The Zulus had watched them for some time, before retiring beyond the crest and out of sight. Pulleine sent scouts up onto the ridge, who reported that the Zulus were, indeed, retiring to the north-west.

The 24th were still lined up when Durnford rode into camp at the head of his men at about 10.30. Durnford allowed his own command – some 250 men of the Natal Native Horse, and a section of two RA 9-pounder rocket tubes, escorted by infantry of the NNC – to off-saddle, while he sought out Pulleine. Technically, Durnford was senior in rank to Pulleine, and he might now have been expected to take command of the camp. Chelmsford's original order had not been clear on this point, however, and there were no fresh orders waiting for Durnford at Isandlwana. It was not clear to either officer what Chelmsford had expected of them in this regard, and Durnford was, in any case, inclined to maintain the independence of his own command. He suggested that Pulleine allow the 24th to stand down, but saw no reason to suppose that Pulleine, aided by the experienced and efficient officers of the 24th, was not in control of the situation.

Durnford was worried, however, that the Zulu presence on the iNyoni heights might pose some threat to Chelmsford. The Mangeni Gorge was about twelve miles away across the plain to the right front; here was a significant body of the enemy on the left front, and much closer to hand. Suppose the Zulus intended to get between Chelmsford and the camp? The general, having no supplies or battalion reserve of ammunition with him, could find himself in serious difficulties. Durnford decided that, rather than wait lamely at Isandlwana, he would take his own command out to search through the iNyoni range, and drive any Zulus he found there away from both Chelmsford and the camp. He asked if Pulleine would lend him some infantry to back up the move, but the officers of the 24th politely pointed out that their orders were to defend the camp. Durnford did not demur, but left with the parting comment that if he got into difficulties, he would expect their support.

Durnford rode out of the camp at about 11.30, an hour after he had first arrived. It is difficult not to conclude that he had used the ambiguity created by Chelmsford's orders to put himself in a position where he might best demonstrate his usefulness. Certainly, Durnford had been impatient, for his baggage wagons had lagged behind on the road from Rorke's Drift, and he had not waited for them to catch him up before riding out again; they arrived in camp after he had left. Not that there was anything intrinsically foolish about Durnford's decision, since the presence of Zulus on the iNyoni had not been anticipated by Chelmsford, and Durnford's command was ideally suited to investigate it.

Durnford had divided his command in two. Two troops of the NNH, under Lieutenants Raw and Roberts, were sent up onto the ridge by a spur closest to Isandlwana itself. A company of the 24th under Captain Cavaye marched up to the top of the escarpment, presumably as a result of Durnford's request that he be supported. Durnford himself took the rest of his command straight out across the plain, hugging the foot of the escarpment as it curved to the left, and out of sight from the camp. The idea was that the two parties would eventually join up, somewhere to the north-east of Isandlwana, beyond the ridge, having caught any Zulus in a pincer movement. It did not quite work out like that.

Once up on the heights, Raw and Roberts found themselves looking across several miles of an undulating grassy plateau. There were no large bands of the enemy in sight, but here and there small groups seemed to be retiring in the distance. The mounted men pursued them at a leisurely pace, until they were perhaps three or four miles from the camp. Then, quite close to them, they saw a group of Zulu herdboys, frantically trying to drive a few head of cattle to safety. Raw's men gave chase, and the Zulus could be seen struggling to drive their charges over a rocky rise ahead, before dropping out of sight on the far side. The pursuers clattered across the rise behind them, only to rein in short.

Below them, the ground fell away sharply into a gentle, open valley. The spot is a beautiful one, hardly altered after nearly 120 years; a soft stream, the Ngwebeni, flows through the valley, and today aloes dot the hillsides. At noon on 22 January, however, the attention of Raw's men was drawn to something other than the landscape. Sitting in the bottom of the valley, the closest of them only 200–300 yards away, were nearly 24,000 Zulu warriors.

That the Zulu army had managed to get so close to Isandlwana without being detected was, perhaps, their greatest master-stroke of the war. Early on the 21st, they had left their bivouac at the foot of Siphezi. Deploying in small groups, making the most of undulations in the ground, they had moved not south-west, where Dartnell would search for them later that day, but north-west, into the Ngwebeni. At one point they had almost been intercepted by a British patrol, but this was driven off by scouts led by

Zibhebhu kaMaphitha, and returned to Isandlwana with no clue as to the danger into which it had so nearly blundered. Opinion is still divided as to whether the Zulus had deliberately lured Chelmsford into dividing his force, but on the whole it seems unlikely. The men encountered by Dartnell were the followers of a local chief, Matshana kaMondise, who had been moving up the Mangeni valley, towards Siphezi, to join the main army; but they were late, for by that time most of the army had already reached the Ngwebeni. But Dartnell's accidental encounter had confirmed Chelmsford's preconceived ideas of how and where the Zulus would move, and had set the British off on the wrong tack.

Once in the Ngwebeni, the main army had sat quietly, not even lighting cooking fires for fear that the British might spot the smoke. Early on the morning of 22 January, there had apparently been mist in the valley, and the great war-shields presented a ghostly spectre as the warriors moved around. The dark patches on the hide appeared to dance of their own volition, earning the valley the name *Mahaweni* – the place of the war-shields. The army did not intend to attack that day, because of the coming new moon, but as soon as Raw's men appeared on the heights above them, it was clear that there could be no more waiting. The warriors of the uKhandempemvu, the regiment closest to the British incursion, sprang to their feet, seized their weapons, and rushed up the slope. With remarkable composure, Raw's men fired a volley, then retired on Roberts's troop, coming up behind, and both began to ride back towards Isandlwana.

The Zulu army spilled out of the Ngwebeni Valley in some confusion, the uKhandempemvu in the van, with other regiments drawn after them on either side. There had been no time to perform the last-minute pre-battle rituals, or for the commanders to address their men. Indeed, the best that Ntshingwayo and Mavumengwana could do was to hold back those *amabutho* who were camped furthest from the initial encounter. These were the regiments associated with the oNdini royal homestead itself, the uThulwana, the iNdlondlo, uDloko and iNdluyengwe. As tradition demanded, Ntshingwayo formed them into an *umkhumbi* (circle), and the specialist *izinyanga* spattered the warriors with the last dose of protective medicines. They were sent out of the valley, to follow in the wake of the main force, and act as the reserve.

Since the surface of the iNyoni heights is not visible from the foot of Isandlwana, Pulleine was unaware of the extent of the force bearing down on him. In the four or five miles from Ngwebeni to the lip of the iNyoni escarpment – the point at which the Zulus would spill over the skyline and come into view of the camp – the *amabutho* regained some of their order.

Guided, no doubt, by men who lived in the locality, they took up the traditional 'chest and horns' attack formation. More by luck than judgement, the youngest regiments – the uVe and iNgobamakhosi – became the left horn, while the slightly older uMbonambi, uKhandempemvu and uNokhenke comprised the chest. The iMbube, iSangqu and uDududu regiments formed the right horn. The *amabutho* advanced at a fast jogging space, the men evenly spaced, and protected by a screen of skirmishers thrown out several hundred yards in front. Quite possibly, some of the girls who had carried food for them followed behind, hanging on any rise to their rear, and encouraging the men with the high-pitched ululating cry which traditionally accompanied any excited occasion.

Raw promptly despatched messengers both to Pulleine and Durnford. Pulleine, when he received his, was sceptical; he could see nothing of the events beyond the ridge, and he, like everyone else in the command, was quite convinced that the main Zulu army was away at the Mangeni, facing Chelmsford. Nevertheless, he sent a further company of the 1/24th, under Mostyn, to support Cavaye's, which was already in place on the ridge. These men, too, were out of sight from the camp, and although Pulleine could clearly hear when they became engaged, he had little idea of what they were firing at. One of the few officers to survive the battle, Captain Edward Essex, accompanied Mostyn onto the hills, and described how he crested a rise, and saw Cavaye's men deployed in open order on the slope below him. They were firing at a long line of Zulus who were streaming round from behind a hill ahead, and moving across their front, from right to left. The 24th, he noted, were placing their shots well, but the Zulu advance was not slowed in the slightest. Ominously, he realised that the Zulus did not seem to have any intention of attacking the 24th, but were trying to move rapidly around their flank. Although he did not realise it, Essex was witnessing the right horn deploying in classic fashion.

Durnford, meanwhile, had ridden out several miles from the camp. Once again, he had been impatient; his rocket battery, escorted by NNC foot-soldiers, had lagged behind, and was out of sight. Durnford had followed the foot of the escarpment, curving round to his left, when Raw's messenger reached him. He was just considering the significance of this report when a large column of warriors – the left horn – suddenly came into view, only a few hundred yards away. Durnford ordered his men into line, and they dismounted, and fired a volley into the advancing warriors. Then they mounted up, and began to retire towards the camp. Every few hundred yards, they stopped and repeated the manoeuvre. A controlled retreat is always a difficult operation in battle, especially when the enemy

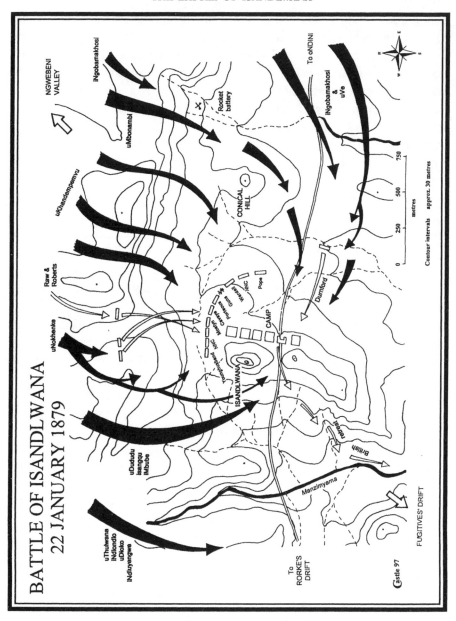

BATTLE OF ISANDLWANA
22 JANUARY 1879

are close behind – the temptation is not to stop and fire, but to keep on going – and it speaks volumes for Durnford's powers of command, and the respect in which his men held him, that he was able to keep them in hand. At times, the pursuing Zulus were only 50 yards away.

The rocket battery, meanwhile, had paid the price of Durnford's impatience. It had just passed an isolated conical koppie, near the foot of the escarpment, when news of the Zulu approach arrived. Durnford had, by this time, disappeared from view, and the battery's commander, Major Russell, decided to turn left, up onto the escarpment. He had just started up the slope when the first groups of Zulus – members of the iNgobamakhosi's skirmishers – appeared on the crest above. Russell ordered his men to set up the rocket apparatus on a slight rise near by. One rocket was fired which passed over the heads of the warriors, without doing any harm, and an anonymous member of the iNgobamakhosi called out 'lightning of heaven! See its glittering flash!', as the Zulus streamed into a donga. They emerged only a few yards to the left of Russell's position, and poured a volley into them at close range. Russell himself was wounded, and his command promptly fell apart. The mules panicked and fled, two falling over a boulder in their terror. Several of the crew were killed or wounded, and the NNC broke. Someone went to help Russell, but as they tried to carry him off the major was hit again and killed. By this time the Zulus had rushed in close, and the position was overrun. Only the gallant stand by one officer and a handful of particularly brave NNC allowed the survivors a chance to escape. The Zulu vanguard, deterred, saw Durnford's men suddenly come into view, and went to ground, waiting for the main body to come up behind them. Durnford's men collected the survivors from the battery, and continued towards Isandlwana.

At the camp, Pulleine reacted to the steady drum-roll of musketry from Mostyn's and Cavaye's companies by sending Major Smith's two guns out to a slight rise, several hundred yards from the tents, which commanded the iNyoni escarpment. Two of the 1/24th companies – Wardell's and Porteous's – were sent in support, and deployed in open order on either side. Although this position was a long way from the camp, it was a good one from a tactical point of view, since beyond it the ground dipped into a slight hollow, scarred by a donga, before rising again to the escarpment. From the camp, this hollow was dead ground; from the rise just above it, Pulleine's men could rake it with fire.

At this point there were still no Zulus visible from the camp, and Pulleine was deploying his men in a line facing due north, the direction from which the threat was apparently developing. To the right of the guns were a company of the NNC and a company of the 2/24th, under Lieutenant Pope, both of whom had been on piquet duty, facing across the plain. Pope's company swung left to form the right anchor of the line, and the NNC company found themselves included almost by accident.

Suddenly, the full extent of the Zulu attack became apparent as the first elements of the chest –the uNokhenke, uKhandempemvu and uMbonambi *amabutho* – reached the escarpment, and spilled over into sight from the camp. Pulleine, realising that Mostyn and Cavaye were in danger of being cut off, sent the adjutant of the 1/24th, Lieutenant Melvill, to recall them. Captain Younghusband's company was positioned at the tail of Isandlwana Hill to cover their retreat. They retired down the slope in some confusion, mixed up with the men from Raw's and Roberts's commands, who had rallied close to them. Indeed, as they fell back, and the artillery in camp opened fire on the Zulus pressing down behind them, there are suggestions that one of the shells struck Roberts's command, killing Roberts himself. When they reached the bottom, however, they reformed, Mostyn and Cavaye falling in next to Porteous, with the Native Horse between them and Younghusband. As the Zulu chest began to push down the escarpment, they came under a heavy rifle and shell-fire, and took such serious casualties that the uNokhenke, on their right, was forced to retire for a few minutes behind the skyline, and redirected its attack from a less exposed position.

By this time, Durnford's men had appeared in view, retreating steadily across the plain, with the left horn close behind them. About 1000 yards from the camp, they reached a large donga, the Nyogane, where a piquet of mounted men from the camp had already taken up position. Here Durnford decided to make a stand. He ordered his men to dismount, and, leaving their horses in the bottom of the gully, they lined the lip, opening fire on the Zulus rushing after them. For the last 50 yards or so the ground sloped gently down towards the donga, and the left horn was fully exposed to Durnford's fire across this distance.

For Durnford, this was the moment of expiation he had been waiting for, the chance to dispel all doubts about his courage or ability. He strode among his men, cheering them on, directing their fire, ignoring their pleas that he should take cover. So heavy was the fire they laid down that the Zulus directly facing them, the young men of the uVe, were driven back, until reinforced by the slightly older iNgobamakhosi coming up behind. Even so, the iNgobamakhosi's attack ground to a halt, the warriors throwing themselves down in the long grass to escape the fire, then advancing in short rushes, alternately rising up and falling prone.

Elsewhere, the chest had also stalled. It had descended from the heights and occupied the dongas below the British line, but the fire was so intense that it was difficult to regain the momentum of their attack and press up the exposed slope. The battle was approaching its critical moment, and superficially the British seemed to be in a commanding position.

In fact, their line was dangerously overstretched. The advance of the left horn, appearing from far beyond Pulleine's right flank, had effectively threatened his rear, a movement only checked by Durnford. Pope's company, on Pulleine's right, had bent backwards to refuse the flank, drawing itself more or less into line with Durnford's command. Yet a yawning gap of several hundred yards separated the two parts of the British force, and bolder elements of the uMbonambi were already trying to slip between the two. For the most part they were checked by flanking fire from both Pope and Durnford, but the red line was nonetheless spread very thin. The 24th companies were deployed in a double line, the men spaced two or three yards apart, kneeling to fire or lying down to take cover behind the boulders. Furthermore, Durnford was also in danger of being outflanked, on his right, by members of the iNgobamakhosi who had extended to their left. His ammunition, too, was beginning to run low, and when he sent back riders into the camp, they were refused supplies from the 24th's reserve wagons – quite rightly, the quartermasters were concerned with their responsibilities to their own men – and could not find where their own wagons, which had arrived after they had left camp, were parked. They returned empty handed.

It was by now somewhere between 1.00 and 1.30 p.m., and within a very short space of time, several events happened very quickly. Pope's company, realising the danger posed by the gap, moved out from its original position and marched smartly to its right, to try to secure Durnford's left flank. The troops had just begun this manoeuvre when Durnford, quite independently, abandoned his position and retired on the camp. As he rode in, he told one officer, who survived the battle, that his position was too extended, and he could not hold it any longer. He rode off to confer with Pulleine. No report of their conversation has survived, but apparently they agreed that the 24th line was now in very real danger. Pope's company was now stuck out on the right, and its fire alone would not be enough to hold back the left horn indefinitely. Pulleine must have given the order for the 24th to retire to take up a more compact position nearer the camp, for according to Zulu sources, a bugle rang out along the length of the British line, and the redcoats stopped firing and fell back in good order.

Shortly before the British withdrawal, the Zulu generals, from a commanding position on the iNyoni escarpment, had become concerned that their attack had bogged down. Directly below them, the uKhandempemvu *ibutho* was pinned down under heavy fire, lying among a line of dongas which drained into the Nyogane. Ntshingwayo sent down one of the *izinduna* of the uKhandempemvu, a man named Mkhosana kaMvundlana Biyela, to stir them into action. Mkhosana was apparently wearing the full finery of his rank, and he strode among the young men lying on their bellies in the dust, apparently untouched by the bullets splashing all around him. In a phrase that has passed into Zulu folklore, he reminded them of their allegiance to King Cetshwayo by reciting the first two lines of Cetshwayo's praises, which dated from his victory at 'Ndondakusuka 23 years before. 'The Little Branch of Leaves that Extinguished the Great Fire kindled by Mantshonga and Ngqelebane,' he cried, 'gave no such order as this!'

Stung by this slight to their courage, the uKhandempemvu rose up and rushed forward. All along the line, the other *amabutho* saw their example, and took heart. On the left, the iNgobamakhosi had not yet recovered from their rough handling at Durnford's hands, and had made no attempt to run the gauntlet of Pope's fire. One of their commanders stood up among them and, recalling the challenges they had issued to the uKhandempemvu before the campaign, called out, 'What was it you said to the uKhandempemvu? There go the uKhandempemvu into the tents!' The iNgobamakhosi, too, rallied and rushed forward.

The general Zulu advance must have taken place only a few minutes before the British withdrew. Setting an example to his men, Mkhosana, the great Zulu hero of the battle, was shot dead, possibly by a stray shot from his own side. At first, the 24th maintained their formations, retiring at a steady pace, and halting every few yards to direct a volley at the Zulus hot on their heels. The NNH and NNC companies, however, who had been interspersed among the 24th's lines, and who had hitherto been steadfastly holding their ground, naturally retired at a quicker pace, and by the time they reached the camp they were running, and there was no one to rally them. Gaps had therefore opened up in the 24th's line, and before they could attempt to block them, the Zulus streamed into their midst. Major Smith scarcely had time to limber up and get his guns away before the Zulus overran his position.

In the few hundred yards between the firing line and the camp, the British position collapsed completely. The uKhandempemvu pushed Younghusband's, Mostyn's and Cavaye's companies through the tents from the north, and Porteous and Wardell's into them from the front. The uMbonambi struck at Pope, and rushed past him into the tents. Durnford had ordered most of his African followers to leave the field, but a small group of Natal Volunteers rallied beside the track, in what had suddenly become the British rear, trying to hold back the left horn. Durnford saw them there, and went to join them; ironically, for the second and last time, he was to face his moment of truth surrounded by the sons of the Natal settler gentry.

As the British line disintegrated, the Zulus streamed into the tents, attacking the camp personnel – cooks, grooms, officers' servants, craftsmen and civilian wagon-drivers – who had suddenly been exposed. For the Zulus, the days of psychological strain, of focusing on the battle ahead, heightened by the experience of lying out exposed to the British fire, were released in a fury of killing. In the smoke, noise and confusion, the Zulus struck at everything that moved, killing soldiers and civilians alike, as well as horses, mules, oxen and even pet dogs.

At the height of the slaughter, nature itself added an apocalyptic touch. The moon passed across the face of the sun, and shortly before 2 p.m. the eerie half-light of a solar eclipse fell over the battlefield. 'The tumult and the firing was wonderful,' a warrior of the uKhandempemvu later recalled, 'every warrior shouted Usuthu! as he killed anyone, and the sun got very dark, like night, with the smoke.'

As the line collapsed, a mob of NNC, civilians, mounted men and camp casuals made for the rear. For a few seconds it looked as if the 24th might join them in the rout, but they were a steady battalion, and they rallied to their officers. As the fugitives crossed the nek, down into the valley of the Manzimnyama behind Isandlwana, they ran smack into a fresh horror: the Zulu right horn, which had slipped into the valley early in the fight, was there before them, and had already cut the road to Rorke's Drift. The uDududu, iSangqu and iMbube, reinforced by most of the uNokhenke from the chest, which had shifted to its right to join them, now poured up over the nek, and into the camp from behind. If there had ever been any hope of the 24th taking up a new position, it was now gone.

The fiercest fighting took place on the nek, and down into the valley of the Manzimnyama beyond. Durnford died by the road, and the Natal Volunteers with him. Among the noise, dust, smoke and confusion, Mehlokazulu kaSihayo recalled a group of men in dark uniforms, gathered around a man with a useless arm, who called out 'Fire!' repeatedly, until the iNgobamakhosi whittled them down with flung spears, and overran them completely. The remnants of two or three companies managed to draw together to make a stand near the wagon park, and Pulleine was probably among them. For a long time these men drove the enemy back with their fire, but the Zulus gradually broke up their formation, and killed them all.

Captain Younghusband's company, which had started the battle on the extreme left of the British line, had retreated behind the tents, and taken up a position on the shoulder of Isandlwana itself. Here the men were safe while their ammunition lasted, for the Zulus were at a disadvantage attacking up the slope, but once their bullets were gone, they had no hope of replenishing the supply. Instead, Younghusband, whirling his sword around his head, led them in a charge down into the chaos below, to try to join the other remaining groups of redcoats still struggling on the nek. Some at least made it; according to one report, Younghusband's body was later found near that of Pulleine.

One group of 24th retired slowly over the nek, putting up such a heavy fire that the Zulus dared not close with them. They were probably hoping to retreat towards Rorke's Drift, but as they descended into the Manzimnyama Valley they were struck by the right horn, and forced away from the road. They retreated slowly down a maze of dongas and boulders, losing men all the way, until they reached the banks of the stream itself. Trapped above the banks, some eight feet high, they could go no further. Here the last organised stand of the 24th was overrun.

Small knots of soldiers continued to fight on for an hour or so after the camp collapsed, wherever they could reach the cover of a wagon, a clump of bush or a rocky outcrop. In truth, there was nothing else for them to do; there was no hope of escape, and the Zulus took no prisoners. At the height of the battle, the killing achieved levels of stark primeval savagery. The soldiers fought with clubs and broken rifles, bayonets, pen-knives, fists, and even stones. The Zulus soon learned to respect the long reach and deadly point of the Martini-Henry bayonet, but there was little hope for a soldier whose bayonet stuck for a second in the body or shield of an opponent, and who was usually brought down by a spear-thrust to the side or back.

Individual fragments of the carnage have come down to us, and tell the story of it all. Seaman Aynsley of HMS *Active*, who was the servant of a naval officer of Chelmsford's staff, set his back to a wagon, and challenged warriors to fight him one at a time, cutting them down with his cutlass, until a Zulu crept under the wagon and stabbed him through the spokes. One man – probably from Younghusband's company – retreated up the slopes of Isandlwana itself, and hid in a cave at the foot of the southern cliff. Here he defended himself for several hours after the camp had fallen, shooting or stabbing anyone who approached, until at last the Zulus grew tired of him, and fired a volley into the cave, and killed him.

In the camp's last moments, Lieutenant Melvill, the adjutant of the 1/24th, took hold of the Queen's Colour of his battalion. Each infantry battalion had two Colours – Regimental and Queen's – which served to symbolise their allegiance and as a focus of regimental pride. Possibly Melvill took the Colour in the hope of rallying the battalion, but if so, he had left it too late; since it was a great disgrace to allow a Colour to fall into the hands of the enemy, he tried instead to carry it from the field. There was no easy route to safety, and survivors were already fleeing across three or four miles of very rugged country in the hope of striking the Mzinyathi downstream of Rorke's Drift. Very few who were not on horseback would make it.

Melvill, who was mounted, fell in with Lieutenant Coghill, also of the 1/24th, and the two managed to reach the river, only to find that it was in spate due to the heavy rains of the previous few days. Both men put their horses into the water, but while Coghill swam across safely, Melvill was unhorsed in the torrent, and swept away downstream. He managed to cling to a large boulder which was just breaking the surface of the water, and Coghill, spotting his predicament, turned back to help him. The Zulus were lining the bank firing at them from close range, but Melvill and Coghill, together with an NNC officer named Higginson, managed to struggle across to the Natal bank; the Colour, however, at last slipped out of Melvill's grasp, and was lost in the river. Exhausted, the three men struggled up out of the valley on the Natal bank, threatened by small groups of warriors lurking in the undergrowth. While Higginson went off to try to catch some stray horses, Melvill and Coghill were overtaken and killed.

Large numbers of warriors followed the fugitives all the way down to the river, and several of their commanders, including Prince Ndabuko kaMpande, urged them to cross over and go on to attack the British garrisons on the Natal side. They were dissuaded by Vumandaba kaNtati, one of the Cetshwayo's advisers, and commander of the uKhandempemvu, who reminded them sternly that the king had ordered them not to cross the border. Most, in any case, were too exhausted to fight for much longer, and they returned to the camp, singing a great victory song which dated from Dingane's day. Only the oNdini *amabutho*, who had served as reserve, and who had taken no part in the fighting apart from killing off a few fugitives, were prepared to disobey the king's wishes, and to cross the river in the hope of finding easy pickings at the British supply depot at Rorke's Drift.

At Isandlwana, once the last survivors had been flushed out, the rest of the army had begun to loot the British camp. The Zulus removed everything of military value, including almost a thousand Martini-Henry rifles, and hundreds of thousands of rounds of ammunition. Boxes and crates were broken open and smashed, food and supplies carried off, and bottles emptied of their contents in a desperate attempt to quench the thirst stimulated by the terrible stress of battle. They tore down the tents, and cut the canvas into convenient lengths to use as blankets, while each warrior took or discarded the rich bounty of the white men's personal possessions, according to his taste: camping equipment, clothes, boots, coins, watches, photographs and trinkets of every description.

There had been just over 1700 British troops and their African allies in the camp at Isandlwana when the battle began. Over 1300 of them were killed; only about 60 Europeans survived. As part of their post-combat rituals, it was necessary for warriors who had killed an enemy to remove part of his clothing, and to wear it until he had undergone a purification ceremony. It was also necessary to disembowel the corpse in the belief that the spirit of a man killed in battle escaped through his stomach; a warrior who had killed a man would remain polluted unless that spirit was allowed safe passage to the ancestors. Most of the British corpses, therefore, presented a ghastly spectacle, partially stripped, stabbed repeatedly, and then cut open. They lay in pathetic heaps surrounded by the Zulu dead, many of whom had been horribly disfigured in turn by the effects of heavy-calibre bullets at close quarters.

As many as 1000 Zulus had been killed outright in the battle, and perhaps 1000 more badly wounded. In addition, most of the 3000 oxen which had been in the camp had been killed in the carnage, together with horses, mules and dogs, and their carcasses lay strewn around among the human bodies. In some places it was impossible to walk a yard in any direction without treading on a corpse of one sort or another, and, as one Zulu witness described it, 'The green grass was red with the running blood and the veld was slippery, for it was covered with the brains and entrails of the slain.' The sheer volume of the dead defied the efforts of scavenging animals and birds to dispose of them. A Zulu boy named Muziwento visited the deserted battlefield a few days after the fight, and left an apocalyptic description of the silent horrors he found there:

> We saw countless things dead. Dead was the horse, dead too the mule, dead was the dog, dead was the monkey, dead were the wagons, dead were the tents, dead were the boxes, dead was everything, even to the very metals.

By late afternoon, the Zulu force had begun to retire back the way it had come, up over the iNyoni ridge, towards the Ngwebeni Valley. Many of the Zulu dead were piled into the same dongas at the foot of the escarpment where the *amabutho* had sheltered from the ferocity of the British fire during the battle, and were covered over with stones and soil; their bones continued to wash out after a heavy rain well into the twentieth century.

Others were simply left on the battlefield, with their great shields placed over them in symbolic burial. By nightfall, most of the army was back in the Ngwebeni Valley. Here it lingered for three days, tending to the wounded, until either many of the mortally wounded had died, or the rest recovered sufficiently to face the long agonising journey back home.

When the army finally returned to oNdini, it looked more like a defeated than a victorious one, and a stunned King Cetshwayo asked, 'When will the rest come before me?' – until he realised that the rest were left behind in the whispering grass at the foot of Mount Isandlwana. In the cleansing ceremonies that followed, many Zulus attributed their heavy losses to the fact that the battle had begun prematurely, without the final administration of protective medicines. Nevertheless, the young *amabutho* were proud of their extraordinary achievement, and it was keenly debated among them who had been the first to 'stab' the enemy – to penetrate the British line. After carefully consulting with his commanders, the king decided the honour had fallen to the uMbonambi regiment, and those of its members who had killed an enemy were allowed to cut sticks of willow-wood, and fashion them into a necklace of small interlocking blocks, the *iziqu*, which served as a recognition of extreme bravery in battle.

The oNdini regiments, however, had not been so fortunate. After leaving the main army at Isandlwana, they had crossed the Mzinyathi in two groups downstream of Rorke's Drift, and had advanced to attack the British post there. But the British garrison – scarcely 150 men, mostly from B Company, 2/24th – had been warned by survivors of Isandlwana that the Zulus were approaching, and had fortified the mission with the stockpile of stores which had been due to go forward to the column that morning. For nearly ten hours the oNdini regiments assaulted the post, carrying and setting fire to one of the buildings – which the soldiers had turned into a makeshift hospital – but they were unable to overrun the last defensive position.

They retired before dawn on the 23rd, having suffered 600 dead, and many more wounded – an extraordinary casualty rate of nearly one in four. To the British, Rorke's Drift represented one small piece of good news on a very bad day, and they showered honours on the defenders. No less than eleven of the garrison at Rorke's Drift were awarded the Victoria Cross. For the Zulu survivors, however, there was a very different reception. They returned home to be mocked by their families for having disregarded the king's wishes, and having achieved nothing but heavy losses as a result.

And Lord Chelmsford? He had spent much of the day searching through the hills above the Mangeni Gorge. Although curious reports had reached him that something was amiss at Isandlwana, his staff officers, looking back at the camp through field-glasses, could see no sign of trouble. It was a hazy day, although the tents were visible as a white smudge beneath the hill, a conspicuous sign of normality, and they undoubtedly allowed themselves to be swayed by their own conviction that the Zulus would never dare attack the camp.

Late in the morning, Chelmsford sent his NNC back to the camp. They were half-way across the plain when the left horn swept across it in front of them, moving to attack Isandlwana; by the time Chelmsford responded to their frantic messages, the battle was over. His own troops were scattered over a wide tract of countryside, and it took some time to assemble them; it was not until late afternoon that he was able to return to the camp. By the time he arrived, it was dark, and only the dead and dying remained. By that time, Chelmsford's own command was exhausted, having covered at least 24 miles in marching to the Mangeni and back, and Chelmsford had no idea of the present whereabouts of the Zulu army; it was only painfully obvious where it had been earlier that day.

Chelmsford ordered his men to bivouac on the battlefield. It was an inevitable decision from a military point of view, but it condemned his men to a harrowing night among the horrors. Men stumbled over corpses in the dark, or awoke the next morning to find they had been sleeping next to the bodies of comrades they had parted from just 24 hours before. Throughout the night there were several false alarms, and nerves were further stretched by the glow of fire on the horizon at Rorke's Drift.

Ordering his command to stand to before dawn, Chelmsford marched them back down the road to Rorke's Drift. Along the way, they encountered large numbers of Zulus crossing their front; these were the men who had attacked Rorke's Drift, in retreat. Yet both sides were exhausted and reluctant to fight, and the two armies passed each other warily, at times only a few hundred yards apart. At the post itself Chelmsford expected to find the aftermath of a further massacre, but his scouts, riding ahead, were greeted by rousing cheers, and Chelmsford knew that Rorke's Drift had held. When his command marched up to the post, devastated by the fight and heaped up with Zulu dead, it was a moment, nevertheless, for mixed feelings; there were none of the garrison of Isandlwana there, as he had hoped, and for the first time Chelmsford realised the full extent, not only of the Rorke's Drift garrison's extraordinary victory, but of his own defeat.

Chelmsford left the remnants of the Centre Column at Rorke's Drift, and rode back to Pietermaritzburg to organise Natal's defences in case of a Zulu attack. Within less than a fortnight, his invasion plan had been destroyed. His main thrust had been decisively repulsed, while his right flanking column was cut off, and effectively neutralised. Of his three original offensive columns, only Colonel Wood's Left Flank Column remained capable of independent action, and that would scarcely be able to prosecute the war on its own. Furthermore, Natal lay open to a Zulu counterattack, and the political consequences of such a disaster would be appalling.

Without doubt, the Zulus had won the first phase of their war. The king's strategy had proved largely successful, and the courage and endurance of the ordinary warriors had been of truly epic proportions. This did not obscure the fact, however, that the Zulus had paid a terrible price for defending their country, and the army needed to be purified and to rest.

Cetshwayo had no intention of mounting an invasion of Natal, hoping to seize instead the chance to negotiate a settlement in the aftermath of his victory, but even if he had, his army was not available to him. The warriors needed to return home to recover, and to reap the crops that needed harvesting across the country. And as they did so, the chance of any lasting success in the war gradually slipped from their grasp, for they allowed Chelmsford time to regroup. The British Government, having been reluctant to embark on a Zulu War in the first place, could nevertheless not allow itself to be defeated by an enemy with a black skin. Whatever policy it might pursue in the future, military success would have to be secured first, and Lord Chelmsford was sent the reinforcements he had been denied before the war began.

With bitter irony, Isandlwana would prove to be both the Zulu kingdom's greatest victory, and the moment at which its destruction became assured. The fighting would soon resume once more.

And in the meantime, the remains of the dead would lie unburied on the battlefield of Isandlwana, exposed to the elements, for months to come.

— 6 —
THE BATTLE OF HLOBANE
28 March 1879
'An awful confusion took place'

The Zulu victory at Isandlwana on 22 January 1879 devastated Lord Chelmsford's original invasion plan. Although the British still had two columns in the field inside Zulu territory, Colonel Pearson's Coastal Column was effectively immobilised without Chelmsford's support, and only Colonel Wood's Left Flank Column retained any capability for independent action.

From the start, it had always been intended that Wood's column would be allowed considerable flexibility within the framework of its ultimate objective, the advance on oNdini. This was largely because the area in which it operated was ruled over by a number of independent-minded chiefs, who had flourished during long years of political instability. On the one hand, the British hoped that, by appealing to the chiefs' own interests, their allegiance to King Cetshwayo might be undermined, while on the other there existed the possibility that, if they remained loyal, they might have to be conquered piecemeal.

Certainly, the area was a cockpit of conflicting loyalties. Although the line of the Mzinyathi and Thukela Rivers had been finally established as the border between Zululand and Natal in the 1840s, there were no such clear-cut boundaries to mark either the north-western corner of the kingdom, in the vicinity of the Ncome (Blood) River, nor, indeed, much of the boundary with the Swazi kingdom further north. Culture and language, too, overlapped in this region, and many of the people who lived here were Swazi by descent, although King Shaka had dislocated the original chiefdoms in the 1820s, and established an *ikhanda* of his own to assert the authority of the Zulu royal house. Called ebaQulusini, this had been ruled over by Shaka's aunt, the formidable Mnkabayi, and over time many of those attached to it had married and settled in the area, so that by the 1870s their descendants, known as the abaQulusi, formed a distinct chiefdom of their own. They considered themselves a section of the Royal House, and were ruled over not by hereditary chiefs but by *izinduna* appointed from among their number by the king.

Shaka, Dingane and Mpande had all attempted to extend their influence into the Swazi kingdom itself, with varying degrees of success. Although the Phongolo River was regarded as the practical border between the two states, the main centres of Swazi authority were further north, and the Zulu kings maintained a nominal claim to territory on either side of the Phongolo, an area famed for its natural mountain fastnesses, which were highly prized as places of refuge.

The reaction of the Swazi kingdom itself to the political crisis of 1879 was of some interest to the British. Because of their past history of conflict, they assumed that the Swazis would be hostile to the Zulus, but the issue was not clear-cut, for the Swazi had learned to be wary of allying themselves too closely to white interests, and they were reluctant to take to the field to support the British for fear of Cetshwayo's wrath if the British were defeated. On the whole, the Swazi king Mbandzeni preferred to hedge his bets, assuring the British of his support while sitting on the fence and awaiting events.

The situation had been further complicated by the spread of Boer farmers into the region from the Transvaal republic in the west. King Mpande had originally permitted the Boers to graze their cattle in some of the comparatively empty north-western reaches of his kingdom at a time when he was attempting to play the Boers and British off against each other, early in his reign. Over the years, a number of Boers had built farms in the area, and they had gradually extended their influence eastwards, to the growing consternation of both Mpande and his son, Cetshwayo. By the 1870s this had led to the so-called 'border dispute', an open rift which occasionally threatened to flare into violence, and which became one of the British grievances against the Zulu kingdom once the British had annexed the Transvaal in April 1877.

Indeed, Wood's supply base was at Utrecht, a small town which the Boers had built in the disputed territory itself, and part of his brief was to protect those white settlements which could fairly be considered to be in no-man's-land once hostilities began. Apart from Utrecht itself, Wood's greatest concern was Luneburg, a hamlet first established by German missionaries in 1869, which lay further north, close to the Ntombe River. King Cetshwayo felt strongly that Luneburg remained subject to Zulu rule, and had repeatedly attempted to exert his authority in the region, without actually resorting to violence. He had sent an *induna*, Faku, to the area with the specific intention of limiting further European encroachment around the site, and under Faku's authority the abaQulusi had built a small royal homestead only a few miles from the town itself to demonstrate their claim to the area.

The overlapping claims of British, Swazi, Boer and Zulu authority had created a climate in which shrewd and aggressive self-seekers could thrive.

Foremost among these was Mbilini waMswati, who maintained two home-steads in the region. One was only a few miles from Luneburg, under the shadow of a large flat-topped mountain, known as the Tafelberg, which over-looked Myer's Drift on the Ntombe River. Mbilini was a Swazi, a prince of the Royal House, the eldest son of one of the great Swazi kings, Mswati Dlamini. Mbilini had apparently been raised as a warrior – on one occasion as a child he was wrapped up in a fresh dog-skin, so that he could assume some of the fierce nature of the animal – and had been among his father's favourite sons; but as the eldest he was ineligible as heir under the complex Swazi laws of succession. When his father died, Mbilini had tried to orchestrate a coup, but found that he did not command sufficient support within the kingdom, and fled to the Transvaal for fear of retribution. In 1867 he left the Transvaal to *konza* (give allegiance to) the then Prince Cetshwayo. He lived for a number of years at oNdini, and when Cetshwayo became king, he gave Mbilini permission to settle on the extreme fringes of the Zulu territory.

Mbilini was a young man, of slight build, but his apparently pleasant personality masked a ruthless and ambitious character. Although he was only of the same age-group as the Zulu uMbonambi *ibutho*, and he was unmarried, Mbilini wore a headring which marked the estate of a married man, since he considered himself the leader of his own household. His position on the Ntombe allowed him considerable freedom of action, and he had raided his neighbours across both the Transvaal and Swazi borders in an attempt to build his prestige, following and cattle.

Although it is probably true that Cetshwayo failed to approve – or even know of – many of Mbilini's actions, Mbilini was careful not to antagonise his patron outright, and it is quite possible that Cetshwayo regarded Mbilini as an ally who could secure a bolthole into Swaziland – as Dingane had once done – should the coming conflict go against him. Indeed, Mbilini had fostered close links with the abaQulusi, and had built the second of his homesteads on the slopes of one of their mountain strongholds, Hlobane. On several occasions both Transvaal and Swazi forces had attempted to punish Mbilini, but they had been unable to do so, and, indeed, Mbilini would prove one of the most daring of the Zulu commanders, with a real flair for guerrilla warfare, once war with the British began.

The Luneburg–Ntombe district was effectively straddled by two British commands. In the north, around the remote village of Derby, Colonel Hugh Rowlands VC commanded a force of several hundred imperial troops, supported by irregulars and locally raised African auxiliaries. Rowlands's command, however, was one of those to whom Chelmsford had allocated a defensive role, and he was expected to keep an eye not only

Above: A Zulu chief and his retainers, photographed in their splendid ceremonial costume, *c.*1865. The formidable appearance and discipline of the Zulu army aroused the suspicion and hostility of the neighbouring white states.

Below: A naive early drawing of the death of John Cane at the battle of the Thukela, 1838.

Above: The final stages of the battle of the Thukela; the Zulu left horn has cut off the retreat of the settler force, herding the survivors into the water, left. The 'Ndondakusuka homestead is on the slope of the hill, centre.

Below: Today, 64 life-sized bronze wagons stand on the spot occupied by the Boer laager during the battle of Blood River. The laager provided an impenetrable barrier against the most determined attack.

Opposite page, top: In the heavy-handed iconography of this bas-relief, part of a monument built to commemorate the centenary of the battle of Blood River, a triumphant Pretorius rides out to smite the retreating Zulu at the end of the battle.

Opposite page, bottom: King Mpande reviewing his *amabutho* in the 1840s. Mpande was a subtle and astute ruler, but his refusal to nominate an heir split Zululand – and its army – down the middle, and resulted in the battle of 'Ndondakusuka in 1856.

Left: King Cetshwayo kaMpande, photographed in captivity after his defeat at the hands of the British. Cetshwayo had personally commanded his army at the battle of 'Ndondakusuka in 1856.

Below: Lieutenant General Lord Chelmsford (seated) and his staff, photographed on the eve of the Anglo–Zulu War. Next to him, with his foot on the chair, is Colonel Henry Evelyn Wood, who commanded the Left Flank Column in 1879.

Above: Colonel Charles Knight Pearson, who commanded the British coastal column in 1879. Pearson won the first battle of the war – at Nyezane – but the subsequent collapse of the Centre Column left his own command stranded at Eshowe. [Tim Day]

Above right: Brevet Colonel Anthony William Durnford, RE, the senior British officer killed at the battle of Isandlwana.

Below: The final stages of the battle of Nyezane; men from the Naval Brigade and Buffs clear the Zulu homestead (left), and drive the remainder of the Zulu left horn away behind Wombane Hill (right). [Canterbury Museum]

Above: The field experience which the 24th Regiment brought to Zululand shows in the faces of this group of the 2/24th, photographed with Captain Glennie, towards the end of the campaign.

Below: British Mounted Infantry (1st Welsh Regiment) visiting the battlefield of Isandlwana, 1884. The cairns mark where the British dead were hastily buried; the cluster of graves and monuments (centre) stands on the position of Durnford's last stand.

Above: In this dramatic contemporary illustration, a small group of British soldiers fight to the last as the Zulus overrun their camp; the picture was actually intended to represent the action at Ntombe Drift in March, but might equally serve to show the last stages of Isandlwana.

Below right: Lieutenant Colonel Redvers Buller, photographed in 1873. In 1879, Buller commanded the irregular cavalry attached to Wood's column; he won the VC for rescuing men during the rout at Hlobane. His smart undress uniform here contrasts sharply with the practical civilian clothes he wore in the field. [Rai England/MOD]

Right: An aerial view of the western end of the battlefield of Hlobane, showing the rocky staircase – the Devil's Pass – connecting the main plateau (left) with Ntendeka (right).

Below right: Although this contemporary illustration contains a number of errors of terrain and uniform, it does nonetheless capture something of the confusion and horror of the terrible descent of Hlobane.

Above: Commandant Piet Uys. Uys was one of the few Boer leaders to join the British in 1879; he was killed during the descent of the Devil's Pass at Hlobane. [Killie Campbell Africana Library]

Right: Two distinguished members of the Frontier Light Horse; Captain Cecil D'Arcy (seated), and Sergeant Edmund O'Toole. D'Arcy was mentioned in dispatches at Hlobane but not decorated; both men subsequently received the award for heroism in a skirmish on 3 July, the day before Ulundi.

Left: Major Robert Hackett, who led the sortie of the 90th which dispersed the Zulu left horn at Khambula. Hackett was hit by a bullet which passed through both temples, destroying his optic nerves and leaving him blind. [Royal Archives]

Below: Three vignettes of heroism at Khambula, as they appeared in the contemporary press. A Zulu warrior stabs himself rather than be captured by a British sortie (left); Lieutenant Browne rescues a dismounted trooper during Buller's foray; and Private Grosvenor of the 13th tends the wounded Colour Sergeant Fricker during the retreat from the cattle-laager.

HEROISM AT THE BATTLE OF KAMBULA

Above: The closing stages of the battle of Khambula; a sortie by the 13th clears the head of the valley up which the Zulu left had earlier advanced. This was the same position occupied by Hackett during the crucial stage of the battle. [Taunton Museum]

Right: Chief Zibhebhu kaMaphitha, photographed at the end of his long and eventful career. Zibhebhu had emerged as one of the most dynamic Zulu commanders in 1879, but was a merciless opponent of the Royal House in the post-war years. [SB Bourquin]

Top left: King Cetshwayo reviews his warriors at his new oNdini homestead in the tense days before the battle of July 1883.

Bottom left: The battle of oNdini, 23 July 1883. The defeated uSuthu army streams away in the foreground, while the victorious Mandlakazi sack oNdini beyond (left). [Rai England Collection]

Above: The Mandlakazi triumphant; Zibhebhu kaMaphitha and two of his white advisers, returning in triumph from the sacking of oNdini. [Rai England Collection]

Below: Troubled times; an *impi* of 'friendly Zulus' on the march in the Reserve Territory, 1884. [Ian Castle]

An Impi of Friendly Natives Zulu Reserve Territory

Opposite page, top left: Dinuzulu kaCetshwayo, who succeeded as leader of the uSuthu cause on the death of his father, and whose alliance with the Boers led to the decisive victory at Tshaneni.

Opposite page, bottom: The Tshaneni battlefield. The skulls and long bones of the Mandlakazi dead are still strewn across the killing ground at the foot of Mount Gaza twenty years after the battle.

Opposite page, top right: Chief Bambatha kaMancinza of the Zondi, the catalyst for rebellion in 1906.

Above: The beginning of the Bambatha rebellion; Bambatha's warriors attack a column of Natal Police on the road in the Mpanza valley during the night of 5 April 1906. [Rai England Collection]

Below: By 1906, most rebels realised that the Zulu tradition of mass attacks in the open was hopelessly outdated in the face of the modern firepower possessed by the Natal troops. Instead, much of the fighting consisted of skirmishes in the bush, like this one. [Rai England Collection]

Above: The Mome battlefield. The view is from the knoll occupied by Barker's guns; the rebel bivouac was on the open spot at the foot of the hills, where the homestead now stands. Barker's men also held the spurs on either side; the rebels fled back into the gorge (centre left), only to find themselves trapped by McKenzie's command.

Below: Chief Sigananda kaSokufa (with bandaged ankles), photographed with McKenzie (second from the right) and his officers after his surrender. Sigananda had been a mat-carrier in the last days of King Shaka's rule; his life, therefore, spanned the rise and fall of the old Zulu kingdom. [Killie Campbell Africana Library]

on the Zulus, but also on republican elements within the Transvaal, the Pedi kingdom of Sekhukhune further north and, indeed, to ensure that, should the Swazis decide to enter the war, they would do so on the side of the British, not the Zulus. With such a huge territory to police, and with too few men to do it, Rowlands was able to offer little more than a supporting role to Wood's column at Utrecht.

Brevet Colonel Henry Evelyn Wood VC was, arguably, one of the more inspiring British column commanders at the outset of the war. A small, slight, heavily bearded man, he had had an adventurous career which had seen him start out as a midshipman in the Navy, and would see him eventually rise to field marshal in the Army. He had experienced a great deal of action, and was both curiously accident prone – he was once trampled by a giraffe, he suffered constantly from bouts of neuralgia, and was going deaf – and rather vain, but he was a shrewd and dynamic commander who excelled in colonial warfare and was popular with his men. The negative face of dynamism, however, is often a certain rashness, and Wood occasionally took more risks than by rights were necessary. The Zulus, who had a knack of summing up a man's true worth, called him *Lukani*, the name of a hard wood from which they made their knobkerries, and this was not only a pun on his name but a comment on his toughness of character.

Wood's commander of cavalry, who was effectively his right-hand man, Brevet Lieutenant Colonel Redvers Buller, was another forceful character, an abrasive bulldog of a man, whose bad temper was matched only by his fearlessness in battle, and who had the knack, rare at the time, of understanding how to use the irregular horsemen under his command to best advantage. Buller was committed to his men's welfare without being in the slightest sentimental about them, and they were prepared to follow him into the jaws of hell as a result. Before the campaign was over, they would be put to the test in that regard.

When Wood's command assembled at Utrecht, it consisted of just over 2000 men, including the 1/13th Light Infantry, 90th Light Infantry, a battery of guns, and a locally raised unit of auxiliaries, called Wood's Irregulars. Like the other invading columns, Wood had no regular cavalry, and his mounted contingent was made up instead of several small irregular units. Unlike the Natal Volunteer Corps – who were part-time soldiers raised by the colony of Natal – the irregulars were full-time soldiers, raised for a specific period and paid for by the British Government. They tended to attract the adventurous and the desperate, and the best of them, such as the Frontier Light Horse, had a reputation for hard riding and tough fighting. Several of them, including the FLH, had served previously on the Cape Frontier.

Britain had annexed the Transvaal under the pretence that a large sector of Boer society supported their intervention. The fallacy of this became apparent when Wood tried to enlist local burghers to fight with his column. Most remained determinedly aloof, and probably relished the prospect of their two greatest enemies – the British and the Zulus – slogging it out. Some frontier farmers, indeed, were prepared to go so far as to support Zulu incursions in the region, in the hope that it would weaken British control and, in the long run, secure their own territorial claims. Only one Boer leader of note, Petrus ('Piet') Lefras Uys, was prepared to join Wood, bringing with him his kinsmen and adherents. The Uys family had a long history of conflict with the Zulus. Piet Uys's father and brother had both been killed by Dingane's army at eThaleni in 1838, and his farm was in the heart of the disputed area. Most of his followers seem to have joined him on the promise of being given cattle looted from the Zulus.

Wood had crossed the Ncome River – the effective border – a few days before the British ultimatum had expired. He built a camp below a distinctive outcrop called Thinta's Kop, and prepared to undermine the allegiance of the local chiefs to King Cetshwayo with a typical mixture of carrot and big stick. He promised that those chiefs who defected to the British would escape the ravages of war, and to reinforce the point he set about enthusiastically raiding Zulu homesteads for cattle. To protect the exposed settlement at Luneburg, an outpost was established there, half-way between Wood and Rowlands.

Once the ultimatum expired, it quickly became obvious which groups would serve as the greatest focus of resistance to the British invasion. Even before the war began, Wood had persuaded an *induna* named Bemba, an official of Chief Sekethwayo's Mdlalose chiefdom, to surrender, with a number of his followers. Once he was actively operating inside Zulu territory, Wood tried to persuade the rest of the Mdlalose to defect, but his overtures were cut short by the arrival of a Zulu force from oNdini, who served to remind the chief where his loyalties lay. Indeed, anyone showing signs of wavering could expect the attentions not only of Cetshwayo's troops, but also of the abaQulusi, Mbilini's followers, and of the adherents of an *induna* named Manyanyoba, who lived near Mbilini, on the upper reaches of the Ntombe. Like the abaQulusi, the origins of Manyanyoba's subjects were distinctly mixed, but Manyanyoba's father had been appointed to rule over them by the Royal House, and Manyanyoba proved surprisingly staunch. Wood therefore faced a twin axis of resistance, from the abaQulusi, whose mountain strongholds lay directly north-east of his camp, and from Mbilini and Manyanyoba, further north still, between himself and Rowlands.

The result was a low-intensity struggle that began almost as soon as the ultimatum expired, a fast-moving war of raid and counter-raid, which would last longer than in any other sector in Zululand. It would be punctuated, too, by two of the greatest battles of the war, fought within a day of each other, and whose outcome was crucial, not only to the course of the campaign, but to the future of the Zulu kingdom itself.

In the first few days of the war, Wood's energetic cavalry raided not only local Zulu homesteads, but pushed down into the northern reaches of the Batshe valley, attacking Sihayo's followers, and securing Lord Chelmsford's left flank. His attempts to persuade local chiefs to defect, however, were countered by the resistance of the abaQulusi, whose strongholds – a chain of flat-topped mountains running roughly west to east – lay only a dozen miles north of Wood's camp.

On 20 January, Buller took a patrol of Frontier Light Horse and Piet Uys's Boers to try to drive the Zulus off Zungwini, the nearest mountain in the chain. He was met by a force of over 1000 warriors who swept down the mountain in perfect precision and nearly surrounded him, forcing him to retreat. This encounter convinced Wood that it was vital to dislodge the abaQulusi, and on the 22nd he set out again with a stronger force, this time including infantry. The Zulus were taken by surprise and driven off the mountain, abandoning their livestock to the British force. Any elation Wood might have felt was tempered, however, by the sight of a much larger force – some 4000 men – drilling on the lower slopes of the next mountain in the chain, Hlobane. Their movements were carried out with such precision that Wood realised that the abaQulusi were not to be treated lightly.

Two days later he led another foray which engaged the Zulus in a running fight between Zungwini and Hlobane. The Zulus once again attempted to surround the British force, but were dispersed with artillery fire, and scattered by Buller's men. Most retired up the slopes of Hlobane. Wood was reluctant to pursue them without careful consideration, but in any case the situation suddenly changed with the arrival of a messenger who carried news of Lord Chelmsford's defeat at Isandlwana. Wood immediately broke off the engagement and returned to Fort Thinta.

News of the disaster obviously affected Wood's position, but he was not as exposed by it as was Pearson at Eshowe. For one thing, he had hitherto concentrated on suppressing local resistance, and had not advanced far into Zulu territory. His line of communication was secure, and, provided he could protect the border settlements from Zulu attack, there was no reason why he could not continue his policy of harassing the neighbouring chiefdoms. This would at least retain some British initiative, and relieve the pressure on Lord

Chelmsford. On the other hand, news of the Zulu victory was likely to stiffen the resolve of local royalists and, indeed, on the 26th Manyanyoba's followers moved out of the Ntombe valley to threaten Luneburg, an action only checked by a vigorous move by the mounted men attached to the Luneburg garrison. Some of Manyanyoba's men took refuge in the caves along the valley to escape the British counter-attack, while others, significantly, moved south to join the abaQulusi concentrated at Hlobane.

Worried by these developments, Wood sent his scouts to search out a more secure position further to the north, which would place himself between the abaQulusi and Utrecht, while at the same time making it easier to coordinate movements with the Luneburg garrison and with Rowlands's column. On 31 January he moved to a spot which fitted those requirements exactly, a windswept ridge fifteen miles north-west of Fort Thinta, known as Khambula Hill.

From Khambula, Wood returned to the war with renewed vigour. On 1 February Buller's mounted men rode out to attack ebaQulusini itself, the *ikhanda* which served as a rallying point for Qulusi resistance. EbaQulusini was situated on the far side of the Zungwini and Hlobane range, in a surrounding basin of hills which made it difficult to approach, but Buller was nothing if not daring, and he took the complex by surprise, setting fire to the huts and rounding up a herd of cattle almost without resistance.

Wood's constant patrolling had undoubtedly demoralised the local Zulus, and both Mbilini and the abaQulusi had sent messages asking the king to send royal troops from oNdini to support them. Nevertheless, this did not discourage them from fighting back on their own account. On the night of 10–11 February, Manyanyoba, Mbilini and a Qulusi *induna*, Tola kaDilikana, combined to lead a joint attack against the white-owned farms near Luneburg. The attack had been carefully planned in advance; some farms, whose Boer owners had given intelligence to the Zulus, were left untouched, while the attack was carried out with spears only, so that the Luneburg garrison was not aroused by the sound of firing. The principal targets were African farm-workers and *amakholwa*, Christian Africans, who were particularly resented for the way in which they had embraced European values, and 41 were killed before the force withdrew.

When the news reached them the following morning, mounted elements from Luneburg sallied out and caught some of the raiders near the Ntombe River. They recovered some of the captured livestock, but this hardly made up for what had been a very successful Zulu attack. Over the following days, Buller led a series of energetic counter-attacks along the Ntombe, but while he destroyed a number of Manyanyoba's homesteads, he could not dislodge him from his caves. Rowlands, in a move designed to support Wood's efforts, also attacked two Zulu outposts which lay between Derby and Khambula, but with similarly inconclusive results.

A more satisfying indication of British success was the fact that Wood finally persuaded an extremely important Zulu notable to surrender to the British. Hamu kaNzibe was a prince of the Royal House, a biological brother to Cetshwayo himself, who, according to the complex Zulu laws of succession, was actually regarded as the heir to his uncle, Nzibe, and therefore at one step removed from the inner circle of the royal family. Nevertheless, he was an extremely powerful *isikhulu*, who was widely believed to be jealous of Cetshwayo's ascendancy. His people, the Ngenetsheni, lived eastwards of Hlobane, towards the Phongolo River.

Hamu had entered secret negotiations with the British before the war began, but the presence of a large force of Zulu loyalists between his territory and the invading column made his position difficult. The British counter-raids in mid-February kept the abaQulusi in their strongholds, however, and Hamu finally plucked up the courage to make his move. He fled into hiding until Wood was able to send out an escort to bring him into Khambula on 10 March. Despite the efforts of troops sent from oNdini to stop them, nearly 1300 of Hamu's followers joined him. The non-combatants were resettled in the Utrecht district, while the fighting men – many of them veterans of Isandlwana – were drafted into Wood's Irregulars.

Mbilini, meanwhile, seemed to be not in the slightest discouraged either by British reprisals or Hamu's defection. He travelled freely between his homestead in the Ntombe valley and the other on the southern slopes of Hlobane, assessing each move as the British made it, conferring with his allies, and keeping out of Buller's reach. Then, in the second week of March, he struck his greatest blow yet.

Towards the end of February, Rowlands was sent to Pretoria to watch for signs of Boer republicanism, which was simmering in the aftermath of Isandlwana, and his column was placed under Wood's control. The colonial irregulars were withdrawn from the Luneburg garrison, whose defence now rested on five companies of the 80th Regiment. These companies were supplied by convoys which travelled regularly down the road from Rowlands's old base at Derby, a road that was considered unsafe for small British parties because it crossed the Ntombe River close to Mbilini's stronghold.

In the first week of March a convoy of eighteen ammunition and supply wagons set out from Derby. Captain David Moriarty of the 80th marched out from Luneburg to meet it on the road, and escort it safely in. The weather was poor, however, and the Ntombe River had risen due to the frequent rains. The convoy reached the northern bank of the Ntombe at Myer's Drift, only a few miles from Luneburg, on 9 March, but only a handful of wagons could be put across before the rising river made the drift impassable. For two days Moriarty's command was stranded, cut in half by the river, and living in a sea of mud. Moriarty had parked the larger portion of the wagons, on the north bank, in an inverted V, with the base resting on the river; at one point the river had risen and flooded half his camp-site, while on another occasion it had perversely dropped, leaving the wagons several yards from the banks.

Frustration, discomfort and the proximity of Luneburg appear to have made Moriarty careless, and he made no further attempt to secure his camp. This was a fatal mistake, for Mbilini's homestead on the Tafelberg overlooked the drift just three miles away. Indeed, on 10 March a civilian wagon-driver claimed to have recognised Mbilini among a group of apparently friendly Zulus who entered the camp. The target was too tempting to miss, and on the 11th, when 71 troops were camped on the north bank and 35 on the south, they were called upon to pay the price of Moriarty's folly.

Under cover of a dense mist that hung in the valley, Mbilini, supported by Manyanyoba's followers and a number of abaQulusi and others – a total of 800–900 men in all – moved down from the Tafelberg and advanced quietly to within 70 yards of the laager before being challenged by a sentry. The Zulus responded with a volley at close range, then threw down their firearms and rushed in with their spears. Most of the men on the north bank were killed as they stumbled out of their tents, Moriarty himself putting up a stout defence before he, too, was overcome. A section of the Zulu force crossed the river, but the British party on the south bank had a few minutes' grace to prepare itself. The officer in charge, Lieutenant Harward, abandoned his men on the pretext of riding to Luneburg for support, and it was left to Sergeant Anthony Booth to rally a handful of men, to try to cover the retreat.

By the time relief arrived from Luneburg, the convoy had lost 79 men killed, including civilian wagon-drivers, and Mbilini's followers had retreated towards the Tafelberg, taking away with them the transport, most of the ammunition and whatever supplies they could carry. Only about 30 Zulu bodies were found on the field, though many more had undoubtedly been wounded.

The action at Ntombe was the greatest Zulu success since Isandlwana, and the first serious British reverse in the northern sector. It left Wood determined to regain the initiative. To this end he was aided by a general shift in the pattern of the wider war, in which both sides were clearly poised to renew the confrontation.

For almost two months after Isandlwana, the Zulu army was concerned only with its purification rituals and with recovery. The *amabutho* had dispersed to their family homesteads, and the young men had been preoccupied with gathering in the harvest. The king had been able to maintain sufficient troops in the field to isolate Pearson's command, but he had not been in a position to mount a fresh offensive. With each day that passed, however, Lord Chelmsford recovered from the setback at Isandlwana. Reinforcements poured into Durban, and made their way to the front. Chelmsford's first concern, to relieve the besieged garrison at Eshowe, and he began to assemble a new column at Fort Pearson on the Lower Drift.

This renewed activity was only too obvious to the Zulus opposite, and in the middle of March the king summoned his *ibandla* to consider the situation. He was extremely angry that Pearson had remained in Zululand, acting for all the world as if the country were already occupied, yet at the same time worried by the constant pressure exerted by Wood, and the defection of Hamu. A new British offensive was clearly imminent, and the council decided upon two apparently contradictory responses. They agreed to summon the *amabutho* once more, while at the same time despatching peace envoys to Lord Chelmsford. The British naturally doubted the faith of the latter under the circumstances, but the king had genuinely been eager to try to come to a negotiated settlement before fighting broke out afresh. This had never been likely, however, if only because Chelmsford was determined to revenge Isandlwana before bringing the war to a close.

Rebuffed, the king and his councillors planned a fresh military response. Once again, as they had in the earlier phase of fighting, they opted to split the main army, sending one portion to the coast, to oppose the Eshowe relief column, but directing the main striking arm northwards. Mbilini and the abaQulusi had regularly petitioned for help from oNdini, and Wood's column was undoubtedly the most dangerous British force still operating on Zulu soil. By attacking Wood, the council also hoped to discourage further defections in the north-west, and it may also have been in Cetshwayo's mind that Wood's force effectively blocked any retreat he might one day want to make into Swaziland.

The army set out in the third week of March. Estimates of its strength vary, but by the time it reached the vicinity of Wood's camp, and had been joined by the abaQulusi and many of Mbilini's men, it totalled at least 20,000 men. This time, the king had been more specific in his instructions.

On no account was the army to attack the British in a defended position; do not put your face into the hole of a wild beast, he said, for you are sure to be clawed. Instead, he ordered them to try to lure the British out into the open by seizing their cattle, or feinting towards Utrecht.

Chelmsford, aware that the Zulu regiments were once again mustering, but uncertain of their plans, also went onto the offensive. He planned to cross the river with the Eshowe Relief Column at the beginning of April, and ordered his remaining commanders to make what diversionary attacks they could to confuse the Zulus. In particular, the garrisons along the Thukela and Mzinyathi borders mounted a series of raids across the rivers, burning Zulu homesteads and raiding cattle. Wood, too, was expected to carry out a diversionary attack, and this coincided with his own hope of striking a blow against the abaQulusi by raiding their stronghold at Hlobane.

Although reports reached him that the main army was heading in his direction, Wood chose to ignore them, sceptical of the time it would take for the army to reach him, and convinced he had time to mount his own attack first. Nevertheless, his despatches before the battle suggest that he was not too hopeful of success, nor, indeed, do they give a very clear idea of what he hoped to achieve. Wood was under no illusions that Hlobane would be a difficult place to assault; he had scoured the western end from Zungwini with a telescope, and even at that distance it was clear that the pass which connected Ntendeka to Hlobane was not only steep, but the path up the middle so narrow that only two or three men could comfortably move up it at any given time. Moreover, Buller and Uys had led patrols along the shoulders of the mountain, and reported that the tracks leading to the summit were difficult, and appeared to be blocked by stone walls.

Nor was Wood obliged to choose Hlobane as a target. Lord Chelmsford had deliberately allowed him some leeway in his choice of diversion, and he might have chosen any number of other objectives. The real reason for his choice of Hlobane may have been shaped by reports that the Zulus were sheltering large herds of cattle there. All irregular troops fighting for the British were entitled to a share of captured cattle and, indeed, this was the main reason why Uys's Boers fought at all. The need to impress Hamu's followers, who likewise understood the significance of cattle raiding, might also have been a factor.

Hlobane Mountain was at the centre of the chain of Qulusi flat-topped mountain strongholds. It was the most impressive of them all, and was situated between two other prominent mountains, Zungwini to the west, and Ityenka to the east. About four miles long, Hlobane rises over 1000 feet from the surrounding plain, its gently undulating summit completely encircled by cliffs, which form an almost impenetrable barrier 200 feet high in places. At the western end of the mountain, where Hlobane comes to a point, it is connected by a narrow staircase of rock to a lower, triangular plateau, known as Ntendeka. Although the southern approaches of the mountain are comparatively easy to ascend, until close to the summit, the northern face is much steeper, broken by a series of high terraces and dizzying cliffs.

Today, mining on the southern flank of the mountain has destroyed the original drainage pattern and opened great fissures on the summit, but in the nineteenth century it was a well-watered spot, with two or three streams meandering across the surface, emptying over the side in crystal-clear waterfalls. The surface is covered with low boulders, worn almost flat like paving stones by aeons of wind and rain, and scattered here and there with bush. In the summer months, the summit is exposed to terrifying electrical storms, so the abaQulusi preferred to live on the lower slopes, using the mountain as a refuge in times of trouble. Several steep, rocky cattle-tracks wound up through the cliffs, and the Zulus had blocked them off with dry stone walls as they crested the summit, to control the cattle and keep out intruders. While Wood had successfully driven the Zulus off Zungwini, Hlobane would prove a tougher nut to crack.

If Wood conceived the attack as little more than a cattle raid, that may, perhaps, explain his lax planning; he was accustomed to leaving command in such expeditions to Buller, who had a talent for it. Wood planned to assault the mountain with two parties, one from either end, and he intended to use only his mounted troops, supported by Wood's Irregulars, and rocket troughs – which could be carried on mules. In retrospect, given the highly broken nature of the terrain, the use of a largely mounted force seems folly, but Wood was well aware that Hlobane was just too far away from Khambula for his infantry to march there and back in a day. His plan was to send one party, under Lieutenant Colonel J. C. Russell, up onto Ntendeka, at the western end of the complex, and, once the summit was clear, to climb the pass to Hlobane. The second party would be led by Buller, and would do most of the work; it would ascend at the far – eastern – end, then sweep along the summit, rounding up cattle, until it met with Russell's command, and retreated via Ntendeka.

The plan depended on an element of surprise, on the assault commanders having a good understanding of this sort of warfare, and the troops being able to work well together. Certainly Buller, and the bulk of the soldiers under his command, fulfilled these criteria, but Russell and many of the men under his command were new to the area, and to this type of warfare. Some, indeed, were survivors of Isandlwana, who had only recently been transferred to Wood's command. Nor indeed, were all the irregulars used to working together, as some of them, too, had only lately arrived at Khambula.

Nor were they fresh at the start of the action. On 24 March, Wood himself had led an expedition north to the Ntombe valley in response to a rumour that Mbilini was preparing to attack the garrison there. The rumour proved false, but the mounted men did not return to Khambula until the 26th, and, indeed, Wood's irregulars camped out in the field to the north of Zungwini. Most of the mounted men were only then appointed to join the two assault columns which rode out from Khambula on the 27th, and who rendezvoused in the veld with Wood's Irregulars marching south to meet them. Neither men nor horses, therefore, could have been rested when they started the fight on the morning of the 28th.

During these manoeuvres some of Wood's Irregulars spotted an ominous sight, although they did not bother to report it to their white officers – who also had eyes – as they had learned from experience that their intelligence was usually ignored. They had seen smoke from a large number of camp-fires rising from behind hills to the south-east, in the direction of oNdini. If any of Wood's officers did spot it, however, its significance escaped them.

Russell's command, consisting of about 200 mounted men, a rocket detachment and 440 auxiliaries from Wood's Irregulars and Hamu's followers, bivouacked that night at the southern foot of Zungwini Mountain. Wood himself rode out that evening and joined them. It seems that he did not intend to take command of the attack; he preferred a supervisory role, riding about the field, accompanied only by his personal escort, and not so much controlling events as observing.

Buller's command, which consisted of roughly 160 FLH, 200 irregulars from other units, nearly 280 men from Wood's Irregulars and another rocket detachment, had further to go, and adopted more elaborate precautions. Passing south of Ntendeka and Hlobane, Buller ordered a halt after dark, while still several miles from his objective, and his men lit a number of camp-fires. They rested for a while, then, leaving the fires burning, mounted up and rode to within four miles of the mountain, hoping to confuse any scouts who might have been watching. The remainder of the night they passed quietly, and in the cold.

Both British groups began their assault at about 3.30 the next morning – the 28th. At the eastern end, Buller's men worked their way to the foot of the mountain, and began the slow and difficult ascent. One unit, the Border Horse under Colonel Weatherley, seems to have become separated

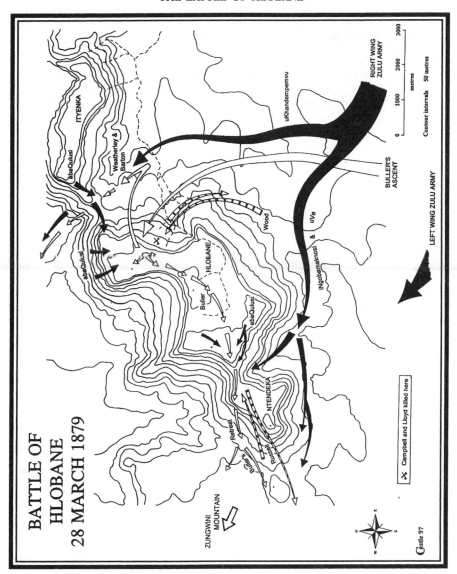

BATTLE OF
HLOBANE
28 MARCH 1879

from the rest of the party in the darkness, and to have lagged behind. As Buller's group approached the cliffs around the summit, a sudden thunderstorm broke over them, and froze them for a moment in the lightning flashes, as the thunder rumbled around the cliffs above them, and the rain lashed down in long, cold spears. No sooner had the storm cleared than they were spotted by the abaQulusi, and came under fire.

The southern slope of Hlobane is curved in a gentle horseshoe, and as Buller's men followed the track up through the centre of the curve, they came under a telling crossfire from both sides. Buller ordered Lieutenant Williams, attached to the FLH, to take a party to a slight rise and return the fire. Williams had just reached his position when a shot from close range struck him clean through the head. Several other men were killed and wounded, and a number of horses were hit. An Austrian adventurer, Baron von Stietencron, was hit and killed by a shot from among the rocks directly above him. Nevertheless, Buller's men spurred their horses up through a jumble of boulders that led to the top of the cliffs. A few Zulus tried to stop them, but Piet Uys shot one dead, and the rest scattered.

It was now about 6.30 a.m., and the first party of British troops was on top of the mountain. Herds of cattle grazed here and there on the surface, but there seemed to be few Zulus in sight. Most of the abaQulusi had taken refuge in the crevices between the boulders among the cliffs below the summit. Ominously, however, one group passed quickly along the foot of the cliffs through which Buller had ascended, cutting off the line of retreat. Buller despatched two troops of irregulars to take up positions around the edge of the mountain as rearguard, and the rest of his command set about rounding up cattle.

Russell, meanwhile, had also achieved his objective. His column had moved up onto Ntendeka, where they, too, found large numbers of cattle. One look at the pass leading up to Hlobane, however, showed that it would be impossible to take mounted men up in any sort of order, and Russell decided to remain on the lower plateau. Instead, he sent a party of Mounted Infantry up the pass on foot, to keep an eye out for Buller.

Wood, meanwhile, had left Russell's bivouac when the latter had moved off that morning. Accompanied by his staff, eight men of the Mounted Infantry, and Prince Mthonga kaMpande – one of Cetshwayo's half-brothers from the Zulu Royal House, who had fled to exile in the Transvaal – Wood proceeded round the southern end of Ntendeka and along the foot of Hlobane, working his way up eastwards, to pick up the track followed by Buller. As Wood reached the foot of the line of cliffs, Buller's route became all too obvious, from the line of trampled grass and dead horses. Here Wood encountered Colonel Weatherley and the Border Horse, who had apparently also been trying to follow Buller, but had been pinned down by the abaQulusi who had cut the track after Buller had passed. Both groups were quite close to the cliffs, and the jumble of huge broken boulders, overgrown with grass and bush, piled up at their foot. The abaQulusi were nestled in among the excellent cover afforded by the rocks, and the British were subjected to a heavy crossfire which would have been more effective if the Zulu weapons had been of better quality.

Nevertheless, the fire would need to be suppressed if the British were to regain the track, and Wood personally led the way forward, towards the rocks, his own escort close behind. The Border Horse followed in their wake. Some 50 yards from the rocks, a warrior fired a shot which struck Wood's interpreter, Llewellyn Lloyd, in the body. Wood, whose relationship to his staff was very close, was horrified by the sight of Lloyd falling. He dismounted and tried to raise Lloyd, but he was clearly dead, and too heavy to lift. Wood's Staff Officer, Captain Campbell of the Coldstream Guards, rushed forward to help, dragging the body back a few yards to the spot where Wood's escort had taken shelter behind the stone wall of a cattle-kraal. Moments later, another shot struck and killed Wood's horse.

Wood told Campbell to order the Border Horse to come up to clear out the rocks, but the position was a daunting one, and the Border Horse held back. Campbell impatiently set out himself, and was joined by Wood's young ADC, Lieutenant Lysons. Seeing them rush forward, Wood ordered his escort to follow in support. Campbell reached the crevice between the boulders whence the firing had come, but as he stepped through, a Zulu inside shot him dead at point-blank range. Lieutenant Lysons and a Private Fowler pushed past the body and fired into the dark recess, sending the concealed Zulus scurrying back into the maze of boulders behind. According to some accounts, Mbilini himself may have been among the number; certainly the incident took place not far from the site of his home-stead, and the cave may well have been his personal refuge.

Lysons and Fowler carried the dead Campbell down to where Wood was waiting with Lloyd's body. Wood was now almost certainly in a state of shock, for his actions over the rest of the day do not appear entirely rational. Determined not to abandon the bodies of his friends to the Zulus, he ordered Weatherley to proceed up the track with the Border Horse. Despite the fact that the abaQulusi were still shooting at them, he then instructed Mthonga's followers to dig a grave with their spears. They cut a shallow scrape in the ground, and Campbell and Lloyd, wrapped in a blanket, were lowered in and covered over. By this stage some of the abaQulusi had skirmished to within 30–40 yards of the party. Wood read a hasty burial service over the grave, then ordered his escort to retire with him back down the mountain, the way they had come. In effect, he was abdicating any further responsibility for the day's events.

On the summit, meanwhile, Buller's command had successfully rounded up much of the abaQulusi cattle. The rearguard, however, were coming under increasing pressure from warriors making their way up through the cliffs. Ominously, a fresh body of Zulus – abaQulusi reinforcements – had appeared on Ityenka Mountain opposite, and were moving towards the nek which connected it to Hlobane.

The events that took place on the top of that mountain are still difficult to disentangle today. The battle became a running fight, in which small groups of men on both sides criss-crossed the plateau surface, most of them – screened by the undulations of the summit – unaware of what was going on elsewhere on the battlefield or on the plain below. Topographic references become confused, men lost their sense of direction, and military terms such as right, centre and left ceased to have meaning. While most of Buller's men drove a huge herd of cattle west towards Russell's command, the rearguard were increasingly exposed to Zulu attack. At one point, the rearguard were directed to abandon their position, only to have the order countermanded a few minutes later as they were compelled to drive off the Zulus who had occupied the site in the meantime. With their lines stretched perilously thin, they were in danger from abaQulusi massing on their flanks, and trying to surround them.

Buller, meanwhile, had become concerned that the body of Lieutenant Williams had been left unburied by the track during the ascent, and he despatched a troop of the FLH under Captain Barton to return and recover it. Barton's men rode back the way they had come. They were close to the original point of ascent when Barton received a fresh order from Buller. In some urgency, it instructed him to abandon Williams's body and retire 'by the right of the mountain'. This must have been confusing, since from Barton's position he was already doing just that. If Barton wondered what had prompted such an inconclusive order, however, it did not divert him, for shortly afterwards he ran into Weatherley's command, heading in the opposite direction. It may well be that both parties had a sense of impending crisis, and decided that Buller's message could be interpreted as instructing them to retire from the mountain by the most direct route. Together, they started to do precisely that – with catastrophic results.

What had prompted Buller's curious message? On the summit of Ntendeka, Russell's command had been the first to realise that the whole military position had suddenly changed. Looking southwards, some members of the column had seen what appeared to be the shadows of clouds moving down from the Inyathi Hills opposite, and into the plain below Hlobane. On close inspection, they proved to be not clouds, but the main Zulu army, en route from oNdini. Russell frantically scribbled a note of warning to Wood, then ordered his own command, hampered by hundreds – if not thousands – of head of cattle, to retreat to the foot of Ntendeka. Meanwhile, Wood had in any case seen the *impi* for himself, as his party worked its way eastwards along the foot of Hlobane. Mthonga's Zulus had been enthusiastically capturing sheep and cattle, and the prince himself, who was on horseback, had ridden further up the mountain to supervise the round-up. Looking back, he had suddenly seen the Zulu army, which was already only a few miles away.

On the summit, Buller was among the last to spot the danger, for there are few places in the centre of the plateau that give a good visibility of the plain below. Once he had sighted the army, however, Buller realised that any escape by the southern side of the mountain, the way they had come up, was extremely dangerous. His immediate reaction was to recall Barton – he later claimed that 'by the right of the mountain' was meant to signify the western end, exactly the opposite of what Barton assumed – and to move his entire command west towards Ntendeka.

Such was the confusion among the British that it is difficult to identify exactly where the enemy army was when they spotted it, and by which route it had come. According to Zulu accounts, the warriors appear to have been advancing in columns, approaching the Inyathi ridge south of Hlobane from between the Black and the White Mfolozi Rivers. The left wing, to the west, seems to have crossed the hills at a spot known as Leeunek, while the right wing was further east. The regiments in the right wing – the uKhandempemvu, iNgobamakhosi and uVe – were all young, eager warriors, and were probably ahead of the rest of the army.

It is unlikely that the Zulu command realised a battle was raging on Hlobane until they crossed the Inyathi range, when they were attracted to the sound of firing. From certain points on the Inyathi Hills, indeed – precisely where the right wing crossed – parts of the summit of Hlobane are clearly visible. As they crested the hill, the men saw the skirmishing in the distance, and charged down to join the fighting. Approaching the mountain, their advance was directed by shouts from the abaQulusi on the cliffs above. Mbilini, of course, knew that the army was in the vicinity, and this must have influenced his command decisions during the battle. He was perfectly placed to catch the British in a trap, and indeed he had. Buller's men were now on the top of a mountain where virtually all the points of exit had been sealed, stranded, with a large army coming to complete their destruction.

As the right wing approached Hlobane, it split in two, the iNgoba-makhosi and uVe turning left towards Ntendeka, the uKhandempemvu turning right towards the nek which connected Hlobane with Ityenka. As Barton's FLH and the Border Horse descended at the eastern end of the mountain, moving out onto the plain to the south, they ran straight into the vanguard of the uKhandempemvu coming in the opposite direction. With their escape route below the mountain cut, they turned back towards Ityenka nek. Here, however, they were blocked by the abaQulusi, who had been moving across from Ityenka to Hlobane, some of whom turned to meet them.

Barton and Weatherley were now effectively surrounded, and had little choice but to try to fight their way through. They rode straight at the abaQulusi on the nek, and a running fight developed as they struck and pushed through the Zulu lines. Many British were killed on the nek itself, while the survivors endeavoured to make their descent on the northern side. But the northern edge of Ityenka consists of a series of steep terraces and cliffs, with no obvious way down, and most of the Border Horse were brought up short. With the uKhandempemvu streaming up to reinforce the abaQulusi, Weatherley and most of his command were killed there, a number of men and horses tumbling over the cliffs.

A few survivors somehow managed to find a path down through the precipice, and fled across the open country north of Hlobane, pursued by some of the abaQulusi and the mounted scouts of the uKhandempemvu. Barton himself was chased for several miles and eventually killed by Sitshit-shili kaMnqandi, an *induna* of the uKhandempemvu. Combined, Barton's and Weatherley's command had numbered about 70 men; only a handful of them escaped alive.

Elsewhere on the summit, Buller's rearguard had collapsed, scattering towards the western end of the mountain. They were harried by growing numbers of abaQulusi who shadowed them, making good use of cover, trying to cut off stragglers and isolated parties. Even by this stage, the British position had dissolved into an ignominious retreat, but it was to deteriorate still further when Buller's command reached the pass leading down to Ntendeka. It was narrow and steep, nothing more than a staircase of huge boulders, overgrown in between with long grass. Although it was just possible for men and animals to wind their way down a narrow track in the centre of the pass, they had more difficulty in crossing the wide gaps separating the higher boulders on either side.

Wood's Irregulars led the way, still driving the precious cattle which, to many, had been the objective of the whole expedition. To add to the confusion, the abaQulusi had built stone walls across the summit, to make the pass defensible, and as they began their descent, the white men had to lead their horses through these barriers. There were already signs of panic, and only the more disciplined irregulars managed to maintain any sense of order. By the time the first troops were half-way down the pass, the abaQulusi had crept onto the rocks on either side, and were shooting or flinging spears at them. At the top of the pass, a rearguard tried to protect the retreat, and their fire kept a large crowd of warriors at bay. They ceased firing for a few seconds, however, when someone mistakenly called out that they were shooting at their own colleagues. By the time they realised the error, it was too late, the abaQulusi were on them, and the stand disintegrated.

The descent of the pass collapsed into utter rout. Here and there a few officers tried to retain some control, directing men to fire at the warriors who were threatening them on all sides. For the most part, however, there was a mad scramble, as the throng of men, horses and cattle slipped, tumbled and crashed down the rocks under a hail of flying spears, gunshot and dislodged boulders.

Individual vignettes have survived to add depth to the picture of horror. A Boer named Andries Rudolph saw Piet Uys running down the pass on foot, with a Zulu following him. Rudolph yelled to Uys to swerve so that he could shoot the warrior, but it was too late, and Uys was speared between the shoulder-blades. One young member of the Frontier Light Horse asked a man standing next to him if they could get down, then recoiled in horror as the man replied, 'Not a hope!', put his carbine into his mouth, and blew out his own brains. Another man slipped and found himself pinned between two large boulders: a woman of the abaQulusi, who had turned out to repel the invaders with her menfolk, spotted him there, stood above him on the rocks, and, as he helplessly flailed his arms for protection, stabbed him in the head.

At the bottom of the pass, Buller attempted to organise another rearguard to cover the descent. By now, however, large numbers of Zulus – possibly the iNgobamakhosi *ibutho* – were streaming up the southern slope of Ntendeka. There was no chance for the British to contain the situation; all they could hope was to get as many of the men away as possible. Buller himself demonstrated that his reputation for personal courage was not exaggerated as he rode several times part-way up the pass to rescue unhorsed troopers; and many other officers and ordinary soldiers followed his example. According to one survivor, at least half the men who got away did so with a wounded or unhorsed man riding double behind them.

Colonel Wood was later vague about his personal movements while all this was happening. He ordered Russell's command to retreat towards Hlobane to escape the approaching Zulu army, and apparently accompanied them. Russell withdrew in good order along the southern slopes of Zungwini. The left wing of the Zulu army, coming up from Leeunek, to the south, but still several miles away, seems to have been in no hurry to close with him, but the iNgobamakhosi and uVe were threatening him from the rear. As he retired, Wood's Irregulars, still reluctant to abandon the cattle, lagged behind. Many of the survivors from Buller's retreat went the same way, and Russell was followed by a long straggling tail of men in outright flight. Probably as many men were killed along the foot of Zungwini, where the iNgobamakhosi and uVe caught up with them, as on the terrible pass itself. Wood's Irregulars suffered in particular, since the Zulus bitterly resented their presence, and were desperate to recover their cattle.

The Zulu pursuit ran out of steam at the base of Zungwini. Russell's command reached Khambula safely, while survivors of Buller's débâcle continued to struggle in throughout the night. In all, no less than 15 officers had been killed, and 79 men, most of them colonial irregulars. Official figures put the losses of Wood's Irregulars at 100 men, but this was probably an under-estimate. Piet Uys's death proved to be serious, for that night at Khambula his followers decided to disperse to their farms. They had joined the British out of respect for Uys and in the hope of cattle, but they had no love for the *rooineks* (rednecks), and now Uys was gone, and their families were in danger of attack from the Zulus. Many of Wood's Irregulars departed as well; in the tense night at Khambula after the battle, their officers had left them to their own devices, outside the protected laagers, and many not unnaturally took this as evidence that their services were no longer required.

On the Zulu side, it is not known how many men died, though the abaQulusi had probably suffered heavily in the initial stages of the fight. According to some reports, Mbilini himself had been slightly wounded in the exchange of fire with Wood's staff. Only those elements on the right wing of the Zulu army had been engaged, and their losses were small. That evening, the right wing moved across to the south of Hlobane, bivouacking on a stream below Ntendeka. The left wing, coming up at a leisurely pace from the south-west, took no part in the fighting, and went into camp at Nseka Mountain. The whole army, therefore, spent the night spread out over several miles of country on a north–south axis.

There is a curious footnote to the story of Hlobane. A fortnight after the battle, a patrol encountered a solitary white man near Zungwini Mountain. He was naked, bruised and exhausted, and he turned out to be a trooper of the Border Horse, named Grandier. He had a strange story to tell, claiming that he had been captured at the height of the battle, and taken to oNdini. Here, constantly threatened with death, he had been interrogated by the king, only to be sent back under guard to Mbilini when Cetshwayo realised he had no intelligence of any value. According to Grandier, Mbilini planned to put him to death, but one night Grandier overpowered and killed one of his guards, drove the other off, and managed to escape. For a while he was treated as a hero until, after the war, evidence emerged to suggest that in fact Grandier had escaped in the confusion of the massacre of the Border Horse, and had only been caught some hours later, as he tried to work his way around Hlobane towards Khambula. The Zulus had generally treated him well, in fact, and the king – who was keen to dispel the myth which prevailed in Natal that he was a bloodthirsty despot – had ordered that he be taken as close to Khambula as his warriors dared, and then released. Although this version of events casts doubt on Grandier's credibility, it does not detract from the distinction he enjoyed as the only white prisoner-of-war taken by the Zulus in 1879.

Although the battle was followed immediately by a British victory, there was a marked reluctance to return to Hlobane, and most of the British dead lay unburied there for months, if not years. In the latter stages of the war, Wood sent patrols who interred some of the bodies lying at the foot of Ntendeka, but it was not until September that any effort was made to bury the Border Horse. Even then, many individual corpses remained undiscovered. Piet Uys's family searched for his corpse after the war, and recognised his remains only because they were held together by a waistcoat, which bore a tell-tale spear hole in the back. A year later, when he revisited the scene, Wood himself was shown Barton's skeleton by Sitshitshili, the *induna* who had killed him.

The British recognised the gallantry of their soldiers by the award of four VCs, two going to Lysons and Fowler, and the others to Buller and a Major W. Knox Leet, who had helped rescue men during the retreat. The courage of the colonial irregulars, however, was overlooked; although Buller mentioned several in his dispatches, none received the award. At least one, Cecil D'Arcy of the Frontier Light Horse, would receive the award for further bravery before the war was out.

No amount of glittering honours, however, could conceal the fact that the attack on Hlobane had been a bloody shambles, and that Mbilini and the abaQulusi had out-generalled Wood at every turn. Yet, as Napoleon once said, luck was a general's greatest asset, and Wood's luck was with him at the end of March 1879. The very next day, the main Zulu army attacked his base at Khambula, giving him the chance to exact his revenge.

— 7 —
THE BATTLE OF KHAMBULA
29 March 1879
'No quarter, boys, and remember yesterday'

The Zulu army spent the night of 28–29 March quietly bivouacking over a large stretch of country between Zungwini Mountain and Nseka Hill. Most of the *amabutho* had not taken part in the attack on Hlobane, and for many of the assembled warriors the battle can have been little more than a curtain-raiser for the main event. They had been sent from oNdini to drive out Wood's column, and they had yet to attempt the task. Nevertheless, news of the events at Hlobane must soon have spread throughout the entire army, and it can only have increased their eagerness for the coming fight. The young regiments of the right wing – the uKhandempemvu, iNgobamakhosi and uVe – all of whom had also been in the thick of the fight at Isandlwana, were particularly sure of themselves, and keen to renew the struggle. Ironically, this self-confidence, exaggerated by the excitement of Hlobane, proved to be their undoing.

Before the great army moved off the next morning, the commanders formed it into an *umkhumbi* (circle), to receive the last-minute instructions and spiritual preparation for battle. There had been no time for these ceremonies at Isandlwana, and many Zulus blamed this for the heavy casualties they had suffered on that occasion. On 29 March, however, there was ample time for the army to undertake all the necessary rituals, and these can only have further heightened their morale.

It was traditional, on such occasions, for commanders to address their men and tell them something of their objectives. Once again, the army had been placed under the command of Ntshingwayo, the victor of Isandlwana, but on this occasion Mnyamana kaNgqengelele, the chief of the Buthelezi people, was also present. The Buthelezi had been one of the most important groups within the kingdom since King Shaka's time, and, indeed, Mnyamana's father had been a councillor to Shaka himself. Mnyamana was an extremely important and powerful *isikhulu*, who had been an *induna* under Mpande, and come to fulfil the role of King Cetshwayo's most senior adviser. He was not, first and foremost, a soldier, and deferred to Ntshingwayo in matters of strategy, but he was undoubtedly the most important man present with the army, and it was Mnyamana who addressed the assembled army that morning.

Mnyamana was only too aware of how much hung on this campaign. The Zulus had so far successfully checked the British advance, but there was no indication that the enemy resolve was weakening, and indeed, reinforcements were massing once more on the borders. If the *impi* could defeat Wood's column, the British would have been repulsed on all fronts; there was at least the possibility that they might abandon military action as being not worth the cost, and listen instead to the king's peace overtures. If, on the other hand, the Zulu army was now defeated, there would be nothing to stop the British completing their reinforcement, and starting the invasion anew. If that happened, there could be very little hope of the Zulus stopping them, and the consequences for the kingdom as a whole would be disastrous. Mnyamana was a good orator, and he spoke with passion, playing on the warriors' emotions. Yet in many ways his speech had the opposite effect to that intended, for although it worked the warriors up into a pitch of excitement, it unsettled them, too, infecting them with a sense of desperation.

This was, perhaps, one reason why the army behaved exactly as Cetshwayo had ordered it not to do. The king, remembering the lessons of Rorke's Drift, had told the *amabutho* not to attack prepared positions, yet the younger regiments, in particular, considered it their duty to strike at the enemy as quickly as possible, wherever they found him. There was no place, in their minds, for subtle feints and strategies to lure the British into the open; their need was to 'eat up' the foe, as they had done at Isandlwana, and this perception was to limit the tactical options available to their commanders.

The ceremonies and speeches over, the army began to advance at about 9.00 a.m., formed up into five great columns, and moved off in a north-westerly direction, towards Khambula and Utrecht.

It had, of course, been equally obvious to Wood's men at Khambula that another battle was imminent. One of Hamu's *izinduna*, who had been on Hlobane with Wood's Irregulars, had sought to escape during the chaos by passing himself off as one of the enemy. He had been lucky enough to fall in with his old *ibutho*, who had no idea that he had defected. He spent the night with his former colleagues, then slipped away to bring Wood the news that the army was heading towards him. In many ways this intelligence was superfluous, however, since the general direction of the Zulu army's advance had been obvious enough since the previous morning. Yet there was still a chance that the Zulus might not attack Khambula, but might bypass Wood altogether, and fall instead on Utrecht. This possibility was particularly disturbing, because Wood had left the town without a significant garrison, and, indeed, the whole Transvaal border lay exposed.

At dawn, therefore, Wood sent his scouts out to determine the exact direction of the Zulu advance. According to local tradition, which is still remembered today, these scouts spotted the *impi* breakfasting along the banks of a stream near Zungwini at about 10 a.m. Only a few regiments had been seen the day before, but now the strength of the entire army was apparent to them, and the scouts realised for the first time the extent of the threat facing them. The black auxiliaries commemorated their expressions of shock – 'Oh my God!' – in the name by which the stream is still known today: amaGoda.

The scouts returned safely to Khambula an hour later, giving Wood several hours' warning of the Zulu approach. His position, in any event, was naturally strong, running west to east along the crest of a narrow ridge. To the north the country was open, stretching down towards a number of streams which fed the headwaters of the White Mfolozi, but to the south it dropped away more sharply into a narrow valley. A stream flowed through this valley, too, and in places the ground was waterlogged and boggy.

Wood had anchored his position on a small knoll in the centre of the ridge, which he had crested with an earthwork redoubt. Long and narrow, this redoubt was fairly typical of the unsophisticated temporary forts built by the British in Zululand, in that it consisted of nothing more than a trench, with the soil piled up inside to form a rampart. Close to the redoubt, on a gently sloping ledge below it, to the south, Wood had constructed a wagon-laager to accommodate the column's cattle. The wagons had been drawn into a square and chained together, and a trench dug around the outside, with the earth piled up between the wheels. Over 2000 cattle were crammed into the laager which could not, indeed, contain them all; a herd of several hundred had to be abandoned outside the camp. The cattle-laager was connected to the redoubt by a wooden palisade, to prevent the enemy moving freely between them. A little more than 100 yards to the west of the redoubt was a much larger wagon-laager, which had also been heavily entrenched.

These three defensive points were able to support one another, and had a clear field of fire to the north, where markers had been set up to help judge the range; to the south, however, much of the approach to the camp lay in dead ground formed by the valley. Wood had moved this camp several times for sanitary reasons. Further along the ridge, to the east, were the remains of an abandoned earthwork, which might provide an enemy with some potential cover, and just below it, on the edge of the valley, an abandoned clump of temporary grass huts which had served as a camp for Wood's Irregulars.

Wood's force had been weakened by the absence of most of the Boers and Wood's Irregulars, who had left the evening before, but he still had an impressive command at his disposal – a total of 2086 men, the core of which were eight companies of the 90th LI and seven of the 13th LI. He had six 7-pounder guns of 11/7 Battery RA, together with two rocket troughs, and his mounted men, although shaken by the events of the day before, still numbered over 500. Most of his troops, moreover, would have known their positions in the event of an attack, and Wood was able to prepare with a minimum of confusion.

Two guns were placed in the redoubt, together with a company and a half of the 13th LI. One company of the 13th held the cattle-laager, while the remaining four guns were unlimbered in the open space between the redoubt and the principal laager, a position that afforded them the protection of the infantry fire, while allowing them sufficient room to change their front to meet attacks from different directions. The main wagon-laager was the most heavily defended. The infantry were deployed along the wagon-walls – 90th on the northern face, 13th on the south – either crouching below the wagon-beds, between the wheels, and firing over the rampart, or kneeling in the wagons themselves, firing over barricades of mealie-bags and biscuit-boxes that had been placed along the outside buck-rails. The mounted men left their horses in the centre of the laager, and found places among the infantry where they could.

The Zulu army came into sight at about 12.30p.m., five miles south of the camp, and considerably west of Zungwini. It was on a course which might easily have taken it past Khambula and on to Utrecht, and Wood watched anxiously as it halted and deployed into attack formation. To his relief, it shifted slightly to the north, on a line that would bring it directly into contact with the camp. Quite why the Zulus abandoned their initial plans remains a mystery, although it probably had much to do with the eagerness of the young men to fight; whatever the wishes of the king or his high command, the battle would take place at Khambula after all. Wood ordered the tents struck, to clear the field, and boxes of reserve ammunition to be opened. The sight of the tents suddenly collapsing was visible to the Zulus several miles away, and it was an encouraging one; they thought the British were packing up to run away.

The Zulu force began its advance again at about 1 p.m. The uKhan-dempemvu were now on the left horn, together with the uMbonambi and uNokhenke. They were all too conspicuous as they moved forward to enter the valley to the south of the camp. The Zulu centre – the more senior iNdlondlo, uDloko, uThulwana, iNdluyengwe, iSangqu, uDududu and iMbube *amabutho* – took up position at the far end of the ridge, directly east of the camp, while the right horn – the iNgobamakhosi and uVe – swung out into the open country to the north.

Wood himself stood watching from a position below the redoubt, by the palisade; according to his account, the army, when fully deployed, covered a front of ten miles; it was an awesome sight, the more so because the regimental masses were marked by different-coloured shields, and moved with a discipline that told on the garrison's nerves. To complete the British discomfort, Zulu speakers in the camp heard the men on the right horn call out, 'We are the boys from Isandlwana' as they came within earshot. When the right horn reached a point about three miles north of the camp, when it was plainly in sight but out of artillery range, it halted, to allow the rest of the army to get into position.

The British, indeed, had expected the first move to come from the left horn, on the opposite front, since the regiments to the south had been manoeuvring into position for some time, and appeared to be mounting an attack. They were surprised, therefore, when the right horn, without any warning, suddenly ran forward, and halted only 1000 yards away, deploying skirmishers and clearly preparing to launch an assault. It was a premature movement, and quite why it occurred is a matter of debate, but the uVe and iNgobamakhosi were the youngest regiments present, with less experience and self-restraint than their more mature colleagues, and the pressure on them was immense. Their preparatory rituals had placed them under a severe psychological strain for several days, while their aggression can only have been heightened by the clash at Hlobane the day before.

Ever since January, moreover, there had been an argument between the iNgobamakhosi and the uKhandempemvu, their great rivals – now on the opposite flank – as to which of these two *amabutho* had entered the camp ahead of the other. Heated words had been exchanged; threats that would need to be honoured at Khambula. From their position to the north of the camp, the right horn could see little of the movements to the south, and may have thought the uKhandempemvu were already in position. To top it all, the words of Mnyamana Buthelezi had inflamed them, stoking their anger against the white man, whose small forts, ahead up the slope, must have seemed to them puny and inconsequential.

Whatever the reason, this development played into Wood's hands. It was now about 1.30 p.m., and from his vantage point outside the redoubt, with a good view of the Zulu position, he could see that the left horn was not about to advance. The opportunity existed, therefore, to provoke the right horn into launching a full attack on its own, unsupported by the rest of the army. Wood sent an order to Buller, telling him to take a mixed force of 100 mounted men out from the north face of the laager, and sting the right horn into attacking.

This was a move that required some nerve, especially among men who had been routed only the day before. Nevertheless, it was the type of manoeuvre to which the irregulars were accustomed, and most of them were keen to exact revenge for their sufferings at Hlobane. Buller's men cantered down across the open, grassy slope to within a few hundred yards of the right horn, and then dismounted to fire a volley into the ranks.

This was too much for the iNgobamakhosi and the uVe, and the spring of tension that had brought them thus far finally snapped. With a great shout of 'uSuthu!', they broke into a charge. Buller's men immediately mounted up and retired, only to halt and repeat the performance further on. As the Zulus swept forward, their skirmishers fell back, revealing the dense mass of the main body. There were as many as 6000 men in the right horn, and at times they chased to within 50 yards of the retreating horsemen. A shallow stream bubbled out of a hollow on the undulating slope, creating a patch of marsh, and as they crossed it, one or two of the horses became bogged down, and at least one man was overtaken and speared to death.

It was during this retreat that the only British VC of the action was won; a private of the 4th Regiment, attached to the Mounted Infantry, had dismounted to fire, but could not remount his nervous horse. Lieutenant Edward Browne of the 24th, commanding the Mounted Infantry detachment, saw his predicament, and rode back to steady his horse, 'thus saving', in the words of one contemporary account, 'his trooper's life at imminent risk of his own'. One party of mounted men, Christian Africans from the Edendale mission in Natal, who had been part of Durnford's command, and survived Isandlwana, preferred to remain outside the laager, and take their chances. They retired off to the west, and kept up a harassing fire on the Zulus throughout the fight. As the rest of the horsemen raced up the slope towards the safety of the laager, the guns opened fire from the crest above them, the shells arcing over their heads and bursting among the Zulus behind.

Once Buller's men had drawn clear and reached the laager, Wood gave the order for his infantry to open fire, and a terrific volley rippled along the northern face of the redoubt and laager. This fire cut down the Zulus by the score, but some elements pressed through it, and crashed against the north side of the wagon-laager, tugging at the wagons in a desperate attempt to break in. The fusillade was so heavy, and at such close range, however, that they could not sustain this position, and fell back. For a few minutes large numbers of warriors tried to hold their ground 50–60 yards from the laager, making the most of a scattering of low, concrete-hard ant-heaps that provided them with their only cover. This proved pitifully inadequate against the storm of fire that continued to rain down on them, and they reluctantly gave way, retiring eastwards, towards the protection of an outcrop of rocks 700 yards away.

Although they could hardly have realised it, the right horn had effectively handed the battle to Wood in that first attack. Although the fighting would last for the rest of the afternoon, the Zulu commanders would never recover the initiative nor be able fully and effectively to coordinate their attacks. Wood had realised that his own force, outnumbered ten to one, was too small to outgun the Zulus if they struck from all directions at once; by provoking and repulsing the right horn, however, he ensured that the Zulu attacks would be made piecemeal, and he was able to move his guns to meet each new assault as it developed. This is not to say, however, that the battle went all his way; several times, before the day was out, the Zulus would come within an ace of upsetting his plans. Khambula would prove the most hard-fought battle of the war.

The terrific crash of gunfire and the huge pall of smoke that rose from the British camp made it all too obvious to the Zulu centre and left that their right had become engaged. The left, however, had been delayed by the terrain, literally bogged down by the marshy ground in the bottom of the valley, which hampered its movements. By the time it reached the foot of the slope that led up to the camp, the iNgobamakhosi and uVe, out of sight beyond, had already retired and gone to ground. The left horn, nevertheless, was in a good position from which to launch an assault. The approach lay in dead ground, and it was not until the warriors burst over the crest of the slope, only 100 yards from the British position, that the British fire could reach them. Once they reached that point, however, they could expect to suffer severely, since the line of their attack brought them out almost between the main laager and the cattle-laager.

The chest's approach was more exposed, since it had to cross the length of the open ridge, but the British were nonetheless impressed by the order in which the Zulus developed their attack. It began at about 2.30 p.m., and Ntshingwayo himself came forward to take up a position on a knoll about 700 yards to the east of the camp. This gave him a commanding view of the southern approaches, and if his presence was obvious to the British, and exposed to their fire – though none struck him – he was equally conspicuous to his own men, and the sight of him there can only have spurred them on.

The attack came on in a very determined manner, the chest making what use it could of the cover afforded by the abandoned camp and huts, or keeping just to the south of the crest line, where the fire could not reach it. The left horn pressed up the valley, and was lost to sight as it massed at the foot of the slope. Wood saw the attacks coming, and was able to reposition his artillery. He moved the guns closer to the main laager, leaving one to cover the northern face, while turning the other three southwards.

The Zulus later admitted that the fire from these guns was quite disheartening, especially at close range, as it seemed impossible to dodge the shells, which struck down whole clumps of men, often mutilating the bodies in a terrifying manner. Nevertheless, they pressed home their attacks right up to the cattle-laager. The palisade on the far side prevented them forcing a way through to the redoubt, but the uNokhenke *ibutho* in particular, managed to reach the wagons on the southern side. This was held by just one company of the 13th, under Captain Cox, and it proved inadequate for the task, since the uNokhenke burst in through the wagons, and hand-to-hand fighting broke out among the cattle. Cox ordered his men to withdraw, but they were exposed to a heavy fire as they fell back. Cox himself was hit, shot through the thigh, while Colour Sergeant Fricker was wounded. Private Grosvenor went back to tend to Fricker, and helped him away, but his compassion cost him his life. Grosvenor was one of the last to leave the laager and, as he retreated, a Zulu ran up behind him and speared him through the back.

Once they had possession of the cattle-laager, the Zulus occupied the barricades the 13th had abandoned, and opened a heavy fire on the main laager and redoubt. For the most part, the guns carried by the Zulus at Khambula were the same antiquated patterns with which they had begun the war; nevertheless, hundreds of British Martini-Henrys captured at Isandlwana and Ntombe had been distributed among the *amabutho*, and there is no doubt that the accuracy of their shooting had improved as a result. In particular, the Zulus in the cattle-laager were able to pour heavy fire into the southern face of the main laager, much to the discomfort of the men stationed there. Moreover, flanking fire from Cox's company had been an important factor in preventing the tip of the left horn, which

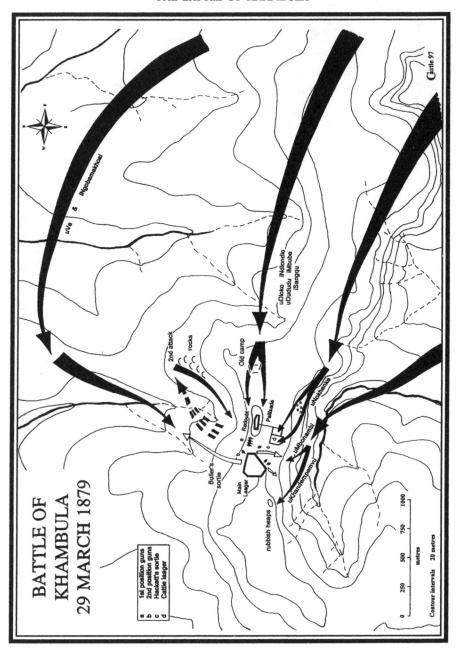

BATTLE OF KHAMBULA 29 MARCH 1879

a 1st position guns
b 2nd position guns
c Hackett's sortie
d Cattle laager

uVe & iNgobamakhosi

2nd attack

rocks

uDloko   iNdlondlo   iMbube
uDududu   iSangqu

Old camp

Redoubt

Palisade

uNobamba

Buller's sortie

uMbonambi

Main Laager

uKhandempemvu

rubbish heaps

Castle 97

0   250   500   750   1000
metres
Contour intervals   20 metres

emerged up the head of the valley only a few yards away, from sustaining any attack. With that fire suppressed, the left horn was free to mount a major assault on the main laager itself. Wood saw some 30 *izinduna*, led by a chief with a red flag, forming one regiment – the uMbonambi – at the bottom of the slope, and realised that the only hope of dispersing them was to send a sortie out to the lip of the valley, and to fire directly into them at close range.

Two companies of the 90th under Major Robert Hackett were given the task. They marched out from the southern corner of the laager as smartly as if they were on parade, a sight that took the Zulus by surprise, forcing their skirmishers to retire on the main body, gathered down the slope. Hackett's brisk advance cleared the open ground at the top of the slope, and here his men deployed into line, and directed a volley into the Zulus massed below. The Zulus were no more than 200 yards away, and at that range the effect was devastating, breaking up the uMbonambi concentration and forcing the regiment to take shelter further down the valley.

Even so, Hackett's men remained extremely vulnerable to return fire, and the Zulus were perfectly placed to enfilade him from both flanks. A couple of hundred yards further west, on the edge of the escarpment, stood a slight knoll, which Wood had used as a dump for the dung accumulated in the horse-lines. The combination of baking heat and heavy rain had produced a fine crop of mealies and grass on the knoll, and Zulus on the extreme left of the left horn had occupied it early in the fight. From here they were able to pour a heavy fire into the south-west corner of the main laager from close range, using a smattering of captured Martini-Henrys to good effect.

Hackett's advance had carried his companies to a line that was level with this position, and the Zulu riflemen were able to rake the length of his companies with fire. Further east, on his other flank, the Zulus in the cattle-laager were able to do the same, and Hackett's troops soon began to suffer casualties. The officers were particularly exposed as they strode about, directing their men; Lieutenant Arthur Bright was struck by a bullet which passed through one thigh and lodged in the other. He was carried from the field alive, but in the confusion the surgeons who attended him dressed one leg, but failed to notice that the bullet had nicked an artery in the other, and he bled to death overnight. Hackett himself was shot through the head, the bullet striking one temple and exiting through the other, missing his brain, but passing behind his eyes and destroying the optic nerves. He, too, was carried from the field, too shocked to realise that he was blinded for life. With at least one man dead and several more wounded, Wood realised that Hackett's position was untenable, and ordered his companies recalled. Two companies of the 13th, under Captains Waddy and Thurlow, were despatched from the main laager to cover his retreat.

Hackett's sortie had certainly discouraged the left horn, but fire from the rubbish heaps and cattle laager remained extremely galling. Two of the guns were ordered to fire shrapnel shells into the cattle-laager to drive the Zulus out, resulting in much carnage, presumably, to the cattle who were still corralled there. Inside the main laager, two companies of the 13th had abandoned their part of the barricade, on the south-west corner, so heavy and accurate was the Zulu fire, and Buller himself took charge of the situation. He organised firing parties and directed them to fire volleys, not at the Zulus sheltering in the mealies on top of the dung-heap, but into the heap itself. The heavy Martini-Henry bullets passed through the light dung, causing mayhem among the Zulus sheltering among and behind it. After several volleys, the heap was shattered, and the following morning no less than 60 Zulu bodies were found lying in the debris.

The repulse of the left horn spurred the right to make a further attempt on the far side of the camp. The iNgobamakhosi abandoned their sheltered position behind the low ridge, and rushed in the open towards the redoubt. Once again, this attack was mounted across desperately exposed ground, the last stretches of which, moreover, rose up steeply towards the redoubt. Here they were met by a veritable storm of shell- and rifle-fire. Some threw themselves down behind the few boulders and ant-heaps that scattered the slopes, while others, pathetically, picked up stones, and carried them forward in front of their faces in a desperate attempt to protect themselves.

Here and there, some parties pressed almost up to the foot of the redoubt before being cut down. It was probably about this time that Lieutenant Nicholson, who commanded the Artillery section in the redoubt, was killed; he stood up on the raised gun platform to see over the rampart to direct the fire, and was shot dead. Nevertheless, nothing could hope to survive in the face of such a fusillade, and the iNgobamakhosi and uVe reluctantly retired once more to the shelter of their rocky outcrop.

It was now about 3.30 p.m., and the main Zulu attacks had been repulsed all along their line. Nevertheless, they were by no means defeated, and the great army still lay in an arc around the camp, clinging to cover near the British positions, and making attacks wherever it could. The chest, comprising the more senior warriors, including the oNdini *amabutho* who had fought at Rorke's Drift, tried several times to assault the camp from their positions along the ridge to the east. Here, the redoubt lay between the Zulus and the main laager, and protected them from much of the fire from it, while the ruins of the abandoned camp, and the huts of Wood's Irregulars, provided a sheltered launching point.

Several charges broke against the rampart of the redoubt itself, and a handful of warriors were killed as they tried to snatch the reins of the artillery horses. Each time they were driven back, however, and the older men proved no more able to sustain the attack than the iNgobamakhosi had been. As they retired to the ruined huts, the guns beside the laager lobbed shells into them, setting fire to the thatch, so that many Zulu wounded who were sheltering there were trapped in the flames, and burnt to death.

By about 4.30 p.m. it was becoming clear to the British that the Zulu attacks, desperately brave as they were, were becoming increasingly disorganised, and that the warriors were tiring. Nevertheless, a heavy fire-fight, punctuated by fresh charges from the left and centre, continued for another hour, until Wood judged it safe to reoccupy the cattle laager. A company of the 13th were sent to drive out at the point of the bayonet those warriors of the uNokhenke who still lingered there. The Zulus retired reluctantly, and only after a flurry of firing, the majority slipping over the rocky terraces and down into the valley below. A company of the 90th, under Captain Laye, was sent to line the edge of the terraces and disperse them as they fell back.

The physical and emotional effort expended by the Zulus had been extraordinary. They had repeatedly assaulted a defended position from all sides, often over difficult terrain, and had endured enormous casualties in the process. For some, the stress and adrenaline had given the battle a hallucinogenic quality, and it seemed that the British had turned nature itself against them. A white trader was later asked by Zulus who had fought at Khambula,

'what it meant that at the beginning of the battle so many birds, such as they had never seen before, came flying over them from the side of the Whites? And why were they attacked also by dogs and apes, clothed and carrying fire-arms on their shoulders?' One of them even told me that he had seen four lions in the laager. They said, 'The Whites don't fight fairly; they bring animals to draw down destruction upon us.'

By late afternoon, even their commanders could ask nothing further of them, and the *amabutho* began an orderly retreat from the battlefield.

Wood was not content to let them go peacefully. He was well aware, even at that point, that he had inflicted an important reverse on an army which constituted nothing less than the Zulu nation's manhood, assembled in its defence. Now he had a golden opportunity to turn that reverse into a crushing blow from which they might never recover. As he wrote:

> When the enemy fell back in the direction in which they had come, they were so thick as to blot out all signs of grass on the hillside, which was covered with their black bodies, and for perhaps the only time in anyone's experience it was sound to say, 'Don't wait to aim, fire into the black of them.'

The British infantry continued to pour a heavy fire into the Zulus as they retired, the guns showering them with shrapnel to a greater distance. The most damage was caused, however, by the mounted men.

Once the Zulus had retired away from the immediate confines of the camp, Wood ordered Buller to get his men mounted, and to chase the enemy from the field. It was a tactical truism that a good cavalry charge could turn a retreat into a rout, and Wood was heard to say, 'Oh, for two regiments of English cavalry!' He had no English cavalry, but he did have the irregulars and the Mounted Infantry, who, exhausted though they were by the events of the last few days, were desperate to exact revenge for the débâcle at Hlobane.

Buller's men rode out of the laager on either side, sweeping across the open slopes where the iNgobamakhosi had first attacked, and driving down the decline into the valley to the south. Here a few warriors still lingered among the grass and bush on the banks of the streams, and the irregulars carefully hunted them out and shot them down. For the most part, however, there was little resistance. Some warriors were so exhausted that they could only drag their shields behind them. The mood of the moment was summed up by Captain D'Arcy of the Frontier Light Horse, who called out to his men, '"No quarter, boys, and remember yesterday!" – and we did knock them about, killing them all over the place.' Another irregular officer, Commandant Schermbrucker, left a vivid account of the carnage wrought by his men:

> They fairly ran like bucks, but I was after them like the whirlwind and shooting incessantly into the thick column, which could not have been less than 5000 strong. They became exhausted, and shooting them down would have taken too much time; so we took the assegais from the dead men, and rushed among the living ones, stabbing them right and left with fearful revenge for the misfortunes of the 28th inst. No quarter was given.

The pursuit lasted for about seven miles, until a heavy mist began to fall at dusk, at about 6.30 p.m. The Zulus had managed to retain some order until they reached Zungwini, but by that time the *amabutho* were falling apart. The abaQulusi seem to have been particularly exposed in the retreat, and their force disintegrated under the British pressure, the warriors slipping away in small groups for the safety of Hlobane. Mnyamana Buthelezi, horrified at the extent of the disaster, made an attempt to rally the *amabutho*, but Zibhebhu kaMaphitha pointed out that it was hopeless. Only the onset of darkness caused the British to give up the chase and return to camp, and saved the Zulus from further losses. Defeated, disheartened, and utterly spent, the great army made its way slowly back to oNdini. Many warriors simply returned to their own homes in their despair.

The following day, the British counted the cost. Wood had lost just eighteen NCOs and men killed, and eight officers and fifty-seven NCOs and men wounded, of whom three officers and seven men would later die of their injuries. A number of black auxiliaries and non-combatants were also wounded, although no one bothered to count them. The dead were buried on the slope below the ground, to the west of the position attacked by the iNgobamakhosi.

Given the intensity of the fighting, these losses were insignificant, and far outweighed by the huge number of Zulu dead scattered around the camp. The British collected 785 corpses from around the laagers and redoubt over two or three days following the battle, dragging the bodies into carts and carrying them three-quarters of a mile away, to where large pits had been dug for them. One of the burial detail wrote:

> A more horrible sight than the enemy dead, where they felt the effects of shell-fire, I never saw. Bodies lying cut in halves, heads taken off, and other features in connection with the dead made a sight more ghastly than ever I thought of.

Many hundreds more bodies lay out on the line of retreat; D'Arcy claimed to have counted 150 on the ground covered by his men, and Schermbrucker 300. Furthermore, many Zulu had escaped from the battlefield with terrible wounds that would kill them before they reached their distant homes. Probably, their losses exceeded 2000 men, and, when all those who eventually died of wounds were taken into account, they may have totalled 3000.

This loss was all the heavier because it was from among the prime of the nation's young men. Even the British commented on the fine physiques and healthy appearance of the dead. Many chiefs, sons of chiefs and *izinduna* had been killed, having exposed themselves in the attempt to urge their men on. British patrols along the length of the Natal–Zulu border reported the sound of wailing and mourning songs from the homesteads across the rivers over the following weeks.

Furthermore, the battle gave the lie to the young men's confident boasts that, whatever the circumstances, they were more than a match for the British. This was the same *impi* which had carried the day at Isandlwana; now, when the battle was fought on the redcoats' terms, there was no escaping the terrible consequences. Cetshwayo was said to be furious that his army had disregarded his specific orders not to attack the 'wild beasts' in their lair.

Indeed, the battle proved the turning point of the war, as the great council had feared it might. Within a few days, it was followed by another British victory, at the other end of the country. While Wood was fighting at Khambula, Lord Chelmsford crossed the Lower Thukela at the head of his Eshowe Relief Column. The Zulu forces mustered to oppose him attacked near the site of the ruined *ikhanda* at kwaGingindlovu on 2 April. Like Wood, Chelmsford met them in a tight formation, protected by entrenched wagon-laagers, and the Zulus were defeated. The following day Eshowe was relieved, and both Lord Chelmsford, and Pearson's command, retired to the Thukela.

British reinforcements flooded into Durban at such a rate that there seemed little hope that the Zulus could stop the British juggernaut. King Cetshwayo tried once more to open negotiations with Frere and Chelmsford, but the British knew that the tide of war was now flowing firmly in their favour, and would only offer him the same terms that they had presented in the ultimatum of December 1878. At the end of May, Chelmsford was ready to begin a new invasion of Zululand.

Wood's column was to play its fair share in the final conquest of Zululand. The British forces were reorganised, but Wood's force was retained intact, and given the new designation of the Flying Column. This was to advance in tandem with a new column, composed of reinforcements and commanded by Chelmsford himself, which was called the 2nd Division. The division crossed into Zululand a few miles north of the line of advance of the old Centre Column, so as to spare the troops the depressing sight of Isandlwana, then linked up with the Flying Column to move on oNdini. In the coastal sector, Pearson's column was replaced by another new column, the 1st Division.

Despite the fact that the British government had grown tired of the cost the war, and sent out General Sir Garnet Wolseley to replace him,

Chelmsford was determined to have his revenge for Isandlwana. The Flying Column and 2nd Division advanced in the face of constant skirmishing, brushing aside Cetshwayo's increasingly desperate peace overtures, and destroying Zulu homesteads as they went. Indeed, the later stages of the Anglo-Zulu War had all the elements of a war of attrition, as Chelmsford tried to erode the Zulu people's will to resist by destroying their homes and food supplies.

On 4 July, both columns finally crossed the White Mfolozi and formed a large rectangle in the middle of the Mahlabathini plain, surrounded by the great cluster of *amakhanda* that included oNdini itself. Here, in a last gesture of defiance, the assembled *amabutho* attacked them once more. Wood, whose troops made up two sides of the British formation, later observed that the Zulu assaults at oNdini were never as ferocious as they had been at Khambula, and in some respects he was right, although he had a vested interest in the claims he made on behalf of his own victory.

The Zulus had at last learned to respect British firepower, and many of the regiments were reluctant to face it. Nevertheless, one particularly determined charge almost struck a corner of the formation and, after it was all over, Zulu bodies were found just a few paces from the British lines. When the Zulus wavered, Chelmsford ordered the 17th Lancers – cavalry at last, newly arrived from England – to pursue them, and they chased them from the field in a style which perfectly illustrated the truth of Wood's remark at Khambula. Buller's mounted men, the veterans of Hlobane and Khambula, followed in the Lancers' wake, shooting down any warriors they had missed, and finishing off the wounded.

Over 2000 Zulu were killed at Ulundi – as the British preferred to call the battle – and the great *amakhanda*, including oNdini itself, were razed to the ground. King Cetshwayo had foreseen the calamity, and had not waited to watch the final slaughter of his young men. With just a handful of attendants, he retired northwards into the Black Mfolozi valley, and it was not until August that British patrols ran him down and captured him. He was taken to the coast and sent to Cape Town in exile.

By that time, most British troops had withdrawn from Zululand. After Ulundi, the majority of the regional chiefs had realised that resistance was futile, and had come in to surrender. Typically, those in the north-west were among the last to accept defeat. Mbilini himself was killed not long after Khambula, in a skirmish with a patrol from Luneburg, but the abaQulusi continued to resist until the king himself was captured. The last shots of the war were fired among the caves and boulders in the hills overlooking the Ntombe; on one occasion, the British, growing weary of their attempts to flush out the Zulus, simply blew up the entrance, with women and children, as well as warriors, still inside.

By September, the last British troops were marching out of Zululand. To all intents and purposes the war was over; the king was deposed, his *amabutho* dispersed. Yet a fresh chapter in the long history of bloodshed in Zululand was about to begin. Although the protagonists changed, and the fighting was often between Zulu and Zulu, the cause of the struggle was basically the same, as the Zulu Royal House strove to recover in the face of determined opposition from the agents of British and Transvaal colonialism.

THE BATTLE OF ONDINI
21 July 1883
'This is what we desire; to die with our king'

The story of the Anglo-Zulu War abounds in tragedies, and perhaps the greatest of them all is the fact that the British had abandoned the cause for which they fought, even before they had achieved their own objectives. Ironically, if the Zulu victory at Isandlwana had guaranteed the ultimate destruction of the army which triumphed there, so it also brought an end to the Confederation policy. Sir Henry Bartle Frere had always relied upon a quick victory in Zululand to obscure the fact that he had exceeded his authority by provoking the war in the first place; Isandlwana, and the protracted resistance of the Zulu people, brought an end to that.

The last stages were played out in the full glare of publicity, and a war that might once have gone unnoticed attracted enormous political and public comment. Far from accelerating the pace of Confederation, the war in Zululand delayed it, and by the time the last shots were fired, the political will in Britain to see it through had evaporated. Disraeli's government fell – given a push by some memorable tub-thumping on the part of Gladstone over the injustice of the Zulu campaign – and the new Liberal government set its heart firmly against further expansion of territory in southern Africa.

The task of devising the settlement of the defeated Zulu kingdom fell to Chelmsford's successor, Sir Garnet Wolseley. Wolseley had been sent out to Zululand in time to supervise the successful conclusion of the war, but to his disgust Chelmsford had managed to reach oNdini and defeat the Zulu army while Wolseley was still trying to reach the front. Chelmsford gladly resigned his command, leaving Wolseley with the thankless task of pacifying the country, and devising a workable settlement.

Given the shift in the position of the British government, Wolseley's brief was brutally simple; he was to establish some form of government in Zululand which would prevent the re-emergence of the Royal House, and therefore the army, and by doing so place Zululand in such a position that it would never again be able to threaten British interests. He was not, however, to annex the country outright, or commit the British to any form of control other than indirectly. The future stability of Zululand itself, and the wellbeing of the Zulu people, was not within his remit.

Wolseley approached his task through the time-honoured colonial method of divide and rule. In this, he was advised by many leading officials in Natal, who clearly had their own agenda. Underlying Wolseley's settlement was the assumption that Zululand was a conglomerate of independent chiefdoms, who had only been held together by the tyranny of the Royal House, and who would welcome British intervention to return to their former status.

This was gross over-simplification which failed to consider the complex role of the monarchy in Zulu society and, indeed, ignored the obvious fact that the vast majority of Zulus had been prepared to go to extraordinary lengths to defend the Royal House against that British intervention. Nevertheless, Wolseley divided the country up into thirteen chiefdoms. Nominally, these bore some resemblance to the old pre-Shakan clans, but in fact Wolseley was motivated rather by the need to appoint chiefs who were broadly sympathetic to British aims. These included men who had either fought with the auxiliary forces for the British, or influential Zulus who had deserted the Royal House before the king was captured.

John Dunn, Cetshwayo's old friend since the days of 'Ndondakusuka, was an obvious choice. Dunn had been torn by divided loyalties to his adopted country and the people of his birth, and had tried to remain neutral in 1879. The British, however, had pressured him into joining them, and he had served with Chelmsford's intelligence department during the Eshowe Relief Expedition. This had damned him in the eyes of the Zulus, and Dunn had little option but to commit himself completely to the British cause. Privately, Wolseley admitted that he would have preferred to make Dunn the 'white king' of all Zululand, but admitted that Dunn's unorthodox lifestyle had compromised him with too many people among the Natal authorities. Instead, Dunn was rewarded with a huge tract of country that not only included his former districts along the coast, but extended along much of the Thukela, so as to provide a buffer zone with Natal.

Prince Hamu kaNzibe, who had defected to Colonel Wood while the war was still in progress, was given control of much of north-western Zululand, while Zibhebhu kaMaphitha was established as his neighbour to the east, north of the Black Mfolozi. Most of the other chiefs were *izikhulu* who had surrendered to the British in the nick of time. Although a British resident was to be posted to Zululand, he was given no means of exerting his authority, and having informed the chiefs of the new regime, Wolseley abandoned Zululand to its own devices, taking the last British redcoats with him.

The settlement was, of course, fraught with tension from the beginning. It had always been intended as divisive, although just how divisive it turned out to be exceeded all expectations. For one thing, although the British had judged correctly that men such as Hamu, Dunn and Zibhebhu commanded tremendous respect among their own followers, many of the chiefs were regarded as collaborators and turncoats by those among their subjects who remained loyal to the king. Furthermore, the British had deliberately drawn the borders of the new chiefdoms so that the most ardent royalist elements were ruled over by the men most resolutely opposed to their cause, in order to keep them in check. In particular, the abaQulusi, who had resisted the British to the last, were given over to Prince Hamu, while many members of the Royal House itself fell under the control of Zibhebhu.

Zibhebhu kaMaphitha was to prove a central figure in the events of the post-war years. His family were closely related to the Royal House itself, being descended from a brother of Senzangakhona, Shaka's father. Zibhebhu's father, Maphitha, had ruled much of northern Zululand on King Mpande's behalf, and his people had become immensely powerful in their own right. They were known as the Mandlakazi ('great strength'), after one of their early homesteads – a phrase that had a particular resonance after the battle of 'Ndondakusuka in 1856.

Many Zulus, indeed, credited the role played by the Mandlakazi at 'Ndondakusuka as being decisive; so much so that Cetshwayo came to fear their potential rivalry. It was the Mandlakazi, among others, whom Cetshwayo hoped to outmanoeuvre politically when he invited Shepstone to his coronation in 1873. When Zibhebhu succeeded his father Maphitha, he proved to be a shrewd, dynamic and strong-minded chief. Moreover, in European minds he was progressive, because in the pre-war years he had cultivated considerable trading links on his own account with the neighbouring colonies. In this he had allied himself both to John Dunn – whose own dealings with Natal were not exclusively on behalf of his patron, the king – and to his western neighbour Hamu. All three had bolstered their personal power and, as a result, the British saw them as a natural counterbalance to the Royal House.

Nevertheless, while Zibhebhu undoubtedly enjoyed his independence, there is no evidence to suggest that he was anything other than loyal to the king in the war of 1879. Indeed, his performance then suggested that he was a man of rare talent; it had been Zibhebhu who, as commander of scouts, had kept British patrols away from the main army on the last stage of the march to Isandlwana, and he had played a prominent part in the battle, where he had been wounded in the hand. It was Zibhebhu who commanded the force which harassed British watering parties on the final approach to oNdini, and, indeed, he it was who had very nearly trapped Buller's mounted men in a skirmish the day before the battle. In the aftermath of the British victory, Zibhebhu had offered sanctuary to the fugitive Cetshwayo at his Bangonomo homestead in the north of the country, and although the king did not take up the offer himself, he did send his son, eleven-year-old Dinuzulu, into Zibhebhu's care, along with many of the royal women and 100 head of cattle.

This incident, apparently, provoked the quarrel with the royal family which was to have such a devastating effect on the kingdom's subsequent history. The presence of the royal party within his territory conferred considerable prestige on Zibhebhu, as well as an obvious bargaining counter with the remainder of the royal family once the king himself had been sent into exile, and Zibhebhu was at some pains to keep them tightly under his control. Dinuzulu, however, who although young was both intelligent and extremely proud of his status as his father's heir, greatly resented Zibhebhu's presumption, and was determined to escape his authority.

To that end, royalist supporters smuggled him away from Zibhebhu's homestead, and delivered him instead to that of his uncle, Prince Ndabuko kaMpande. Ndabuko's own standing among the Royal House was high, and he was a staunch supporter of his brother, Cetshwayo, but he was a headstrong man who, typically, had been the one Zulu commander who had urged the army to cross the Mzinyathi river in the aftermath of Isandlwana. Unfortunately, Ndabuko held no authority in British eyes, and his followers had been placed under Zibhebhu's control. Zibhebhu demanded the return of young Dinuzulu, and Ndabuko, acting as if he were still a man of consequence and not Zibhebhu's subject, refused. In retaliation, Zibhebhu refused to give up the royal women and cattle. Friction broke out between the Mandlakazi and the royalists living in their districts – who called themselves by the name which had been associated with Cetshwayo since before 'Ndondakusuka, the uSuthu – and within a year of Wolseley's settlement, the first violence erupted in Zululand.

The British, meanwhile, had been pondering the fate of King Cetshwayo himself. He had been taken on ship to Cape Town, and there lodged in apartments in the old Dutch castle, where the British hoped he would simply fade away. That he distinctly refused to do. Once he had recovered from the depression that marked his first few months in captivity, the king began to orchestrate a campaign to allow him to return to Zululand. He received a steady stream of visitors, many of whom believed that the Anglo-Zulu War had been unjust, and who kept him informed of events in Zululand.

Cetshwayo fretted at the tales of the growing tension between his own supporters and Zibhebhu, and argued that the only way to ensure peace in Zululand was to restore royal authority. At first, the home government refused to listen to his arguments, but as the situation inside Zululand became increasingly tense, it began to consider whether some sort of partial restoration of the monarchy, carefully controlled by the British, might not be in the long-term best interests, not only of Zululand, but of its white neighbours. Certainly, both Hamu and Zibhebhu were now engaged in constant skirmishing with the royalists living within their own boundaries, while leading uSuthu had led a deputation to Pietermaritzburg to appeal for the king's return. They had received little enough sympathy – indeed, the British Resident in Zululand considered it his duty to uphold the integrity of Wolseley's settlement by supporting Zibhebhu and Hamu in the face of royalist intrigues. Inevitably, both chiefs became increasingly contemptuous of uSuthu notables living in their territory, and openly raided them for cattle. Nevertheless, Cetshwayo proved to be a tireless, patient and subtle petitioner, and at last, in August 1882, three years after his capture by British dragoons, he was given permission to visit London to argue his case before the Colonial Office.

Cetshwayo's visit to London was a particularly bizarre twist in a story rich in ironies. The British public had by no means forgotten about the war, but curiosity about the victor of Isandlwana – who had been portrayed in some British papers at the time as an ape-like savage – coupled with sympathy for a brave enemy, and a vague sense of unease about the justice of the war, combined to produce crowds of sightseers on the king's arrival. When they found not the scowling barbarian they had imagined, but an imposing man with a polite and regal manner, smartly dressed in European clothes, curiosity turned to delight, and the king was cheered wherever he went. High society queued to pay its respects at the king's London lodgings, and Queen Victoria herself granted Cetshwayo an audience at Osborne House. The meeting was a little cool – the queen had had many friends among the officers of the 24th – but she presented the king with a three-handled silver drinking cup, and the royal portrait-painter was commissioned to paint Cetshwayo's portrait.

Moreover, the serious part of the king's visit was at least a limited success. The Colonial Office agreed that Cetshwayo might be returned to Zululand, but only under strong constraints. Not only was he to be forbidden to revive the *amabutho* system, and a British resident placed near by to ensure his compliance, he was to be given only a part of his original territory. It was clearly impossible to return men such as Hamu,

Zibhebhu and Dunn to his rule, especially as all Wolseley's chiefs had accepted their positions on his specific assurance that Cetshwayo would never be allowed to return. Both Hamu and Zibhebhu were confirmed in their positions, and their territorial integrity guaranteed; and Dunn was allowed to retain his authority over his own followers, but his territory was brought more firmly under British control, in an area designated the Reserve Territory.

Cetshwayo was, in effect, hemmed in both to north and south by his rivals, an invidious position which the British justified on the grounds that such enclaves provided a necessary refuge for ordinary Zulus who no longer wished to live under their king. Some adjustment of boundaries was made in an attempt to restore uSuthu supporters living in the king's new territories, but since the whole country was rapidly sliding into pro- and anti-royalist factions, any kind of simplistic geographical partition soon became unworkable. Cetshwayo, of course, was bitterly disillusioned at the limitations placed on him, but was realistic enough to accept them with only token complaint. They were, after all, the only terms on offer.

King Cetshwayo landed at Port Durnford, a small landing place amidst the crashing surf on the coast of the new Reserve Territory, on 10 January 1883. He had expected his people to be gathered to greet him, but he was disappointed; instead, there was only Sir Theophilus Shepstone – the same man who had supervised his parody of a coronation in 1873, and schemed against him ever since – and an escort of dragoons. Shepstone had deliberately not informed the uSuthu of the date of the king's return, so as to prevent any such demonstrations. Instead, the king was to meet his followers on the Mthonjaneni heights, overlooking the emaKhosini valley, in the heart of Zululand, a week later.

For Cetshwayo, the meeting must have been full of ironies; British dragoons had once escorted him from Zululand, and now they escorted him back, in the company of the same Shepstone who had 'crowned' him just a decade earlier. How much had happened in that decade; and how very different times were now. At the end of the month the king was finally installed once more in a ceremony attended by some 6000 prominent Zulus, including Mnyamana Buthelezi, and members of his family, like Ndabuko and Dabulamanzi, who had remained so loyal to him in his absence. Inevitably, none of the chiefs opposed to his return were present; Zibhebhu had ridden to join the meeting at Mthonjaneni, but had pointedly ignored Cetshwayo, and paid his respects only to Shepstone.

The ceremony over, Cetshwayo returned to the Mahlabathini plain. None of his old homesteads there had survived the battle with the British four years previously, and their charred remains were steadily disappearing beneath a growth of dark bush. Nevertheless, the king still regarded the spot as his home, and he directed his followers to begin construction of a new oNdini, on a rise less than a mile to the east of the old one. This was to be the third such settlement by that name, and all reflected his fluctuating fortunes; the first had been built for him near Eshowe by his father, in the days of his youth. The new oNdini followed a similar pattern to the old, though it was slightly smaller, containing about 1000 huts.

Yet in truth the new settlement sharply highlighted the king's ambiguous position. The old *amakhanda* had been an integral part of the nationwide manifestation of royal control; the previous oNdini had been busy with *amabutho* and with great men and *izinduna* coming to pay their respects from across the country. Now, although most Zulus continued to think of themselves as members of an *ibutho*, the practical infrastructure that had supported them was gone. Many of the younger men had already married, without waiting for the king's permission; the king was prevented from summoning them for military purposes, and he could no longer supply shields to protect them and cattle to sustain them. Indeed, many thousand head of royal cattle had been appropriated by the king's rivals, who had no intention of returning them, and without them he was effectively impoverished. Although many Zulus continued to visit the new oNdini, often slipping away from their homes in the territory of his rivals and the Reserve to do so, it remained something of an anachronism, a symbol of a power whose base had already and effectively been undermined.

Trouble followed the king's return almost immediately. Both the British Resident in the Reserve, and Zibhebhu in the north, reacted to the restoration by insisting that the people living in their districts should declare their loyalties; they must either submit to their authority or move into the king's territory. For many, this meant abandoning the lands of their ancestors, and was not acceptable. Such people, together with diehard royalists like the abaQulusi, looked to the king for support, and many were encouraged by the simple fact of his return to attack their tormentors. Cetshwayo could not openly succour them, but neither could he abandon them without irreparably damaging his own prestige. Two of his staunchest allies, realising his dilemma, took matters into their own hands.

Throughout the last week of March, Prince Ndabuko and Mnyamana Buthelezi assembled a large army at Mnyamana's homestead on the Black Mfolozi. It was loosely organised into divisions based on regional chiefdoms, rather than the old *amabutho*, but it numbered some 5000 men –

the largest force yet put in the field by the uSuthu. Mnyamana's territory bordered the Mandlakazi district, and his aim was to strike north-west into enemy territory, and to destroy Zibhebhu's principal homestead, Bangonomo.

Although its objectives were clear enough, however, the army lacked the cohesion and sense of common purpose which had been such a feature of the *amabutho* system, and morale was further undermined by Zibhebhu's reputation as a skilled and ruthless general. That reputation proved to be wholly justified when the uSuthu army entered the Msebe Valley on 30 March. Although Zibhebhu's force was only one-third the size of his enemy, he held them under much tighter control, and had carefully deployed them in ambush, among the long grass and broken terrain of the valley. When the uSuthu were perfectly placed, Zibhebhu rode along his line, urging his men to rise up and attack. They swept down on the uSuthu with such determination that the royalists immediately collapsed, and fled back down the valley. The pursuit was ruthless, and several thousand uSuthu were killed, for the loss of just a handful of men on Zibhebhu's side. Only the fact that the uSuthu generals had been marching in the rearguard enabled them to escape the carnage.

The defeat at Msebe proved to be a disaster of the first magnitude for the king. Zibhebhu and Hamu continued to attack royalist supporters with impunity – many uSuthu living outside the king's territory were forced to take refuge in caves, and remained there for many months – while British hostility towards the king deepened. With no possibility of outside help, the only solution for the beleaguered royalists was to continue the fighting, which spluttered on inconclusively throughout the next three months. Although the uSuthu gained some success in bringing relief to their beleaguered compatriots, particularly in Hamu's territory, they never managed to regain sufficient confidence to stand before a Mandlakazi army in open fight.

By July, the king and his supporters were becoming increasingly desperate. The country was now in the grip of a full-scale civil war. Any lingering hope that Cetshwayo might one day be able to reunite the country under his authority had gone, and, indeed, the uSuthu needed a decisive victory if they were to retain any credibility at all. Zibhebhu's prestige, by contrast, had risen through a seemingly endless succession of victories.

So far, the British had steadfastly refused to become involved, but it was clear that they blamed Cetshwayo for the situation which had developed since his return, and if they did intervene, it would probably be to depose him. This was a scenario that left Cetshwayo with little to lose, and towards the end of June he baldly informed the British Resident camped near oNdini that he was going to muster his forces and decide the matter once and for all. Although his animosity towards Hamu dated back to the latter's desertion to the British in 1879, it was widely hoped among the uSuthu that Hamu could easily be defeated in isolation; the real problem – and therefore the true object of the king's attack – was Zibhebhu.

Throughout May and June, the king's messengers summoned his supporters to oNdini, including hundreds who crossed over from the Reserve Territory to join him, much to the Resident Commissioner's annoyance. Part of the army was sent north, once more under the command of Ndabuko and Mnyamana, to rendezvous with northern uSuthu, and establish a presence on the Mandlakazi borders. The greater proportion, however, remained at oNdini with the king, and it is interesting to consider its composition.

Unlike the force defeated at Msebe, there was a deliberate attempt to revive the *amabutho* system among the men gathered at oNdini. The Anglo-Zulu War was only four years old, and the vast majority of men still considered themselves bound to their former regiments. Of course, only those who presently supported the king responded to his summons, and the *amabutho* were a fraction of their original size, since many members were now fighting for Zibhebhu or Hamu. To the uSuthu, these people were known as *amambuka* – renegades who had deserted their king. Those regiments who mustered in some strength were the iNgobamakhosi, their old rivals the uKhandempemvu, the uThulwana, uDloko, uNokhenke and uMxhapho. The regiments associated with Cetshwayo's old kwaNodwengu homestead – the iSangqu, iMbube and uDududu – also appeared to have rallied together.

In addition to the old, pre-war regiments, King Cetshwayo had formerly enrolled the regiment of youths who had been cadets in 1879. Wryly, he had named them uFalaza – the 'storm clouds' – reflecting the way the fortunes of the Zulu people had been tossed around by the whirlwinds unleashed by the British. Without proper *amakhanda* to house them, and cattle to supply shields, few of these regiments retained anything of the uniform appearance they had once enjoyed, and to identify themselves as royalists they had adopted a badge known as the *tshokobezi*, a piece of stiff white cowhide worn upright over the forehead, or hanging from a necklace over the shoulders, with the bushy part of a tail attached to the tip. Most were well armed with their own shields and spears, and many still had the antiquated firearms they had carried into war against the British.

The uSuthu high command, too, represented an almost nostalgic reunion of the great men of the former kingdom. Chief Ntshingwayo kaMahole, the victor of Isandlwana, was given charge of the uDloko *ibutho*, and Chief Godide kaNdlela, who had commanded at Nyezane, led the uMxhapho. Hayiyana kaMaphitha, the eldest brother of Zibhebhu himself, who had fought for Cetshwayo at 'Ndondakusuka, and deserted his brother's cause through loyalty to the king and family rivalry, commanded the uThulwana. Vumandaba kaNtati, who had been the senior *induna* at the presentation of the British ultimatum in December 1878, and had later dissuaded the regiments from crossing into Natal after Isandlwana, was present with his old command, the uKhandempemvu. Prince Dabulamanzi, the defeated Zulu general at Rorke's Drift, was there, together with a number of other important sons of Mpande, including Ziwedu, who had watched the first battle of oNdini on the king's behalf, Sitheku, whom Zibhebhu had captured and released once before, at Msebe, and Shingana.

The assembly of this impressive host was all too obvious to Zibhebhu. Being the dynamic and aggressive commander he was, Zibhebhu decided not to wait lamely for the uSuthu to attack him, but called up his own supporters to strike first. USuthu spies soon brought news to Cetshwayo of the Mandlakazi preparations, but although the great council deliberated on the matter, the general feeling was that Zibhebhu was bound to strike at the uSuthu army in the north, which, led by Ndabuko and Mnyamana, was hovering on his borders. Although no one under-estimated Zibhebhu's daring, the uSuthu leadership thought it impossible that he could ignore so immediate a threat, and cover the huge distance necessary to attack the king himself. This was a fatal misjudgement; Zibhebhu planned exactly that.

On 20 July Zibhebhu mustered his army at his ekuVukeni homestead on the Nongoma ridge, in the south of his territory. He had only about 3000 men at his disposal – significantly fewer than the uSuthu ranged against him – but they were a much more formidable force than the enemy. Most were veterans of dozens of skirmishes, and some had been present when Zibhebhu had slaughtered the uSuthu at Msebe. They had the greatest confidence in their leader, who kept them well in hand. All carried their traditional weapons, but many had some sort of firearm, since Zibhebhu had secured the services of five white 'advisers', who not only procured guns for him, but were also prepared to fight for him. Foremost among them was Johan Colenbrander, a young adventurer who had fought with the British forces in 1879, and whose daring, marksmanship and horsemanship had earned him the nickname of 'The White Whirlwind'. Zibhebhu, too, was an accomplished horseman – he rode a white horse, so that his men could always spot him in a fight – and a crack shot. After they had undertaken the necessary rituals, the Mandlakazi marched out that evening on a route that would keep them east of Ndabuko's uSuthu on their borders, heading towards oNdini.

The speed of Zibhebhu's advance is not the least remarkable aspect of the extraordinary events that followed. His army had some 30 miles to cover before they reached the Mahlabathini plain, and they covered it in a single night's march. Much of the route lay along the valley of the Black Mfolozi, a wild, rugged, and sparsely populated part of the country. With no one to spot them and raise the alarm, the Mandlakazi reached the hills to the north-east of the Mahlabathini plain before dawn the following morning. Here Zibhebhu halted his men and formed them into the usual chest-and-horns formation, before continuing the advance. According to some accounts, he timed his last approach so that his warriors would be silhouetted against the dawn sky, knowing that this would strike terror into the hearts of his enemies.

The uSuthu, for their part, were completely unaware of the impending catastrophe. In addition to the military commanders, a great many important chiefs and *izinduna* had gathered at oNdini to discuss the situation with the king, but none of them were expecting to fight. At dawn the great homestead came alive with men and women going about their everyday business. The young uFalaza regiment assembled at the gate, where many of their womenfolk, who had come to bring them food, were preparing to depart for their own homes.

It is not entirely clear who first spotted the Mandlakazi approach; according to some sources, it was a group of envoys of the Swazi king, who had come to discuss a possible alliance with Cetshwayo against Zibhebhu, and who had been lodged at the homestead of Chief Mfanawendlela, a mile or two from oNdini itself. They spotted the *impi* about five miles away, and rushed to oNdini, calling out, 'Is the king going to die in his hut, then? The *impi* has arrived, and it is upon us!' A different account credits the honour to a Zulu woman, who had gone out to relieve herself before dawn, and spotted the Mandlakazi cresting the hills in the distance. Either way, the message soon reached oNdini, where it caused complete consternation.

The uSuthu leadership seemed to collapse in shock. The great men hurried to confer with Cetshwayo, but none could agree on a course of action. Several of them urged the king to flee, but Cetshwayo replied indignantly, 'Am I to run away from my dog?' Indeed, the king appeared to be one of the few who kept his head. Seizing the initiative, he ordered Godide to rouse those *amabutho* who had not yet awoken, and appointed Ntuzwa kaNhlaka as senior commander, with several of the Royal House as lieu-tenants.

The *amabutho* began to assemble outside the main gate, but their movements were slow and uncoordinated, partly because so many of their commanders were still locked in discussion with the king. By the time they were in some sort of order, the Mandlakazi were only about a mile away, and approaching rapidly. Hayiyana kaMaphitha, at least, was aware of the danger they were in, but faced it resolutely. Calling to a boy who attended him, he remarked, 'Bring those weapons, boy, bring them here. This is what we desire, to die with our king.' He calmly ate some of the beef which had been cooked for breakfast, took a drink of sorghum beer, then went out to fulfil his boast.

The uSuthu force moved eastwards along the rise above oNdini to meet the Mandlakazi. Typically, the young regiments were on either flank, the uFalaza on the left and the iNgobamakhosi and uKhandempemvu on the right; and the more mature men, the uThulwana, uDloko, uMxhapho and uNokhenke, in the centre. A message was sent to the Nodwengu contin-gent, which was camped several miles to the west, to hurry forward in support. This, however, was a hopeless request. The uSuthu had not advanced far, and were still sorting themselves out, when the Mandlakazi struck them.

Despite their exhausting night march, the left horn of the Mandlakazi rushed forward without pausing, calling out its ominous war-cry, 'Washesha' – 'make haste' (to the fight). The iNgobamakhosi and uKhan-dempemvu responded with a half-hearted cry of 'uSuthu!', and a volley of badly directed shots. The Mandlakazi left was neither deterred nor deflected, and rather than advance to meet the uSuthu, continued to stream round to their left, outflanking them in traditional style. This was too much for the uSuthu right. The once-proud *amabutho*, who had braved the terrible firestorm unleashed by the British to triumph at Isandl-wana, collapsed, and began running back towards oNdini. Years of defeat had demoralised them, and Zibhebhu's reputation was sufficient in itself to overawe them. The Mandlakazi struck them as they went, killing them as they ran, and shepherding them away from the nearby safety of the White Mfolozi valley.

In the centre, the senior men were more resolute. Here they were stiff-ened by the presence of the uSuthu commanders, and they opened a heavy fire on the men opposite them. These were a contingent of Hamu's Ngenetsheni people, supported by several companies of Mandlakazi. Zibhebhu's men, however, made no attempt to return the fire, but

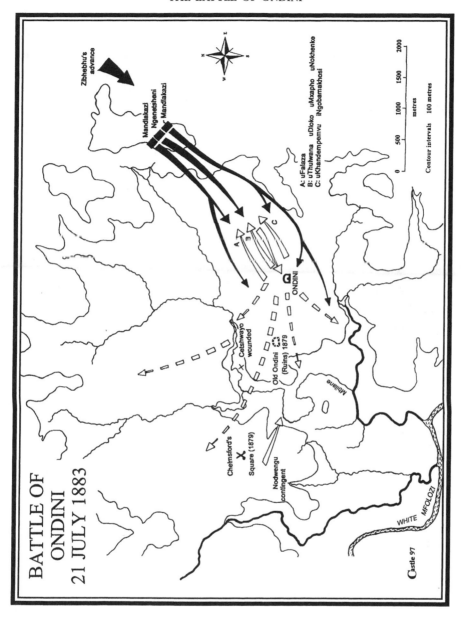

BATTLE OF
ONDINI
21 JULY 1883

advanced steadily towards them, hoping to close with their stabbing spears. Discouraged by the rout of their right, the uSuthu chest, too, crumpled in the face of this intimidating sight. Most of the warriors broke before the Mandlakazi reached them, but a few tried to make a stand, and a flurry of fighting broke out. Among them was Godide kaNdlela, who was killed trying vainly to rally his men. With the chest and right horn gone, the inexperienced uFalaza gave way, and the whole force streamed back in panic towards oNdini.

Some of them, particularly the older men of the uThulwana, attempted to rally at oNdini himself. Several miles away to the north, the British Resident, Henry Fynn Junior, 'observed the huts on the right-side of the entrance to be on fire, and could hear the gunshots among the scattered people running and covering the country westward of Ulundi [oNdini]'. The uThulwana made a desperate stand in the huts, and fierce fighting ensued. Large numbers of Mandlakazi broke off the pursuit to join the struggle, and streamed into oNdini through the side gates.

The battle continued until many of the uThulwana were wiped out. It was probably here that the redoubtable Vumandaba was killed, 'who stabbed the Mandlakazi until they lay in heaps, until they finally overcame him by showering him with a flight of spears, and he fell, the great warrior'. Many of the chiefs, who had stayed in the homestead, came out to find the enemy among them. Too middle-aged or fat to run, many of them were overtaken and killed. According to Colenbrander, 'Being all fat and big-bellied they had no chance of escape; and one of them was actually run to earth by my little mat-bearers.' Seven men tried to hide under the wagon of Fynn's assistant, which was parked at oNdini, but the Mandlakazi found them, and killed them all.

The rout continued across the Mahlabathini plain. The Mandlakazi left horn had effectively succeeded in cutting off the retreat from the river, and instead a great horde of refugees fled past the site of Cetshwayo's old oNdini, and down the slope, across the spot where Lord Chelmsford's troops had caused no less carnage four years before. Here they met the Nodwengu contingent, hurrying to support them; by this time the rout was so general, however, that the Nodwengu *amabutho* gave way without making a stand and joined the fleeing mob. Most of those who got away were the fit young men of the junior *amabutho*; their older comrades lagged behind and were killed. As the Mandlakazi rampaged across the plain, they set fire to every homestead in their path. The wind fanned the flames into the grass, and soon patches of the veld itself were on fire. For the second time the heart of King Cetshwayo's kingdom had, quite literally, gone up in flames.

The king himself barely escaped the slaughter. He lingered in oNdini until the last minute, and only when defeat was inevitable did he allow himself to be led away. His attendants could only round up one horse, and it fell as Cetshwayo tried to mount it. Instead, he hurried off on foot, and took refuge in a small clump of trees near the Ntukwini stream. The Mandlakazi were in hot pursuit, and some of the royal attendants courageously tried to decoy them away. Nonetheless, a group of Mandlakazi warriors spotted him crouching in the undergrowth. Guessing he was a man of importance, they called upon him to stand up, and simultaneously hurled four spears at him. Two missed, but the other two struck him in the thigh.

Amazingly, under the circumstances, Cetshwayo recognised one of his assailants, and called out, 'Do you stab me, Halijana, son of Somfula? I am your king!' The Mandlakazi warriors were immediately overawed; the king's person was widely held to be sacrosanct, the embodiment of the great ancestral spirits of the nation, and to strike a blow against him, even in time of war, was a heinous crime. The Mandlakazi warriors put down their weapons, and, addressing the king by a royal salute – 'Ndabezitha!' – approached him at a respectful crouch, helping him remove the spears still embedded in his thigh, apologising that they had mistaken him for one of his brothers. One of them cut a reed, and blew water through it into the king's wounds, to wash them out, while the others collected mimosa bark, to bind up the cuts. The injuries were not serious, and his attendants helped him away, the Mandlakazi pointing out the safest route to take in order to avoid their army.

Some of the king's family, too, had managed to escape. Dabulamanzi slipped away, while Cetshwayo's heir, fifteen-year-old Dinuzulu, was led to safety by Sitshitshili kaMnqandi, who had once distinguished himself by killing some of the survivors of the Border Horse at the battle of Hlobane. Prince Sitheku found himself captured, for the second time, while the king's younger son, Nyoniyentaba, was killed in his mother's arms.

The slaughter of Zulu dignitaries was, indeed, appalling. Godide, Vumandaba and Hayiyana kaMaphitha were all dead, as was Ntshingwayo, the victor of Isandlwana, who lay stretched out on his war-shield, covered with stab-wounds. One careful count suggested that no less than 59 important men had perished, and between them they represented all that survived of the heart of the old Zulu order. Representatives of all the great royalist lineages were killed, many of them individuals who had been powerful in Mpande's time, and had distinguished themselves in the war of 1879. Zibhebhu had broken the old Zulu kingdom in a way that the British never had.

Zibhebhu himself is said to have regretted some of the deaths, although the battle was his most astonishing victory, and his losses were negligible. His men rounded up what cattle and captives they could find, and retired north towards Mandlakazi territory. They managed to snatch some loot from among the burning ruins of oNdini; someone took the silver mug

Queen Victoria had presented to Cetshwayo the previous year, but dropped it during the retreat. Curiously, it turned up again in the 1930s, washed out of the side of a donga during a sudden flash-flood.

The king and his attendants slipped away, and retired south, hiding for a few days in a cave in the White Mfolozi valley, until it was safe to proceed. From there he made his way to the Reserve Territory, to throw himself on the mercy of the British Resident, Melmoth Osborn, who was based at Eshowe. For a while he lingered among the Cube people of Chief Sigananda kaSokufa, in the dark Nkandla forest, a traditionally safe place of refuge. Across the country, the uSuthu followed his example as Zibhebhu and Hamu attacked them with impunity. Cetshwayo realised that his fortunes were so low that he could only attempt to recover with British help, but Osborn refused to assist him in any way unless he placed himself directly under his protection. In October King Cetshwayo surrendered himself at Eshowe, once again a fugitive at the mercy of the British.

Osborn lodged the king in a small homestead on the outskirts of Eshowe. Over the following months, the more important of his family and followers came out of hiding to visit him and pay him their respects. Then, suddenly, just after lunch on 8 February 1884, King Cetshwayo kaMpande, the last independent king of the Zulus, collapsed. A military doctor was rushed to attend him, but he was already dead. The king's attendants refused permission to conduct an autopsy, and the doctor entered the cause of death officially as a heart attack.

Privately, he suggested that Cetshwayo might well have been poisoned.

The king's supporters conducted the traditional burial rites, tying his body in a sitting position, then wrapping it round with a fresh bull's hide, and a blanket. They placed it in his hut and watched over it for several days, before loading it onto an ox-wagon. They had hoped to bury him alongside his ancestors in the emaKhosini valley, but the distance was too great, and the country was not safe. Instead, they took the body westwards, into the Nkandla forest north of the Thukela Valley, far away from the prying eyes of the white men who, one way or another, had destroyed him. Close to the homestead of Chief Sigananda they buried him, and Sigananda's descendants watch over his grave to this day.

With his death, however, leadership of the royalist party fell to a new, younger generation. For them, the war with the Mandlakazi was by no means over.

— 9 —
THE BATTLE OF TSHANENI
5 June 1884

'I wonder I have lived so long, but oh, my poor children'

The death of King Cetshwayo brought royalist fortunes in Zululand to their lowest ebb. The deliberately divisive policies of the British Government had succeeded to a degree which had alarmed even them, and produced a bitter crop of bloodshed. If it is true that Cetshwayo's defeat at the hands of Zibhebhu was far greater than that inflicted by the British, the British nonetheless bore the responsibility of creating the circumstances for that defeat, and of weakening the royal position beyond its ability to withstand it. Now the king was dead, the royal family was scattered, and uSuthu supporters in hiding throughout the length of the country. The uSuthu begged the British Commissioner in the Reserve to intervene and bring a halt to the suffering, but he was still of the opinion that the war had been Cetshwayo's fault, and that the uSuthu had nobody but themselves to blame. The Colonial Office in London was, in any case, determined that British troops should not be employed in Zululand, and the most that it would sanction was the deployment of small garrisons at strategic points within the Reserve, which were intended chiefly to safeguard the border with Natal.

Clearly, the uSuthu could not retrieve the situation alone, and in the absence of British intervention, they looked elsewhere. There was one obvious source of assistance, but the uSuthu knew that it came at a price. Even before Cetshwayo's disastrous defeat at oNdini, some elements among the Transvaal Boers had approached him to offer their help in defeating Zibhebhu. The king had thanked them politely, but declined; he knew too well that the Boers' interest was not philanthropic, but that they were hoping to be rewarded by greater access to Zululand's rich grazing lands. The idea had cropped up again after the battle, when Ndabuko suggested to the king, then hiding in the Nkandla forest, that he should take up the Boer offer. The king remained resolute. 'If you once get them into the country,' he said, 'you will never get them out again.'. Mnyamana Buthelezi, the greatest of the surviving *izikhulu* who adhered to the royal cause, was also against the notion of Boer intervention, but once the king was dead it seemed that there was nothing else left to them.

The uSuthu leadership had, in any event, passed to a younger, less cautious, generation. Among the king's own family, his brother, Ndabuko, who had always been headstrong, had seized something of the initiative in the vacuum that followed Cetshwayo's death. It is said that in his last moments Cetshwayo had given over care of his son, Dinuzulu, to another brother, Dabulamanzi. Dabulamanzi, too, had a reputation as an aggressive and rash man – it had been he who led the unsuccessful attack on Rorke's Drift in 1879 – while Dinuzulu himself was by no means a mere pawn in the power games played by his elder relatives. Although still a teenager, he had already earned a reputation for his sharp mind, decisive temperament, and a fierce pride in his status which had made him a bitter enemy of Zibhebhu. Dinuzulu looked to his uncles for advice, but also cultivated the company of a new generation of younger men, such as Chief Ndabankulu of the Ntombela, and Mehlokazulu kaSihayo.

Mehlokazulu was also a dynamic and assertive man; it had been his expedition to Natal to recover his father's wives in 1878 which had provoked the British ultimatum, and he had played a prominent part in the subsequent fighting. He was typical of a generation that remained fiercely loyal to the Royal House, but who had been hardened by war and suffering, and did not scruple to use tough methods if necessary. They had grown up at a time when the European penetration of Zululand was a commonplace, and they lacked their fathers' awe of the white world. To them, the whites were merely another political element to be exploited; an element, moreover, that was better armed than most. In March 1884 Mehlokazulu and Ndabankulu led a deputation which approached Boers living on the Zulu borders, and opened direct negotiations with Coenraad Meyer and Jacobus van Staden.

The effect of this contact made itself immediately felt. In April Prince Dinuzulu vanished from the Reserve and reappeared on a farm in the Transvaal. Word spread throughout Zululand that a Boer–uSuthu alliance was imminent and, typically, Dabulamanzi took encouragement from this to launch an attack on the Reserve Commissioner's camp in the Nkandla forest. He was met with a resolute defence conducted by the Reserve Territory Carbineers – a police unit recruited from among the Zulus, with white officers – and was easily repulsed, but the country was alive with the excitement of a coming clash. None of this was lost on Zibhebhu, but he remained defiant, and continued to harass uSuthu supporters living in his territory. Ironically, however, his appeals to the British to intervene on his behalf – and they had always treated him as a favourite – were no more successful than Cetshwayo's had been a few months earlier.

By May 1884 the nature of the new alliance was becoming clear. Although the Transvaal government was at pains to distance itself formally, a number of its officials in the border regions were involved in the movement to support Dinuzulu, which was joined initially by some 200 farmers in the Utrecht and Wakkerstroom districts – areas that nursed long-standing ambitions to extend their territory into Zululand, which in some cases dated back to the old pre-war 'disputed territory'. Many of these farmers were of long standing, whose livelihoods had been threatened by the continuing turmoil on their boundaries, and they were interested not only in acquiring more land, but also in re-establishing some sort of stability in Zululand. Once their intentions became known, however, they were joined by dozens of young adventurers, men for whom the alliance offered the hope of a first farm, with little to lose in return, or simply the prospect of being involved in a good fight. They were not all Boers, and included English, Irish and Scotsmen, as well as a handful of Germans.

In mid-May, the Boer forces under the command of Lucas Meyer assembled in north-western Zululand, not far from the old battlefield of Hlobane, and on the 21st they formally installed Dinuzulu as the new king of the Zulus. It was the third time in Zulu history that the whites had played a role in such an important Zulu event, and the significance was not lost upon those present. It had been the Boers who had confirmed Mpande's claim to kingship after his battle against Dingane nearly half a century before, while scarcely ten years earlier Theophilus Shepstone had placed his tinsel crown upon Cetshwayo's head. There had been many Zulus on that occasion who had not approved of white intervention, and that situation had not changed under his son.

The traditionalists had been at pains to lead Dinuzulu through the purely Zulu ceremonies the day prior to those planned by the Boers, so once again the faintly absurd efforts of the whites were largely a question of show. Mnyamana, undoubtedly the most senior among the wider uSuthu leadership, signalled his disapproval by being absent. Nevertheless, the Boers made the best of the occasion. Two wagons were drawn together to form a platform, while an up-ended box served as a throne. About 350 Boers formed a semicircle on one side, faced on the other by the great men of the uSuthu. Beyond them were gathered some 9000 Zulus, including women and children. Dinuzulu, who was in European dress, knelt, while four Boers placed their hands on his head and swore to protect him from his enemies. One of them then anointed him with castor oil – the only vaguely appropriate substance available – and then formally announced that Dinuzulu was the new king. The Zulus responded with a great shout of 'Bayethe!', the royal salute.

It seems likely that a specific plan to attack Zibhebhu only emerged after the coronation. Zibhebhu himself refused to acknowledge Dinuzulu as Cetshwayo's successor, defiantly declaring that he was not a king but 'a dog and when he is hungry he may come to me'. The uSuthu reaction to this was predictable and, within a few days, Dinuzulu had committed himself to rewarding with farms any Boers who fought for him. Ominously, the Boers insisted on being allowed to make their specific claims after the event. The uSuthu leadership then set about gathering its forces, calling warriors together from their hiding places across the country. As they assembled, one white observer noticed that the uSuthu fighting men were 'gaunt and lank from long privation and hardship'. They were, however, greatly encouraged by the prospect of Boer support, and possessed a fierce desire to revenge themselves on the Mandlakazi for the humiliations they had suffered.

Zibhebhu responded to the looming crisis by trying to galvanise his allies. Once again he appealed to the British for support, reminding them that 'he always depended on you, his father, for help; and thought that when he died, you would be near at hand', but concluding ominously that 'fighting against the whites he does not like, but he will never give in to the Boers; he will be killed by them first'. But the British, who had set him up, and connived at his attempts to suppress the Royal House, now deserted him in his hour of need.

Prince Hamu's Ngenetsheni continued to offer him support, since they were also clearly at risk, but elsewhere in the country most of Zibhebhu's friends found it convenient to remember appointments elsewhere. Zibhebhu appealed to his old trading partner, John Dunn, who was also bitterly opposed to any restoration of royal power, but Dunn's territory now lay within the British Reserve, and he was not prepared to take to the field except to defend his own borders; an attitude which Zibhebhu took as a betrayal.

Many of Zibhebhu's white advisers, too, deserted him, despite the fact that they had long profited by supplying him with guns, and had been happy enough to share in his victories. Johan Colenbrander stuck by him, and in desperation rode down to Natal to try to raise a mercenary force to counter the Boers. His advertisement in a local paper was nothing if not to the point:

All able-bodied men of good character who can ride and shoot well are required at once. Applicants must be prepared to provide their own horse, carbine, etc., such as they may require for field service. Satisfactory remuneration offered.

According to his own account, twenty men responded to this advertisement, although other sources suggest he could only muster eight Europeans and two coloured men. Certainly, the adventure can have had only limited appeal, since the smart money was on Dinuzulu and the Boers, and many of those who might have been attracted by such an offer had already joined the other side. In any case, Colenbrander's efforts brought down upon him the wrath of the Natal government, which was opposed to any intervention in Zululand's affairs, and he was forced to disband his pocket army. Nothing if not resourceful, The White Whirlwind then tried to make his way back to his chief alone, but found that the whole country was in uproar, and that his road was effectively blocked by uSuthu supporters.

The combined uSuthu–Boer force assembled at Mnyamana's homestead, on the borders with Mandlakazi territory, at the beginning of June. There were about 120 Boers, under the command of Lucas Meyer, all of them well-armed, mounted, and equipped for life in the field. The uSuthu had been able to muster about 7000 warriors in all, and they were led by Dinuzulu himself who, although young, was a fearless warrior who would never miss an opportunity to take to the field in person against his enemies.

The invading army crossed gingerly into Mandlakazi territory, following a course that led it past the battlefield of Msebe, where the bones of their dead comrades were still strewn across the veld. Although morale was higher than in most previous expeditions, both the uSuthu leadership and the ordinary warriors were only too aware of Zibhebhu's almost unbroken record of victories, while the majority of the Boers were determined that any serious fighting should fall to their allies. On 3 June they arrived at Bangonomo to find that Zibhebhu had abandoned his favourite homestead, and was apparently retiring north-east. This was dry, arid country, particularly so in the winter months, and the uSuthu army followed the obvious signs of Zibhebhu's retreat at a slow pace. Water was in short supply, and the Zulus suffered as a result, although they were inured to deprivation. The Boers, of course, seem to have been well provided with water.

The situation eased when the army reached the Mkhuze River, even though this, too, was almost running dry. Zibhebhu's trail moved east through the open country beside the river, until it disappeared into the

Mkhuze Poort. Here the river had cut a pass through the Lebombo Mountains, which rose up suddenly from the flats on either side, as if to block its path. It was now 5 June, and the heights were such an obvious spot from which to mount an ambush that Lucas Meyer approached them with the greatest caution.

He was quite right to be careful. Deserted by most of his allies, Zibhebhu had been able to muster no more than 3000 warriors, supported by a handful of whites. With these he had to protect a great crowd of civilians, and a cattle herd which exceeded 60,000 head. He decided quickly enough that Bangonomo was indefensible in the face of a combined Boer–uSuthu assault, and fell back instead to the Mkhuze Poort. He knew that the uSuthu would track him, and made no efforts to conceal the trail his followers made in the long, dry grass. That, indeed, was part of his plan. More than any other Zulu commander, he had a flair for using terrain to its best advantage, and the hills on either side of the Mkhuze Poort were ideally suited to his purpose.

The river flowed through open country to the west, to the point where the Lebombo Mountains cut across it at right angles, from north to south. On the northern bank of the river there was a succession of rocky ridges, while to the south lay two distinctive outcrops known as Gaza and Tshaneni, with a grassy amphitheatre between. Gaza was crowned with a jagged pinnacle of rock, while Tshaneni was topped with an exposed, bald dome. Both peaks had mystical associations. Gaza was said to be the traditional burial ground of the chiefs of a section of the Ndwandwe people, who had been great rivals of the Zulu in Shaka's day, and the shades of their spirits were said to inhabit the summit. In later times, the novelist, Rider Haggard, would draw on these stories to create the legend of the 'Ghost Mountain' as a backdrop for his tales of adventure and romance. The lower slopes of Tshaneni and Gaza were broken by dongas and overgrown with thick bush that would hamper the movement of horses and limit the field of fire.

Zibhebhu positioned his forces carefully. His cattle and women and children he hid behind a ridge on the north side of the river, but his fighting men he deployed a safe distance away, on the south bank. Here a long donga flowed into the river from the south, bisecting the track which led into the pass. Zibhebhu placed his vanguard behind the donga, close to the river. He concealed the remainder of his force in the bush further back, at the foot of the two mountains. His plan was for the uSuthu to follow the trail and suddenly encounter his advance guard. After putting up a token flight, these were to fall back towards the pass, and as the uSuthu lost formation, pursuing them through the broken ground close to the river, the remaining Mandlakazi would rise up and fall on them. It was a classic Zulu ambush; similar tactics had destroyed the Boers at eThaleni nearly 50 years earlier, while Zibhebhu himself had used them to chase off Buller's horsemen on the eve of the first battle of oNdini in 1879.

For its success, however, Zibhebhu's plan depended on the uSuthu allowing themselves to be drawn into the trap, and on the Mandlakazi having sufficient discipline to remain hidden until the right moment. Sadly, in both regards, Zibhebhu's luck at last ran out.

The combined uSuthu–Boer force approached Mkhuze Poort along the south bank of the river on 5 June, already deployed in battle array, and clearly expecting an attack. The left wing, consisting of uSuthu under the command of Mamese, supported by the abaQulusi and stiffened by sixteen mounted Boers, advanced close to the south bank. The main uSuthu body was in the centre, further back, and supported by Meyer and the main Boer force, which rode behind it; the Boers had no intention of being in the front line if they were about to be ambushed. The uSuthu right was also thrown out some way ahead, further to the south.

The two horns struck the donga at more or less the same time, and Mamese's left horn blundered into the Mandlakazi vanguard concealed behind it. Fighting immediately erupted, but before the Mandlakazi had time to break off the attack, as planned, a shot rang out from among Zibhebhu's men concealed in the foothills. Afterwards there was much debate among the Zulus as to whether this was deliberate treachery on the part of one of the Mandlakazi, and lurid tales began to circulate of the terrible revenge wrought on him by Zibhebhu; it is more likely, however, that in the excitement of the moment someone simply put too much pressure on a sensitive trigger. At any rate, the shot was enough to destroy the element of surprise, and without waiting for Zibhebhu's orders, his main body rose up out of the grass and streamed down towards the uSuthu, the warriors drumming their shields with their spears, and thundering the grim war-cry, 'Washesha!'

The Mandlakazi charge was all too familiar to many in the uSuthu ranks who had faced it before, and had barely escaped with their lives. The Mandlakazi fell upon the uSuthu right, which immediately crumpled under the pressure and was driven back on the centre. For a few moments, it looked as if the entire uSuthu line might collapse, and the Mandlakazi carry the day despite their premature attack. The line of uSuthu retreat, however, took them towards the Boers in their rear, and

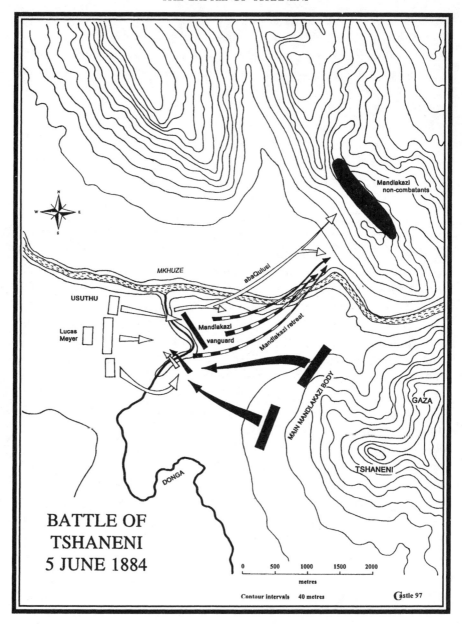

**BATTLE OF
TSHANENI
5 JUNE 1884**

MKHUZE

USUTHU

Lucas
Meyer

abaQulusi

Mandlakazi
non-combatants

Mandlakazi
vanguard

Mandlakazi retreat

MAIN MANDLAKAZI BODY

GAZA

TSHANENI

DONGA

0   500   1000   1500   2000

metres

Contour intervals   40 metres

Castle 97

as the struggling mass of men rolled in their direction, Lucas Meyer ordered his men to open fire from the saddle, firing over the heads of the uSuthu, and into the ranks of the Mandlakazi beyond.

This was a dangerous move, for the Boers made little effort to distinguish between their enemies and their allies, both of whom were shot down in the confusion. Nevertheless, the fire was heavy enough to check

188

the Mandlakazi charge, and stiffen the resolve of the uSuthu, who were quite literally caught between two fires. As the Mandlakazi tried to regroup, the Boers poured a heavy fire into them, as Zibhebhu himself recalled:

The left wing of my force closed with the right wing of the enemy, and drove it back in confusion onto the breast. While this was going on, the Boers, having taken up a favourable position, opened a heavy flank fire on my men, and it soon became impossible for them to stand it and they gave way; they retreated, pursued by the Boers who shot down many in their retreat!

As the Mandlakazi left gave way, the uSuthu returned to the attack, concentrating their efforts on the centre and vanguard until they, too, broke and fled. Most of the Mandlakazi made their way to the river, to try to get across and join their womenfolk on the opposite ridge. It was here that much of the bloodshed took place, as the uSuthu, released at last from the fear of an enemy who had oppressed them for so long, hunted the Mandlakazi down, cutting off whole groups in the dongas and broken ground, and killing them all. Many more were slaughtered in a deep channel of the Mkhuze itself, since, as Zibhebhu recalled, 'the river was deep, and the drift not very practicable'.

Indeed, the uSuthu left horn made a desperate attempt to try and cut off the Mandlakazi retreat by the river. No sooner had the Mandlakazi collapsed than the abaQulusi charged out at great speed, crossing the river at an easier point, outpacing the fleeing enemy, and turning the rout back down the valley and through the Mkhuze Poort. The reason for the direction of the Mandlakazi flight soon became obvious as the abaQulusi reached the ridges to the north, and blundered into the Mandlakazi non-combatants concealed there. Many of these people were uSuthu, who had been captured in earlier raids by Zibhebhu, and they were delighted to be reunited with their menfolk, but the fate of the others was grim. In the excitement of battle, the uSuthu charged straight into their midst and many were slaughtered.

The whole battle had lasted scarcely fifteen minutes from the initial encounter to the Mandlakazi rout. Unusually, and perhaps because of the speed of his collapse, Zibhebhu himself had not been prominent in the fight. Certainly, the uSuthu searched for him during the pursuit, but it was only when the battle was over that a group of three horsemen were spotted looking down from one of the hills to the north. Two were white men, believed to be Zibhebhu's advisers, John Eckersley and Grosvenor Darke, and the third was Zibhebhu himself. The extent of the calamity, which had occurred despite his usual meticulous planning, was only too obvious to the Mandlakazi chief. 'I have had my day,' he exclaimed in despair. 'I wonder I have lived so long, but oh, my poor children.'

There was no assessment of casualties after the battle, although many hundreds of the Mandlakazi were dead, and there were rumours that at least one of Zibhebhu's white friends had been killed. The uSuthu, too, had suffered significant losses, not only in the initial Mandlakazi attack, but also from the heavy and indiscriminate Boer fire. The remains of the dead littered the site until the early years of the twentieth century; when the first road was later built through the battlefield, the local magistrate gave instructions for the skulls, which still lay, overgrown by the grass, to be collected together and placed along either side of the highway. The Boers had suffered no losses, but they had undoubtedly played a decisive role in the battle, even though no more than 70 of them had actually been engaged in the fighting, and they had fired only a few rounds each.

The main Mandlakazi retreat took them through the Mkhuze Poort and then to the north. The uSuthu pursued them as far as they dared, and spent most of the day rounding up cattle and captives. Between 40,000 and 60,000 head of livestock were captured, and the Boers did not stint in claiming their share. In the Mkhuze valley, along the banks of the river, the Boers came across some wagons abandoned by Zibhebhu's white advisers, and took great pleasure in looting them thoroughly.

Zibhebhu and those of his followers who stuck with him retired north, into the territory of Chief Sambane of the Nyawo people. These were the same people among whom Dingane had taken refuge in similar circumstances, and Zibhebhu's warriors were scarcely more welcome. A week later Zibhebhu rode into Eshowe, accompanied by Darke and Eckersley, to seek the protection of the British Commissioner. Officials in Natal and Zululand were certainly sympathetic to his plight – he had, after all, been the main instrument of their dirty work in independent Zululand for half a decade – but the British government at home was less understanding. Determined not to become embroiled in further fighting, the Colonial Office firmly declared that Zibhebhu was not a formal British ally, but an independent ruler whose misfortunes were directly related to his own policies. The best that the British were prepared to do was offer Zibhebhu and his followers sanctuary in the Reserve Territory.

In September, Zibhebhu duly organised the exodus of about one-third of the Mandlakazi to British territory. This was a long and difficult march, from one end of the country to the other, and through areas controlled by the victorious uSuthu. The spectacle was witnessed by a senior British officer, and his description of the refugees is one of the enduring images of the civil war period:

> The sight was one of the strangest and saddest imaginable. They numbered 5 or 6000 souls; the men as lean as greyhounds; sleeping mats and blankets on their heads; all fully armed with spears, but with few guns; the women with enormous loads on their heads, weary and tired; children of all ages to the infant at the back. They also had a great many cattle. How such a host managed to pass through a large extent of hostile territory unmolested is a mystery.

The uSuthu, meanwhile, counted the cost of their victory. The triumphant army returned to the Boer laager near Hlobane, only to find that many more Boers had joined the expedition once an easy victory had been assured. Although the steering committee which decided Boer policy accepted that these men were hardly entitled to the same reward as those who had actually taken part in the fighting, it nonetheless decreed that they should be given smaller farms. With the tide clearly flowing in their favour, and the uSuthu quite unable to object, the Boer demand exceeded a million hectares. The claims extended over almost all of Zululand north of the reserve, including a corridor which ran down to St Lucia Bay, on the coast, where the Boers hoped to achieve a long-standing ambition to build a port, and open a road to the wider world. The uSuthu were horrified, but powerless to resist, and on 16 August 1884 Dinuzulu signed a document agreeing to Boer demands. In their desperate attempts to cling on to a last vestige of their independent identity, the Zulu people had been forced to sign away their birthright.

Ironically, it was this agreement that at last stirred Britain to act, and accept some of the responsibility for the events it had unleashed in 1879. The British reaction was not, however, prompted by concern for the Zulu people, nor, indeed, by the worries of settler society in Natal, who felt the Boers had cheated them of land which by rights should have fallen to them. What worried the British was increased German activity in the colonial sphere, and the possibility that Germany might extend its interests into southern Africa by forming an alliance with the Boers through Lake St Lucia. Britain therefore intervened to put pressure on the Boers to restrict their influence to northern Zululand, promising to recognise about half their claims if they abandoned the rest. In the event, that meant splitting what remained of Zululand on a north–south axis, with the Boers taking the western slice. This was simply to be annexed to the Transvaal, but was to be a new country – the New Republic – with its capital at the new settlement of Vryheid ('freedom'), which lay between Hlobane Mountain and Khambula.

The eastern slice was taken by the British, and incorporated into the Reserve Territory. In May 1887 Zululand finally became a British colony.

Unfortunately, the extension of British authority did not mean that peace finally returned to Zululand. Dinuzulu, Ndabuko and many of the uSuthu leadership might have preferred British authority to that of the Boers, but their real hope was for the restoration of the monarchy. This the British refused to consider, and, indeed, permission was given in due course for Zibhebhu to return from exile in the Reserve to take up his old territory in northern Zululand, as a check to royalist aspirations. While he had been away, however, many uSuthu had settled his lands, and both they and the uSuthu leadership were filled with foreboding at his return. Sure enough, Zibhebhu had scarcely arrived in Bangonomo when he called up armed men to evict uSuthu supporters squatting on his location.

In this tense situation a British magistrate was established at Nongoma, which lay between Mandlakazi and uSuthu territory; but rather than calm tensions, he found himself caught up in a new wave of fighting. When Dinuzulu finally snapped and attacked the Mandlakazi, fighting broke out around the walls of the magistracy itself. British redcoats were once more marched into Zululand to restore order, and the uSuthu rose in revolt. After a series of sharp encounters, their position became insupportable, however, and Dinuzulu and Ndabuko again attempted to play the Boer card. The Boers, however, were too shrewd to risk a direct confrontation with the British, and refused the uSuthu leaders sanctuary. For the last time, the representatives of the House of Shaka had little choice but to surrender themselves to white enemies.

Dinuzulu and his uncles Ndabuko and Shingana were found guilty of rebellion and sentenced to exile on the island of St Helena. The British had, at last, begun to question the wisdom of their support for Zibhebhu, and he, too, was called to face charges for his role in the violence. Although the sympathy of the Natal officials led to his acquittal, he was relocated in the Reserve, away from his own lands.

A decade later, in 1898, Both Dinuzulu and Zibhebhu were allowed to return home. British officials insisted that the two meet and stage a public gesture of reconciliation, but in truth the bitterness between their supporters lingered for many years, and further violence might yet have flared had Zibhebhu not died in August 1904. Even by that time, the world had changed a good deal for the African people of Natal and Zululand, bringing with it new pressures to add to existing tensions. Bloodshed would break out again in 1906, but this time its reasons had as much to do with resentment at the establishment of a new order, as with the traditional rivalries engendered by the passing of the old.

THE BATTLE OF MOME GORGE
10 June 1906
'An ox driven to the slaughter-house'

When Dinuzulu kaCetshwayo returned to Zululand in 1898, following his exile on St Helena, it was to a world already vastly different from the one in which he had grown up.

His own position, for one thing, was ambiguous. Nearly twenty years of civil war and colonial interference had created such deep divisions within Zulu society that there was little hope of restoring the jurisdiction of the monarchy across the country as a whole. Gone, too, were the institutions upon which royal power was based; the *amabutho* system, and the huge herds of royal cattle which sustained it. Nor was it ever likely that the colonial authorities in Natal would allow Dinuzulu to assume the potent symbols of royal power, since it was still widely held there that the Royal House was the greatest single threat to settler interests.

In this the colonial attitude differed from that of the government in Britain, who, in the aftermath of the 1888 uprising, had at last come to different conclusions, and realised that the roots of the turmoil and bloodshed lay in the deliberately divisive policies pursued since 1879. Dinuzulu's return had been approved in the hope that, rather than struggle against the prestige of the Royal House, the British might turn it to their advantage, using Dinuzulu as a tool of colonial rule. Significantly, the Natal authorities had blocked the move until the British had agreed to give effective administrative control of Zululand to Natal, a move that greatly increased the influence of the settler lobby. Under such circumstances, Dinuzulu was emphatically denied the right to call himself king; his return was conditional upon him accepting the position of a government-approved and salaried regional chief. His direct authority was confined to Nongoma, where the greatest number of uSuthu followers were located, in a move that was calculated to limit and control his prestige.

Of course, Dinuzulu undoubtedly resented this situation. He had grown up in the last days of the Zulu kingdom's pre-colonial glory, and in the knowledge that he was his father's favourite son. He had always been fiercely proud of his royal status, and, indeed, the majority of Zulus across the country still regarded him as their king. No sooner had he installed himself in his new homestead than a steady stream of chiefs and important men began to make their way to him from across the country, to *konza* him, to give him allegiance and pay their respects. Nevertheless, Dinuzulu was only too aware that the practical authority which he did command was held by sufferance of the Natal authorities, and he had seen too much of the power of the white military machine ever to hope that he could restore his birthright by force. Instead, he existed in limbo, recognised as king by thousands of his people, yet deprived of any real means of fulfilling their expectations of him.

Indeed, the extent to which the Natal government manipulated traditional forms of authority, and subverted them to their own ends, was a feature of colonial rule. Under the system first devised by Sir Theophilus Shepstone in Natal proper, half a century before, the role of the monarchy, the ultimate form of authority, was taken over by the colonial administration, while local forms continued unchanged. Whereas the district chiefs had once been responsible to the king, they were now responsible to the government. Since the whites had shown themselves more than capable of using force to depose chiefs who failed in this regard, the rest were forced to accept a role that effectively made them the front line in a process of creeping colonialism. The chiefs became responsible for implementing white laws, and for raising taxes from among their followers.

This was a move that turned most chiefs into government collaborators, and had incalculable effects on the traditional lifestyle of people in Natal. Taxation was an important part of the process by which Africans were drawn into the settler economy, since it not only raised funds for the government, but forced the Africans to work to raise cash to pay taxes, thereby satisfying the insatiable settler demand for cheap labour. In traditional society, young men had been required to give service to their chiefs or kings, and since they were the most productive members of society, it was upon them that the chiefs depended to provide the money for taxation. In effect, from 1888 when the first hut tax was levied in Zululand, the young men found themselves required to give service not to the *amabutho*, but to the developing white economy.

At that time, there was little European enterprise in Zululand, and most of these men had to travel to Natal, or the mines of Kimberley or the Witwatersrand, to seek employment. This in itself weakened the bonds that held traditional society together, a process exaggerated by the fact that many young men kept a proportion of their wages to raise *ilobola* and marry, without the consent of their chiefs. They now possessed a degree of independence that they had never previously enjoyed. Thus the authority of the chiefs was compromised at a time when the communal checks and balances, which were such a feature of established society, were severely disrupted. The consequences were widespread unease and inter-generational tensions within communities, further exacerbated by the government's shrewd manipulation of the political situation, in which favoured chiefdoms were allowed to prosper, while chiefs considered hostile were deposed, fined or relocated.

With the implementation of colonial rule, too, came alienation from the land. The settler community had long harboured ambitions to extend their rich grazing grounds, and once Zululand had been incorporated into Natal it became inevitable that much of the country would be opened to white settlement. Between 1902 and 1904, the Zululand Lands Delimitation Commission effectively parcelled the country up between those areas to be made available to white farmers, and those to remain as 'locations', reserved for the exclusive use of the black population. Roughly one-third of the country was given over to white settlement, and since the commission had been guided by the need to release only viable land, that third included almost all of the best farming land in the country. The Zulu either found themselves confined to the cramped and unproductive reserves, or squatting on land now owned by whites. In the latter case they were usually forced to provide labour by way of rent, or were expelled, often from lands that their ancestors had occupied since long before the time of Shaka.

The unsettling effects of these profound changes were exaggerated by a series of natural calamities which befell the region in the last few years of the nineteenth century. In 1895, large parts of both Zululand and Natal suffered a severe plague of locusts, which destroyed much of that year's harvest, and the problem was to recur several times in the following years. To compound this problem, the area was stricken by one of its occasional periods of drought. Most devastating of all, in 1897, the cattle disease, rinderpest, swept through southern Africa from the north. While white farmers were able to contain their losses by isolating their herds and practising inoculation, the Africans, with their tradition of communal grazing, were devastated. Up to 85 per cent of the animals in black ownership died. In communities where cattle represented not only food but wealth, status and an important part of religious ritual, the effects were devastating.

By the early part of the twentieth century, then, African society in Natal and Zululand was approaching a crisis, its customs undermined by an unsympathetic colonial administration, its traditional forms of authority and support eroded, and its economy all but destroyed. Into this mix was added a final element: war.

Between 1899 and 1902, the white settler groups in southern Africa were torn apart by the Anglo–Boer War. Although some of the heaviest fighting of the early stages of the campaign took place in Natal, it was largely confined to thinly inhabited areas, and the effect on the black population was limited. Indeed, for a while some areas profited by the war, since although both sides maintained the myth of the 'white man's war', neither could, in fact, function without thousands of black wagon-drivers, labourers and scouts.

Zululand was largely untouched by the fighting, until towards the end, when Louis Botha mounted a raid into central Zululand, and some guerrilla commandos operated in the north-eastern districts around Vryheid. The British were keen to secure Dinuzulu's support, at least passively, and for much of the war he was allowed to exercise more than his legal authority For the most part, the Zulus did not take an active part in the fighting, but in the last few weeks of the war, a Boer commando raided and taunted the abaQulusi, with disastrous results; it was attacked one night at a place called Holkranz on the side of Zungwini Mountain, and almost wiped out. The incident nearly derailed the peace process, which was by then under way, and raised once again the fear of a Zulu revolt, which was always a potent one in the settler consciousness. Thus, instead of emerging with some recognition for his support, Dinuzulu found himself under suspicion at the end of the war – again – and his powers reduced to their former limits.

By 1905 most African groups in the area felt under pressure, and for many, even those who had never been a part of it, the old Zulu kingdom was beginning to assume a deep, nostalgic significance, the embodiment of a golden age of glory and independence. In May that year a fierce storm swept through the country, bringing hail and snow, and the word spread that this had been unleashed by Dinuzulu, who, as head of the Zulu Royal House, was accredited with rain-making powers, as a sign that he was about to reclaim his inheritance. It was a time of rumour and portents, and against this background the Natal government made a disastrous error of judgement.

The colonial government, too, was suffering economic hardship in the aftermath of the Anglo–Boer War, and one obvious solution was to tax the black population still further. In August 1905 it introduced a poll tax of £1 to be paid by all adult males. From the beginning, this tax was bitterly resented, largely because it fell equally on unmarried men as well as on wealthier family-heads, who had borne the burden of the hut tax. Many young men refused to pay, and the chiefs found themselves caught between the threat of government retaliation and the defiance of their own people. Anger was expressed in strange millennial rumours, and many people began to destroy pigs – which had been introduced by Europeans – white fowls, and European utensils, in the belief that foreign rule was about to come to an end. Attempts to collect the poll tax were greeted with sullen resistance.

Violence first flared in February 1906, near Richmond, in the Natal midlands. A police patrol was sent to arrest a group of young men who had refused to pay the tax, and a skirmish broke out which left a police inspector and one trooper dead. The incident revived all the latent fears of a widespread uprising, and the Natal government reacted harshly. Local militia units were mobilised, and rampaged through the disaffected area, burning huts and crops, and rounding up suspects. A group of men implicated in the murders were found guilty of murder and, despite protests by the British government – including the young Winston Churchill – they were executed by firing squad on 2 April.

Far from quelling the disturbances, however, this incident seems to have increased the sense of desperation among many of those contemplating resistance, and left them with the feeling that violence was the only means of escape. It is true that most of the subsequent fighting took place in Natal, rather than Zululand, and that the term commonly used for the subsequent troubles, 'The Zulu Rebellion', is a misnomer; nevertheless, discontent was common in both areas, and if feelings ran higher in Natal, that was simply because most people there had suffered for a longer period at the hands of government policy. Indeed, those groups who took to arms later in the rebellion included a number who had recently crossed into Natal, and who had close historical associations with the Royal House; for such groups the reality of European rule seemed particularly harsh. Moreover, the rebels looked to Dinuzulu as their natural leader, and constantly drew on the symbols of the Royal House as a means not only of spreading the revolt, but also of providing a common sense of identity. It is no coincidence that the rebels adopted the royalist war-cry 'uSuthu!', and wore the *tshokobezi* badge, which since the 1880s had been the sign of those who had 'crossed over' to fight for the king.

When the uprising did come, it crystallised not around one of the great leaders of the Royal House, but upon a minor chief named Bambatha kaMancinza, who ruled over a section of the Zondi chiefdom, on the Natal bank of the Thukela, near Greytown. Bambatha was in his early 40s, and had suffered the full weight of the recent years' hardships. He was heavily in debt, was unpopular with his white farmer neighbours, and his chiefdom was split by a succession dispute which had led to faction-fighting, and drawn down the disapproval of the local magistrate. Bambatha refused to pay the poll tax, and many of his young men supported him. Police were sent out from Greytown to arrest him, and he fled to Zululand. Like many in similar difficulties before him, he made his way to Dinuzulu. Privately, Dinuzulu may well have sympathised with him, but as a government chief, already under close scrutiny, he could do nothing in public but advise Bambatha to pay. Nonetheless, when Bambatha went back to his ward, he left his wife in Dinuzulu's keeping.

When Bambatha returned home, he found that the government had deposed him and made his uncle chief in his place. His situation was now intolerable, and he had little to lose; as one eloquent African witness later put it, Bambatha 'was very much like a beast which on being stabbed rushes about in despair, charges backwards and forwards, and, it may be, kills someone that happens to be in his path'. His followers declared that 'the chief should not be shot as a buck [nor] as a beast or an ox driven to the slaughter house'. Instead, they took up arms, and drove out Bambatha's uncle.

The government responded by sending a strong police patrol into the area to escort local whites to safety, and on the night of 5 April, as they rode back to Greytown through the Mpanza valley, not far from Bambatha's homestead, they were ambushed. Bambatha and his men had taken up a position among the bush on either side of the road, he himself sitting on top of a large rock, and carrying a shotgun. As the police passed between them, Bambatha fired his gun, and his warriors, yelling 'uSuthu!', rushed out to attack. They were driven off after fifteen minutes of heavy firing, and the police party managed to force its way through to Greytown, but four were killed. One was found later, his body mutilated and parts removed by Bambatha's war-doctor, Malaza, as *intelezi* medicines.

The government reacted quickly, sending troops into the Mpanza valley, shelling Bambatha's homestead, destroying crops and rounding up members of his chiefdom. In fact, Bambatha had long since fled, slipping into the Thukela Valley, then crossing into Zululand. Here he and his small band of followers made for the territory of the Cube chiefdom, nearly 50 miles away from his own ward. Along the way, he picked up a few sympathisers from the Ntuli people, whose lands he crossed. The chief of the Cube was Sigananda kaSokufa, a venerable old man who had been a member of King Dingane's uMkhulutshane *ibutho*, and had been present at the massacre of Piet Retief nearly 70 years earlier.

The Cube were closely associated with the Royal House, for they had joined the kingdom in the days of Shaka, not by conquest, but as allies.

Sigananda had fought for Cetshwayo at 'Ndondakusuka, although, after attracting the wrath of Mpande, he had later crossed into Natal, where he had been given hospitality by Bambatha's grandfather. Cetshwayo had later recalled Sigananda and installed him as chief; and when Cetshwayo had been defeated by Zibhebhu at oNdini in 1884, it had been to Sigananda's territory that he had fled. Sigananda had built him a homestead, on a spur overlooking the steep Mome Gorge, which he had named eNhlweni, 'the poor man's retreat', in honour of the incident. When Cetshwayo died, just a few months later, it was in Cube territory that he was buried.

Bambatha hoped to persuade Sigananda to join the rebellion, and, through him, involve other influential Zulu chiefs. Sigananda sent a message to Dinuzulu, asking for advice, but the latter refused to commit himself, remarking that Bambatha's troubles were no concern of his. He could hardly do otherwise, but Bambatha argued persuasively that the true king of the Zulus had privately given his backing. Moreover, Bambatha's easy victory at Mpanza, and the powerful medicines prepared by Malaza, suggested that he enjoyed the approval of the spirit world.

Sigananda decided to throw in his lot with the rebels. His support was immensely important to them, since he soon began to circulate messages to many other leading Zulus, urging them to join him. Although few chiefs were prepared to declare themselves openly, many allowed their young men to make their way to the Mome Gorge, to join the army of resistance that Bambatha was beginning to assemble there. Once the Natal authorities got wind of the situation, they were consumed with the fear that another old-style Zulu War might break out.

The Natal government was, nonetheless, reluctant to call upon the imperial power for assistance. Natal had only recently been granted 'responsible government' – which essentially meant independence from London rule, under Crown authority – and was eager to prove that it could handle what it considered a purely internal affair. This resolve became all the more determined once the British government let it be known that it might have responded to the crisis in a very different way. No appeal, there-fore, was made for British troops; instead Natal called out its militia once more. Because there was some concern that fighting in Zululand might leave Natal vulnerable, several new units were raised to augment those already established, while both the Transvaal Republic and the Cape, to show their solidarity with a fellow white state, under threat from within, also volunteered some of their own units.

The forces were placed under the overall command of Colonel Duncan McKenzie, a Natal farmer who had a distinguished military record. Having joined the Natal Carbineers – one of the country's first volunteer units – as a trooper, he had served in a number of African campaigns, and throughout the Anglo–Boer War. An impressive man with a commanding personality and a distinctive white moustache, McKenzie was a firm believer in using harsh methods to suppress the rebellion, so much so that he had earned himself a simple but chilling Zulu name – Shaka.

Militarily, the scales of war had tipped further against the rebels even since 1888. Whereas most of the insurgents were still armed with shields, spears and, at best, antiquated firearms, the whites no longer fought in red coats with single-shot rifles. Khaki had become the universal field dress even before the Anglo–Boer War, where many of the Natal troops, although no more than part-time soldiers, had gained valuable military experience. Most were now armed with bolt-action magazine rifles, like the Lee-Enfield, and, despite the fact that it contravened the Geneva Convention, many did not scruple to use soft-nosed 'dum-dum' bullets. There was a general feeling that the rules of 'civilised' warfare were not applicable when fighting an African enemy, where the 'stopping power' of such bullets was greatly valued. In addition, the troops were armed with quick-firing artillery, including the 1-pounder 'pom-pom' which had proved such a success in the Anglo–Boer War, and a variety of machine-guns, including the deadly Maxim. Apart from the Durban Light Infantry, most of Natal's troops were mounted, which added greatly to their manoeuvrability.

Despite the widespread nervousness of the white population at the prospect of a Zulu revolt, the troops were generally confident of their ability to defeat the enemy on the ground. The general mood was summed up by one volunteer who, referring to the generous bounties offered for enlistment, told a friend: 'I'm out after the natives ... it's a good deal better than farming, I can tell you!'

In Natal, the Indian population, keen to demonstrate its loyalty to the Empire, raised a volunteer stretcher-bearer company, which included in its ranks one Sergeant Major Mohandas K. Ghandi. To assist the white forces, the government also called upon the services of 'loyal' chiefs, who were expected to provide a levy, in the manner of the old Natal Native Contingent. Despite the festering resentment – which had often found bitter expression on the battlefield in the past – between chiefdoms favoured by the government and those who suffered its disapproval, the rebels and levies in 1906 sometimes showed a distinct reluctance to fight one another.

The rebels were not entirely unaware of the disadvantages they faced. Although Bambatha's followers placed great faith in the spiritual power which he had apparently harnessed by his victory at Mpanza, they had nonetheless learned something of the practical limitations of the old Zulu fighting techniques. To succeed, the traditional 'chest-and-horns' assault, mounted in the open, needed large numbers and tight discipline, and even then it was acutely vulnerable to concentrated rifle-fire. In 1906 the rebels had neither overwhelming numbers nor anything like the discipline of the *amabutho* system, while the firepower of the government forces was even greater.

The intentions of the rebel high command, as far as they can be guessed, were to wage a guerrilla war instead, fighting in terrain which best suited them, but which would hamper the movements of European armies. In that regard, Sigananda's territory was ideal, situated as it was in one of the great primordial forests of Zululand, the Nkandla. The Nkandla consists of a maze of sharp ridges and dizzying valleys, covered with patches of thick, ancient forest, interspersed with dense bush. It had always been something of a place of magic and mystery – the Cube were renowned iron workers, an art in itself which had potent magical associations – and a place of refuge. Moreover, King Cetshwayo's grave lay in the Nkandla, and the rebels evoked its symbolism to provide the perfect rallying place.

As the rebels gathered at Nkandla, so the government forces moved to intercept them. McKenzie's aim was to encircle the forest, to prevent the rebels either entering or leaving, so that the supposed sanctuary became a giant trap. His main force was sent by rail to Dundee – the nearest railhead close to Nkandla – then marched south through Nquthu, until it established a camp at eMpandleni, north of the forest. A further column, consisting largely of police and the Durban Light Infantry, was assembled at Eshowe, and marched westwards to a base at Fort Yolland, on the eastern side of the Nkandla. A third force was positioned on the southern bank of the Thukela, near Middle Drift, to prevent the rebels escaping back into Natal. Given the general fear of a widespread uprising, small garrisons were maintained at key points along the Zulu border, and reacted sharply at the first sign of any disaffection among the local troops.

The first serious action occurred on 5 May. A column of troops from Fort Yolland had marched out in the direction of Cetshwayo's grave, probing for Bambatha's whereabouts. As it descended the steep Bobe ridge, not far from the grave, it was suddenly attacked by rebels massed on either side of the track. They put in a determined charge, but were driven off by heavy fire at close range. About 60 rebels were killed, and the incident had a very detrimental effect on the survivors' morale. It proved that Bambatha's *intelezi* medicine was not effective after all, and the supernatural power which he had been thought to wield since the outbreak at Mpanza had deserted him. Bambatha himself traced the blame to a more pragmatic cause, Sigananda's bad generalship, and the rebel forces scattered, Sigananda and his men hiding out in the Mome Gorge, while Bambatha and his followers retired west to Macala Mountain.

In the aftermath of Bobe, troops from Fort Yolland moved forward to establish an advanced camp near Cetshwayo's grave. The burial place itself aroused some curiosity among the men; since it was forbidden to burn grass on the grave, a thicket had sprung up all around, and the remains of the wagon which had served as the king's hearse could still be seen among the tangled undergrowth. Unfortunately, while troops were sweeping through the surrounding area, they discovered some temporary huts erected by the rebels, and set fire to them, the flames spreading rapidly through the grass, burning close to the grave. Although damage to the site was limited, the incident was deeply shocking to many Zulus, and probably encouraged many to join the rebel cause who had so far remained uncommitted.

Over the next three weeks, McKenzie attempted to coordinate a series of sweeps through the bush. The combined total of government troops operating in the Nkandla was about 1700, most of whom were mounted, supported by about 2000 levies. It was difficult to assess the rebel strength, since a number of groups moved through the bush under the command of different leaders; their numbers in any given battle, however, seldom reached 1000 men. Indeed, there were few enough pitched battles, as the rebel strategy was to avoid open conflict, forcing the troops to sweep through the rugged, heavily forested country, only attacking small parties who became separated from the main body. Although there was continual skirmishing, most of it was light, and few rebels were killed. In an attempt to force them to submit, McKenzie destroyed local homesteads, including Sigananda's eNhlweni residence. For the most part, the rebels remained secure in their hiding places between the narrow ridges, and the troops often found themselves shelling and machine-gunning patches of bush for several hours, and at the end of it having no clear idea of the result.

Under this constant pressure, however, cracks appeared in the rebel coalition. Sigananda himself was losing stomach for the fight, and took to hiding in the Mome Gorge. He made tentative efforts to surrender, although many of his young men were keen to continue the struggle. Bambatha and one of his commanders, Mangathi, slipped away from the Nkandla to visit Dinuzulu at Nongoma. If anything, however, Dinuzulu's attitude towards the rebels had hardened; he had already felt obliged to make a public offer of support for the government, and Bambatha's lack of clear military success could scarcely have encouraged him to change his mind.

Bambatha and Mangathi returned with no concrete offer of support, and it was probably from that moment that the rebellion was really lost. Had Dinuzulu decided to risk everything on a last, reckless gamble, it is possible that a general uprising might just have persuaded the British government to intervene and address some of the rebels' grievances, but the cost in Zulu lives would have been colossal, and Dinuzulu had come to view armed resistance as futile. Without his backing, however, the rebellion had no hope of success.

When Bambatha returned to the Nkandla, however, he found that at least one Zulu chief of note had risen to join him. This was none other than Mehlokazulu kaSihayo Ngobese, the veteran royalist. Mehlokazulu, too, had had a chequered career since 1879, and had suffered both because of his reputation, and because of his attachment to the Royal House. Despite the fact that his father, Sihayo, had been killed by the Mandlakazi at oNdini in 1883, Mehlokazulu had been refused permission to assume the role of chief until 1893, when British attitudes had begun to thaw. He lived with his people not far from Isandlwana. His followers had been unsettled by the passage through their territory of McKenzie's column in early May, and Mehlokazulu had been reluctant to supply levies when called upon to do so. He was summoned to the local magistrate to explain himself, but instead fled to the bush, a move that may have been influenced by the fire at Cetshwayo's grave, which took place about that time. He passed Qudeni, picking up followers along the way, travelling towards Nkandla. He was intercepted by troops who crossed over the Thukela from the south and attacked him at Mpukinyoni on 28 May; but despite being defeated, his forces kept together and slipped into the forest from the west. Here they managed to link up with the rebels under Bambatha's direct command. This made them potentially the most dangerous rebel concentration in the field, since Mehlokazulu's prestige was considerable, but far from striking a serious blow for the uprising, they blundered into a disaster of such magnitude that it effectively crushed the rebellion in Zululand in one fell swoop.

On the evening of 9 June, McKenzie received information from his intelligence department that Bambatha and Mehlokazulu had joined forces, and were hidden in dense bush about fifteen miles west of the Mome Gorge. Their combined forces were said to number 20 *amaviyo*, or companies; although the strength of a company could vary wildly, from 50 to 150 men, this clearly amounted to a considerable force. According to McKenzie's sources, they were about to move towards the gorge that same night, to join up with Sigananda's people. The gorge itself was very steep and narrow, and once the rebels had slipped into it, it would be almost impossible to drive them out.

Although it was already late – about 9 p.m. – McKenzie, typically, decided to take immediate action to cut the rebels off. His own camp was situated several miles to the north of the gorge, closest to the head, where it ended in a series of sharp ridges and a tangle of forest: country so difficult that it was known as Sigananda's Stronghold. The troops at Cetshwayo's grave, east of the gorge, who were under the command of Lieutenant Colonel W. F. Barker of the Transvaal Mounted Rifles, were much closer to the mouth. McKenzie's plan was for Barker to try to intercept the rebels as they entered the mouth of the gorge, while his own force converged from the north. Speed was essential, and it would be necessary for the troops to move into their positions, across very steep country, in darkness, and without being spotted. McKenzie's messengers set out from his camp to take the order to Barker, fifteen miles away, and arrived there at 1 a.m. on the 10th, after a nerve-wracking ride through pitch-black forest, held mainly by the enemy.

Barker immediately grasped the importance of the situation, and had his force on the march by 3 a.m. It consisted of three squadrons of his own regiment (TMR), the Natal Police, one section of the Natal Field Artillery (equipped with two 15-pounder guns, one Maxim and one Colt machine-gun), the Nongqayi (the quasi-military Zululand Native Police) and about 800 levies. The troops had already swept through part of the gorge on previous occasions, and had no difficulty in reaching its mouth at about 4 a.m. On approaching it, the Nongqayi and levies were sent off to the right, so as to take up a position on one of the steep ridges overlooking the entrance on its eastern side. As the remainder of the force crossed in front of the mouth, at a distance of about 1000 yards, the officers spotted a cluster of camp-fires burning off to their right, at the entrance. This was the rebel army; they had already arrived at the gorge, and it was too late to cut them off.

The gorge is a remarkable topographical feature, and it seems extraordinary that any campaigning could have been carried out within its confines, since even today it is accessible only to the most adventurous traveller. The Mome itself is little more than a stream, flowing down from the upland to the north, and ultimately into the Nsuze River below. In the course of that journey it drops some 3000 feet, tumbling into the top of the gorge as a waterfall, then twisting and turning sharply through the steep, high buttresses on either side. The gorge itself is over a mile long, and in some places the sides descend steeply for nearly 2000 feet. The bottom of the gorge is seldom more than a few hundred yards wide, and here and there the walls crowd in almost upon the banks of the stream itself. Most of the floor is covered in bush, which thickens towards the top. Sigananda's eNhlweni homestead had been built on a spur jutting out to the east of the waterfall, and secluded footpaths led down to a cave behind the cascade, which was the most secret hiding place of the Cube. Midway along the western face, nestling in a curve between two spurs, a thick forest, the Dobo, shaped like an inverted pear, climbed almost to the top of the ridge. The only practical way into the gorge was at the mouth, where it opened out into the comparatively flat terrain of the Nsuze valley. Some 1000 yards from the mouth of the gorge, and commanding the entrance, was a solitary kopje. Barker was close to this kopje when he spotted the camp-fires within.

In retrospect, the rebel decision to camp at the mouth of the gorge, rather than enter it immediately, appears suicidal. In fact, the difficulty of the terrain under darkness was such – even for the rebels, who were accustomed to it – that they had decided, after the exertions of the march, to delay their entrance until the following morning, when it was light. Sigananda was reputedly hiding near the stronghold, and some care would be needed to find him. Mehlokazulu, moreover, who was now in his 50s, was feeling his age, and dismissive of any threat from the government forces; he argued that the troops did not know where they were, and even if they found them, would hardly be able to manoeuvre in such country in the dark. In the bitter words of Mangathi, who survived the subsequent débâcle, Mehlokazulu refused to go further 'because he was very stout and wore boots and was tired'.

The rebels agreed instead to bivouac on an old mealie-field at the mouth of the gorge. Confident that their position was unknown, they posted only a handful of sentries. When a young mat-carrier reported that he had heard wagons in the night – the 15-pounders and their carriages – Mehlokazulu dismissed the report as nonsense. After the battle was over, most Zulus took this as proof that Bambatha's *itonya* – the mystical force which assured him of success in battle – had deserted him, and that his *intelezi* medicines were desperately inferior to those of the government.

Indeed, there does seem something curious about the way the government forces were able to deploy so effectively without the rebels having the slightest inkling of their presence. Even Barker felt it, and recalled afterwards that his men had encountered a black cat on the road, and that it had led them all the way to the gorge. When Barker spotted the rebel camp, he placed his two guns on the kopje, looking straight down the mouth of the gorge. Two squadrons of the Transvaal Mounted Rifles, with a Maxim gun, were placed on the hills immediately to the right of the entrance, and one TMR squadron and 50 Natal Police, with the Colt gun, were positioned on the heights opposite. Barker kept the rest of his troops behind him, in case the rebels attempted to break out the way they had come. These deployments were made before dawn.

Barker hoped to delay the attack for as long as possible, in order to allow McKenzie to reach the far end of the gorge, and cut off any retreat. Clearly, however, there was a good chance that the rebels would discover him when the sun came up, in which case he ordered his men to pour as much fire into the enemy as possible, before they could escape. The signal to open fire would be a shot from one of the 15-pounders.

After two tense hours, the sun began to rise, only to reveal a thick mist hanging in the bottom of the gorge, and obscuring the entrance. As Barker anxiously watched for signs of rebel movement through his field-glasses, the mist lifted suddenly to allow him a glimpse of a dark black circle, standing where the fires had flickered the night before. For a second he thought it was the remains of a burnt-out homestead, before he suddenly realised that it was the rebel force, formed up in the traditional *umkhumbi* to receive last-minute instructions before battle. Clearly, the troops had been spotted, and there was no time to be lost; but before Barker could give the order to fire the first shot, a burst of Maxim fire, ripped out from the hills to the east. The Transvaal Mounted Rifles, stationed there, had also seen the rebel force preparing to deploy. They had held their fire until it was obvious that some of the enemy companies were crossing the low nek which led into the gorge itself, and rather than let them escape, they had decided to 'have a go'. Within a few seconds, the whole of Barker's force had opened up in a great arc of fire, sputtering in the pink dawn light.

The rebels had become aware of the presence of Barker's men shortly after dawn. Scouts had been sent up onto the western spur, and had hurried back with the news that the bivouac was overlooked by whites. Bambatha had apparently panicked, and it was left to his commanders to try to impose some order on the warriors. They were formed up by companies, and were preparing to advance against the ridge to the west when the firestorm broke over them. Exposed in the open, they scattered in confusion as shrapnel and bullets rained down on them, abandoning blankets, sleeping mats and many weapons in their haste.

Any possibility of an organised resistance collapsed in the first few minutes, and instead the rebels streamed across the nek and into the gorge, hoping to escape the devastating fire. Once there, however, they found themselves under fire from a new direction. The Nongqayi and levies had lined the ridge on the eastern side of the gorge a few hundred yards further up from the TMR, and as the rebels poured up the narrow entrance, they ran directly across the Nongqayi's front, 400 feet below them. Many warriors were shot down as they ran the gauntlet, while the remainder, making what use of cover they could, fled upstream towards the sanctuary of the stronghold.

The advanced parties of McKenzie's force, meanwhile, had started out from his camp at 3 a.m. His force consisted of one squadron each of the Natal Carbineers, Zululand Mounted Rifles and Northern District Mounted Rifles, 450 men of Royston's Horse, the Natal Rangers, a detachment of the Durban Light Infantry, the Natal Field Artillery with one 15-pounder, two pom-poms, a Maxim, and several hundred levies. While his main force advanced south, on a course that would bring them out on the western heights above the gorge, McKenzie detached the Natal Rangers with orders to circle further east, beyond the head of the gorge, and occupy the upper reaches of the eastern heights. McKenzie himself had reached the head of the gorge just before dawn. Convinced that Sigananda was hiding near the stronghold, he had just begun to deploy his troops to sweep down from the heights when he heard the burst of firing from the far end of the gorge. His first thought was that Barker had succeeded in preventing the rebels from entering the gorge, and that they would therefore probably try to escape up the Nsuze valley. He cancelled his order to sweep the head of the gorge, and ordered his command instead to ride along the narrow razor-backed crest of the western heights, following them down into the Nsuze valley. They had not gone far, however, when they saw Barker's troops in the distance, firing into the mouth of the gorge, and realised the true situation.

It was now imperative that his troops seal off the top of the gorge to prevent the rebels reaching the stronghold, and McKenzie ordered his men to dismount. That they had managed to ride their horses thus far was a remarkable tribute to their horsemanship, but it was dangerous enough to proceed further on foot. The ground dropped away alarmingly, and was covered with long grass which was slippery underfoot. A false step might send a man sliding down 1000 feet into the valley below. Nothing daunted, McKenzie himself set the pace, racing down the side of the hill at a speed that took his own men by surprise. He stopped half-way down on a shoulder which gave a commanding view of the gorge below. The tangled country around the stronghold was upstream, on his left; to his right was

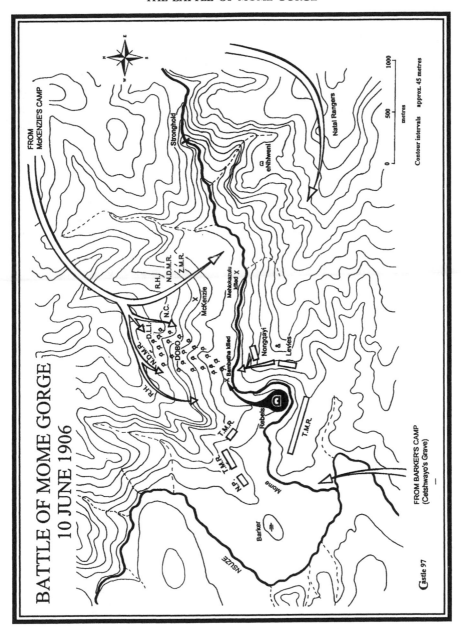

BATTLE OF MOME GORGE
10 JUNE 1906

the Dobo forest. Beneath, the first rebels were just beginning to hurry up the gorge towards him.

There was no time to lose, and McKenzie immediately ordered detachments of the Natal Carbineers, Northern District Mounted Rifles and Royston's Horse to continue down the slope to the bottom of the gorge, and cut off the retreat. They reached the stream just ahead of the main body of rebels, and opened a heavy fire into them. Some warriors attempted to rally on a patch of open slope on the opposite side of the gorge, but fire from the rest of McKenzie's force above dispersed them. Cut off from the stronghold, most had no choice but to go back the way they had come, and take refuge in the gorge. As they retired in confusion, Mehlokazulu himself was shot. He was wearing European clothes, but running in his socks; his personal attendant was carrying a new pair of tanned boots – the very ones, presumably, that had caused his delayed entry into the gorge the night before. Those new boots had lost him the rebellion.

McKenzie was well aware that the Dobo was the only way out of the trap, and he ordered the remainder of his force to line the ridge at the top of the forest. Although they could see little of the rebel movements within, they effectively sealed off any escape route. The rebels were completely surrounded, with only the slender protection of the forest for cover. It was now about 9 a.m., and the initial phase of the fighting was over. The mist had lifted, and it was light enough for McKenzie to open communications with Barker. Most of the rebels were now in the Dobo, although isolated pockets were still hiding near the entrance, or trying to force their way through the cordon. McKenzie ordered Barker to move his guns forward to the mouth of the gorge – the very spot occupied by the rebels at the start of the battle – an experience that must have given the gunners a chilling insight into the effect of their fire. Here they were positioned across the nek, and at maximum elevation began systematically to shell the Dobo forest.

With no obvious targets in front of them, Barker ordered the rest of his men forward from their original positions, and down into the gorge itself. As they advanced, driving through the bush like beaters raising game, they discovered many rebels hidden in thickets or pretending to be dead, and shot them all. This slow, deadly progress took several hours, and it was midday by the time they had swept through the entrance. Once they reached the stream itself, the Nongqayi crossed over, and began to probe the narrow foot of the Dobo. McKenzie immediately sent an order to recall them, for not only were they advancing uphill against a concealed enemy – a position that made them unnecessarily vulnerable – they were likely to be hit by his own men as they descended the ridge. Instead, McKenzie formed them into a line with his own men, and the whole force began to drive through the bush from above.

The advance started early in the afternoon, and lasted for the rest of the day. It was dangerous work, because the ground was steep, the bush thick, and the rebels desperate. Having caught their enemy after so many frustrating weeks of searching, the troops were not inclined to be merciful, and dozens of rebels were turned out of the thickets and shot down. At about 4.30, when only a small portion of the foot of the forest remained to be swept, the Nongqayi were seen to be outpacing the rest of the force, and in danger again of being shot by their own men. Their officer gave the order to sound the retire, and the whole force, thinking the call applied to them, abandoned the drive. It was a frustrating end to an extraordinary day, but in truth only a few hundred square yards had remained unsearched. To this mistake many of the rebel survivors owed their lives.

Since it was now getting dark, and there was no point in trying to pursue the rebels further, McKenzie ordered his men to break off the engagement, and to march back to their respective camps. It was quite clear to all of them that they had won a decisive victory; quite how decisive would only become apparent over the next few days. Losses on the government side were negligible – one officer killed, probably shot by his own side while pushing too far ahead – and another officer and trooper mortally injured. Eight other white troops and an unknown number of levies were wounded.

By comparison, rebel losses were appalling, probably in the region of 600 killed. The engagement was hardly a battle; it had all the characteristics of a massacre. For many years afterwards, Africans living near the gorge avoided walking near by at night, for it was widely known to contain ghosts. These ghosts took an unusual form; although they looked like men, they had no mouths, and could only make their presence felt by a low, howling wail – the wail of suffering, sorrow and grief.

McKenzie continued to sweep through the Nkandla bush over the next few days, hoping to locate Bambatha and Sigananda. On the 13th, a rebel who had surrendered identified himself as Bambatha's personal attendant, and revealed that his master had apparently been killed on the banks of the Mome. Since it was imperative that Bambatha's death be proved, McKenzie sent a patrol back into the gorge to find the body. The attendant led them to a corpse lying on the banks of the stream near the foot of the Dobo. This man had been killed when Barker's Nongqayis and levies had first reached the area, and the manner of his death suggested something of the brutal nature of much of the slaughter. He had been spotted walking up the middle of the stream, unarmed, wearing a white shirt, by a levy who was 60 yards ahead of him on the opposite bank. The rebel turned to run, unaware that another levy had approached him from behind. The second man then struck at him with a stabbing spear. The rebel fell, but was still alive, despite the fact that the force of the blow had bent the blade in his body, and the levy could not pull it out. While the two figures were struggling, the first levy approached, and tried to stab the rebel in his turn. The fallen man, however, caught the blade as it lunged forward, and tried to twist it out of his enemy's hands. For a few seconds this macabre and desperate struggle continued, until a Nongqayi came past and, placing his rifle against the wounded man's head, blew his brains out. Having no clue as to the identity of the victim, the levies then abandoned the corpse to rejoin the fight.

The body had been badly disfigured by its injuries, and had already been lying in the open for several days. The attendant, however, was positive that it was Bambatha's and, since it was impossible to drag the corpse out of the valley, the sergeant in charge of the party decided instead to cut off the head. It was taken back to McKenzie's camp, and displayed as proof of Bambatha's death. According to official reports, the head was treated with respect, and only relevant personnel allowed to see it; the existence of photos, however, showing troops posing with it in triumph, tend to suggest otherwise. Eventually, the head was sent back to the gorge, and buried near the rest of the body.

Although the Natal authorities were greatly relieved by this apparent proof of the rebel leader's death, there is a good deal of evidence to suggest that they were duped. Most Zulu sources suggest that Bambatha's servant was directed by the surviving rebel leaders deliberately to mislead the whites, and that he identified a body with no more than a passing resemblance to Bambatha. Certainly, none of the officers in McKenzie's command had met the chief while he was alive, and to this day Bambatha's descendants believe that he escaped the massacre, and fled to Mozambique for sanctuary. According to their story, he returned to Zululand a few years later, and lived with his wife under an assumed name until eventually he died of natural causes.

The slaughter in the gorge cut the heart out of the rebellion in Zululand. On 13 June, the last Zulu rebel of consequence, Sigananda, surrendered unconditionally with his sons and supporters. Ancient and dignified, Sigananda aroused some sympathy, even among his enemies. He had a vivid memory of the history of Zululand, and entertained McKenzie and his officers with stories of the great Zulu kings. One of his captors, not otherwise moved to pity by the plight of the rebels, wrote of him:

> He was a man looked up to by his tribe not only with respect but with veneration; and in the sere and yellow leaf of his life to have lost all for the grim walls of a prison was a poor exchange indeed.

Sigananda's ruin was complete; he was tried under martial law, but died on 23 July of natural causes, before the sentence could be carried out.

With the collapse of the uprising in Zululand, the focus of the rebellion shifted to Natal. Less than a fortnight after the battle of Mome Gorge, two important groups living in Mapumulo district, along the southern bank of the lower reaches of the Thukela, rose in revolt. These were sections of the Qwabe and Zulu chiefdoms, who had been located in Natal. Both had long and proud histories, and had suffered impoverishment and harassment under the colonial system. Their districts, however, were not so well suited to open warfare as the Nkandla, and McKenzie was able to disperse them with ease.

The final months of the rebellion were characterised by a ruthless effort on the part of the government troops to suppress any lingering trace of dissent. Huts were burned, cattle confiscated, and suspected rebels arrested, beaten and sometimes shot. By the time the rebellion was officially declared over, at the beginning of September, as many as 4000 'rebels' had been killed, and 7000 imprisoned. Many of the latter were used to provide forced labour for the Public Works Department. One source estimated that at least 700 had been subjected to the lash, but commented that there were no records of the hundreds who had been flogged by troops in the field.

By contrast, just eighteen white troops had died as a result of enemy action, and a further six had died of other causes while on campaign. Six civilians were also killed. Thirty-seven white troops had been wounded, and six levies were killed. The official records list thirty levies wounded, but this figure may have been higher. No European women and children had been harmed, while missionary societies complained that their missions in the troubled districts, while untouched by the rebels, were often vandalised by passing white troops. The disparity in casualties prompted Churchill, who had thoroughly disapproved of the Natal government's actions throughout, to comment, when an imperial medal for the campaign was mooted:

> There were, I think, nearly a dozen casualties among these devoted men in the course of their prologued operations and more than four or even five are dead on the field of honour. In these circumstances it is evident that special consideration should be shown to the survivors. But I should hesitate to press upon them an imperial medal in view of the distaste which this colony has so strongly evinced for outside interference of all kinds. A copper medal bearing

Bambatha's head, to be struck at the expense of the colony, seems to be the most appropriate memento of their sacrifices and their triumphs.

That Natal's reaction to the disturbances had been harsh reflected the deep-seated fears of settler society, fears that found expression in their suspicion of the Zulu Royal House. To many whites, the fact that there had been a rebellion at all was in itself proof of the lingering hold which the old Zulu kingdom still held over the imagination of many blacks. Dinuzulu was therefore guilty because of what he represented, rather than his actual complicity. He was the son of Cetshwayo, and the heir of the House of Shaka, and for that, once again, he had to be punished. Once the rebellion ended, many whites expected Dinuzulu to be arrested, and he was finally charged with high treason in December 1906. After a highly publicised trial, in which the prosecution failed to prove on twenty counts that Dinuzulu had either authorised or supported any act of overt rebellion, he was nonetheless found guilty of three other charges, that he had at various times given shelter to Bambatha's followers.

In truth, Dinuzulu's position had always been ambivalent; whereas he knew, more than most, the folly of taking up arms against the whites, he had a duty, too, to those who considered him their king, and he was further trapped between government attempts to reduce him to the level of a stooge and his own belief in the destiny of the House of Shaka. His sentence – four years' imprisonment – seemed paltry in comparison to the position with which his enemies credited him, and the crimes he was alleged to have committed. Perhaps more significantly, he forfeited his role as a government *induna* and, as official leader of the uSuthu, his royal homesteads were demolished, and his followers dispersed and given into the charge of neighbouring chiefs.

Dinuzulu served most of his sentence in Natal, but in 1910, when South Africa became a Union, its first premier, Louis Botha, released him onto a farm in the Transvaal. Botha remembered Dinuzulu from his youth; he had been one of the Boers who had rallied to the uSuthu cause to defeat Zibhebhu in 1884. Yet the future had little to offer Dinuzulu, the last warrior king of the Zulus; the government had taken away what little had remained of his power, his health was broken, and he was removed from his supporters and the lands of his ancestors. He died in October 1913, probably from rheumatic gout and Bright's disease, and the government granted his last wish, that he be taken back and buried in the heart of Zululand.

He left to his heir, Solomon, the difficult task of trying to find a role for the Zulu monarchy in a world which bore little economic or political resemblance to the glorious days of the nineteenth century. The old kingdom had passed into the shadows, and its successors could only draw strength from its memory to find their way in a world dominated, for the next 80 years, by the harsh reality of dependence on white rule.

FURTHER READING

Bulpin, T. V., *Shaka's Country*
(Cape Town, 1952)

Castle, Ian, and Knight, Ian,
*Fearful Hard Times; The Siege
and Relief of Eshowe, 1879*
(London, 1994)

Emery, Frank, *The Red Soldier;
Letters from the Zulu War, 1879*
(London, 1977)

Knight, Ian, *Brave Men's Blood;
The Epic of the Zulu War*
(London, 1990)

Knight, Ian, *Zulu; The Battles of
Isandlwana and Rorke's Drift,
22/23rd January 1879*
(London, 1992)

– *Nothing Remains but to Fight;
The Defence of Rorke's Drift,
1879* (London, 1993)

– *The Anatomy of the Zulu Army;
From Shaka to Cetshwayo*
(London, 1994)

– *The Zulus* (London, 1989)

– *British Forces in Zululand, 1879*
(London, 1991)

– *Zulu, 1816-1906* (London, 1995)

– *Rorke's Drift; Pinned Like Rats
in a Trap* (London, 1995)

Knight, Ian, and Castle, Ian, *Zulu
War 1879; Twilight of a Warrior
Nation* (London, 1992)

– *The Zulu War; Then and Now*
(London, 1994)

Laband, John, *Rope of Sand; The
Rise and Fall of the Zulu
Kingdom in the Nineteenth
Century* (Johannesburg, 1995;
also published London, 1997,
under the title *The Fall of the
Zulu Nation*)

– *Kingdom in Crisis; The Zulu
Response to the British Inva-
sion of 1879* (Manchester and
New York, 1992)

– *The Battle of Ulundi* (Pietermaritzburg and Ulundi, 1988)

– *Fight Us in the Open; The
Anglo–Zulu War Through Zulu
Eyes* (Pietermaritzburg and
Ulundi, 1985)

Laband, John, and Knight, Ian, *The
War Correspondents; The
Anglo–Zulu War* (Gloucester-
shire, 1996)

Laband, John, and Matthews, Jeff,
Isandlwana (Pietermaritzburg
and Ulundi, 1992)

Laband, John, and Thompson,
Paul, *Field Guide to the War in
Zululand: the Defence of Natal*
(Pietermaritzburg, revised
edition, 1987)

– *Kingdom and Colony at War;
Sixteen Studies on the
Anglo–Zulu War of 1879*
(Pietermaritzburg and

Constantia, 1990)

Laband, John, and Wright, John, *King Cetshwayo kaMpande* (Pietermaritzburg and Ulundi, 1980)

Lock, Ron, *Blood on the Painted Mountain; Zulu Victory and Defeat, Hlobane and Khambula* (London, 1995)

Marks, Shula, *Reluctant Rebellion; The 1906–08 Disturbances in Natal* (Oxford, 1970).

Stuart, James, *A History of the Zulu Rebellion, 1906* (London, 1913)

Taylor, Stephen, *Shaka's Children; A History of the Zulu People* (London, 1994)

INDEX